THE ENGLISH PRESS
1621–1861

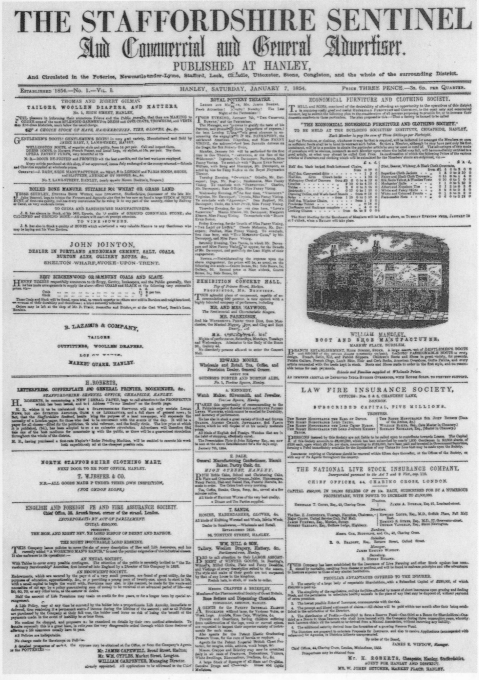

Front page of the Staffordshire Sentinel, *1854.*

THE ENGLISH PRESS

1621–1861

Jeremy Black

SUTTON PUBLISHING

First published in 2001 by
Sutton Publishing Limited · Phoenix Mill
Thrupp · Stroud · Gloucestershire · GL5 2BU

British Library Cataloguing in Publication Data
A catalogue record for this book is available from the British Library.

ISBN 0-7509-2524-8

For Geoffrey Holland

Typeset in 10/12pt Baskerville
Typesetting and origination by
Sutton Publishing Limited.
Printed and bound in England by
J.H. Haynes & Co. Ltd, Sparkford.

Contents

Abbreviations   vi

Preface   vii

1   The Development of the Press 1621–1750   1

2   Politics to 1750   25

3   Balancing the Contents   50

4   Continuity and Change 1750–1833   72

5   'Improvement': The Social Politics of Morality   96

6   The Development of the Provincial Press   110

7   Politics 1750–1789   127

8   Reporting the Revolution   143

9   Politics 1800–1833   161

10 A New World of Print   177

Selected Further Reading   204

Index   205

Abbreviations

Add.	Additional Manuscripts
AE, CP, Ang.	Paris, Archives du Ministère des Affaires Etrangères, Correspondance Politique Angleterre
BB	Bland Burges papers
BL	London, British Library
Bod	Oxford, Bodleian Library
Cobbett	W. Cobbett (ed.), *A Parliamentary History of England . . . 1066 to . . . 1803* (36 vols, 1806–20)
CRO	County Record Office
EHR	English Historical Review
HL	San Marino California, Huntington Library
HMC	Historical Manuscripts Commission
PRO	London, Public Record Office
RA	Windsor Castle, Royal Archives, Stuart Papers
SP	State Papers
Weston	Iden Green, Kent, home of John Weston-Underwood, papers of Edward Weston

Unless otherwise stated, all works are published in London.

Note on Currency
Prices are given in pre-decimal currency: £1 = 20 shillings (*s*) = 240 pennies (*d*).
Therefore 6*d* = 2½ new pence; 1*s* = 5 new pence.

Note on Dates
Until the 1752 reform of the calendar, Britain conformed to Old Style, which was eleven days behind New Style, the Gregorian calendar used in most of the rest of Europe. Until the reform all dates given are Old Style apart from those marked (ns). The convention by which the English New Year began on 25 March has been ignored, and it is given as starting on 1 January.

Preface

For several months past I have resided in the country, with a very agreeable family, about forty miles from London, where we had plenty of shooting, fishing, walking, and riding. But as the weather was frequently such as obliged us to keep within doors, we then endeavoured to amuse ourselves with cards and newspapers. Cards for those who love play, are a vast fund of amusement, but this is by no means the case with regard to newspapers; for when you have once read the pages of unconnected occurrences, consisting of politics, religion, picking of pockets, puffs, casualties, deaths, marriages, bankruptcies, preferments, resignations, executions, lottery tickets, India bonds, Scotch auctioneers and quack doctors, this abrupt transition from one thing to another, is apt to overload and confuse the memory so much, that, after reading two or three newspapers, people generally throw them down, with the usual complaint of, Not a syllable of News; to silence this complaint, and to show that newspapers, as well as cards, are capable of entertainment, I shall mention one improvement, which we practised in the country with great success; and that was, after we had read the paper in the old trite vulgar way, i.e. each column by itself downwards, we next read two columns together onwards; and by this new method, found much more entertainment than in the common way of reading, with a greater variety of articles curiously blended, or strikingly contrasted.

'A New Method of reading Newspapers', *Gentleman's Magazine*, 1766[1]

To record these events as they occur, and to deduce from them reflections and principles that shall improve the past experience, and regulate the future, is the province of the journalist; and whether these events are national or local, his duty is equally obvious and important.

Birmingham Chronicle and General Advertiser of the Midland Counties,
2 January 1823

Given the opportunity to write again on English newspaper history, I set aside the invitation to produce a second edition of my *The English Press in the Eighteenth Century* (1987). Instead, I have tried to rethink my approach to the subject, to expand my scope in order to cover the period from the foundation of the newsbook press in London to the abolition of the last of the newspaper taxes, and to draw on both my own subsequent work and the insights offered by the fine works of others. I would particularly like to direct readers' attention to the latter, which are cited both in the footnotes and in the selected further reading. It is valuable to consider these works both because they are first-rate in themselves and because several differ in their assumptions and/or conclusions from my own effort.

As will emerge in the book, I am less inclined than many other scholars to emphasize both the modernity and the impact of the eighteenth- and early nineteenth-century press. This reflects my own work on the newspapers and on English society and politics in this period. It also contributes to and stems from a wider view, seen for example in my *Eighteenth-Century Europe* (2nd edition, 1999), in which I stress a late onset for modernity and am less inclined than many others to stress the role, impact and consequences of earlier change. An assessment of the press in this light is important, as it has generally, sometimes uncritically, been seen as cause and means of change.

Clearly there is no simple dichotomy of change and continuity, and it would be naïve to deny that there was change in the late seventeenth and eighteenth centuries. My emphasis on other elements, however, is intended to encourage a re-examination of the role of the press and of the teleological assumptions that have been frequently expressed. I know that this view will be rejected by many, but I hope that I contribute to a pluralism of interpretation that matches the variety of its subject.

This book contains chapters that offer a chronological perspective and others that are thematic. Such an approach has its problems, but to offer a work that was entirely chronological or totally thematic would be misleading. As is appropriate for a work tackling the press, there is a particular emphasis on quoting passages from newspapers in order to convey the character of content and tone. In addition, the text is illuminated by vignettes: particular episodes serve as examples for more general trends.

I am grateful to the large number of friends, fellow-scholars, archivists, librarians and owners of manuscripts without whom it would have been impossible to write this book. I am most grateful to Her Majesty the Queen, Earl Waldegrave, Lady Lucas, the trustees of the Wentworth Woodhouse collection, and John Weston-Underwood for permission to consult archival holdings they own. Grayson Ditchfield, Bill Gibson, Bob Harris and Ian Maxted made helpful comments on an earlier draft, and Nigel Aston, John Belchem, John Derry, John Hargreaves, Ian Machin, Donald Read and David Taylor gave advice on particular chapters. The Huntington Library appointed me to a visiting fellowship in 1988, and the Beinecke Library to another in 1991.

I have benefited from the opportunity to present papers at symposia on newspaper preservation and access in London in 1987 and Durham in 1994, the third annual Cultural History Conference held in the University of Aberdeen in 1988, the conference on the French

Revolutionary press held at the Museum of the Revolution at Vizille in 1988, the Second Münster Symposium on Jonathan Swift in 1989, the bicentennial conference on the French Revolution held at Paris in 1989, the Literature and History Conference at Newcastle in 1989, three conferences on newspaper history held at the German museum of newspaper history in Meersburg in 1987, 1989 and 1994, the eighth seminar on the British book trade held in Durham in 1990, the international conference on the Enlightenment held in Bristol in 1991, the fourteenth annual conference on book trade history at the Birkbeck College Centre for Extra-Mural Studies in 1992, the conference on Eighteenth-Century Britain held at Paris in 1995, and a Liberty Fund colloquium on censorship held at Indianapolis.

Christopher Feeney continues to be a supportive publisher. It is a great pleasure to dedicate this book to a colleague whom I much admire.

NOTES

1. *Gentleman's Magazine* (1766), p. 587. Item by 'Papyrus Cursor'. Many humorous examples were provided.

CHAPTER ONE

The Development of the Press
1621–1750

With its strong sense of change through time, the essential constituent of
news, the newspaper press was and is necessarily a medium whose
contents are not static. There were and are, also, powerful organizational
reasons encouraging change: newspapers wished and wish to obtain,
publish and distribute news as fast as possible; they seek an attractive
layout; as profit-making concerns, they need constantly to be conscious of
costs. Changes in the 'press' as a whole are in part the result of, and are
certainly closely related to, the continual effort of individual titles to
probe the market and improve their own product in order to maximize
profits.

There are therefore important reasons, inherent to the press, why it
should be continually changing. In addition, change in the press can be
related to contextual transformations, both those that are general,
affecting much of society, such as rising literacy in the late nineteenth
century, and those that more specifically influence the press, either
because they alter its *modus operandi*, for example the invention and
spread of the railway and telegraphy, or because of their competitive
impact, as with modern developments in radio and television. Furthermore, the press has been greatly affected by changes in its regulatory
framework, with legal developments determining what can be reported,
and how, and with fiscal legislation, which can either directly alter the
cost structure of newspapers or, through tax changes, affect the conduct
and profitability of newspaper businesses.

Change is therefore a central theme in newspaper history, not only
because of its occurrence, and the speed of its occurrence, but also as the
awareness of change creates a sense of transience and opportunity. Each
period of English newspaper history can be presented as one of
transformation, shifts in content, production, distribution, the nature of
competition, and the social context.

A variety of media has generally characterized news reporting and
commentary in England in recent centuries: newspapers have had to
compete not only with each other (a central feature of English press
history), but also with other means of conveying news. These means can
essentially be divided into two types. First, there have been other
capitalist agencies, both those involving the culture of print, such as

1

magazines, and, more recently, those using different technology, such as radio and television. In England over the last three centuries, these agencies of news formulation and transmission have been produced by distinct, coherent, capitalist entities. In contrast, there are the far less readily grasped non-institutional and non-capitalist agencies for formulating and disseminating news, and ones which pre-date newspapers. These can essentially be described as community agencies: families, kindred, localities, confessional and economic groups.

The relationship between the two was obviously not one of simple competition. Community agencies can serve for the assessment and transmission of news received from elsewhere through the first type of agency. And yet, there is and was a basic tension. Though local communities can influence, through their values, the impact of the news from external agencies on the local recipients of it, they play a more limited role than in the creation and discussion of local issues – local being understood to refer to a specific group and not necessarily being a geographical term. In contrast, external agencies mediate between localities and the outside world, in particular creating or sustaining expectations, hopes and interests that are not those of the locality. External agencies therefore offered and offer a source and means for independence: democratization. Knowledge is not so much freedom, but rather a cause of the demand for freedoms.

Early-modern England was a society that, by present-day standards, was, in practice and ideology, inegalitarian, religious, hierarchical, paternalistic, patriarchal, male-dominated and reverential of the past, although in each case there were tensions and conflicting definitions. The culture of print represented a potential threat to this cultural, social and political order. However, it is necessary not to see this order as rigid and unchanging, nor to exaggerate the degree of tension between society and the culture of print, most particularly by abstracting this culture from society, and thus thinking in terms of rivalry and an opposition of *mentalités* or consciousnesses. The threat was most potent in the religious sphere. The printing of vernacular bibles had given concerned individuals an opportunity to consider God themselves and to defy traditional teachings from the zealous perspective of scriptural authority.

The development of printing, economic growth and the Reformation all contributed to, and indeed defined, a shift in which society in the sixteenth century became more literary and less oral or visual. Literacy, print-reading and print-purchase all rose. Initially, this had nothing to do with the establishment of an English press. Instead, religion was central. The first complete translation of the Bible to be printed, that by Miles Coverdale, was dedicated to Henry VIII in 1535. Henry argued that the 'word of God' supported the idea of royal supremacy over the Church, and this encouraged the translation of the Bible. An official English Bible was produced (1537), and every parish church was instructed to purchase a copy (1538), a marked extension of the authority of print and a testimony to the effectiveness of the publishing industry. Printed devotional books were very important too. Print also drew on more recent ecclesiastical developments. For example, John Foxe's *Acts and Monuments of the Church* (1563), popularly known as the *Book of Martyrs*, was extremely influential in propagating an image of Catholic cruelty and Protestant bravery that was to sustain a strong anti-Catholic tradition.[1]

Other current developments were important in the new culture of print: they were both discussed in it and encouraged demand for it, helping to make print attractive as well as authoritative. Learned treatises, chapbooks, printed ballads and engravings all commented on witchcraft, with works such as Reginald Scot's *The Discoverie of Witchcraft* (1584), George Gifford's *A Dialogue Concerning Witches and Witchcraftes* (1593) and John Cotta's *The Triall of Witchcraft* (1616), and accounts of trials, such as the *Most strange and admirable discoverie of the three Witches of Warboys* (1593) and *The Witches of Northamptonshire* (1612).

The world of print also predicted the future. The publications of popular astrologers, such as William Lilly, author of *The Starry Messenger* (1645), sold thousands of copies.[2] Belief in astrology declined in the eighteenth century, but this should not be exaggerated. Very large numbers of astrological works were still being sold in the 1790s, a decade in which apocalyptic beliefs were widely aired. Prominent almanacs, such as John Partridge's *Merlinus Liberatus* and Cardanus Rider's *British Merlin*, had also been very successful earlier in the century. In addition the press repeated popular superstitions. *Drewry's Derby Mercury* of 10 September 1775 noted of a fatal accident in Staffordshire: 'it is very remarkable that a bird hovered over the head of the deceased for a considerable time'.

Whether this particular example reflected a belief in the occult or that it could have been providential, and thus in keeping with Protestant theology, or both, this is an unconventional introduction of the newspaper. It is not, however, obviously less appropriate than the habitual chronology which securely places the press in a political context and one that is at once modernizing, 'rational' and readily comprehensible in our terms. In short, the rise of the press is seen as an adjunct of the defeat of Stuart authoritarianism in the seventeenth century. This was indeed important, although it is far from the whole story.

Belief in witchcraft, astrology and providentialism were all, although in varied ways, aspects of the interaction of human and sacred space, and of the extent to which this interaction was continual, and thus a subject for regular report and commentary. News helped to explain life. It was of, as much as a counterpart to, a religious culture that put a greater stress than prior to the Reformation on explanation, not least through use of the vernacular and of print. Much news was not as we would know it today. Instead, news could be repetitive and cyclical, telling and retelling familiar tales and superstitions. Perhaps this afforded some security in an insecure world. A sense of news as frequent, even diurnal, did not represent a secular rejection of a religious world view, but, instead, was a common theme in society, offering explanation in the form of narrative continuity. Both print and great interest in recording and 'telling' time were aspects of a significant cultural shift. Time-based forms of publication, such as astrological publications, news pamphlets and newspapers, were part of this shift, which was shaped by government regulation, entrepreneurial activity, and the purchasing and reading decisions of many for whom both were acts of political and/or religious affirmation as well as expressions of interest.[3] Standards and conventions in publication and content, for example the persona of the writer, developed.

For part of society, as an aspect of the rise of the so-called 'public sphere', print became more authoritative than the handwritten word, as well as functionally better able to reach this sphere; although, until the eighteenth century, printed news complemented rather than replaced its manuscript counterpart. Nevertheless, the general authority of print helped ensure its use as the medium for news. In another key development, the nature of printed news production and distribution in serials was commercial and for profit. Regular sales and low costs combined to make the product a desirable one for producers and distributors.

An active world of newspapers drew closer in the Elizabethan period with the publication of news pamphlets, especially by the publisher John Wolfe. These and other pamphlets fostered a lower-cost marketplace of print and encouraged entrepreneurs to seek profit in ephemeral publications.[4] In 1620, the first English-language newspapers were imported from Amsterdam, a testimony to greater interest in foreign news at the time of the Thirty Years War. They encouraged the publication of 'corantos' (newsbooks or newspapers) in London from 1621, and Michael Frearson has argued both that the scale of production and the profitability of the news trade was greater than hitherto appreciated, and that London corantos were widely distributed in the country using weekly postal services. Publication once a week reflected the demand for frequent news: more frequent publication would not have been feasible given the time taken for printing, the extent of the market, and rate of news transmission from the Continent. By 1622 newsbooks were appearing in a numbered sequence. This helped create a sense of location in time: news was placed in a sequence, and later items in a sequence qualified what had gone before.[5] Location in a sequence also contributed to a sense of the enduring character of news.

The development of newspapers can be related to more than entrepreneurial activity and market demand for regular news. In addition, this development can be located within a wider cultural shift that focused attention on what could be presented as news. As has recently been noted: 'By the reign of James I we find prodigies and prophecies becoming pawns and weapons of sectarian conflict with the Protestant establishment, and the journalistic genre of "strange newes" being hijacked as a vehicle for articulating topical grievances'.[6] This genre had been used to provide accounts of providential tales, and this had attracted entrepreneurial publishers.[7]

News serials focused on developments abroad. This reflected not only the role of trade, particularly in London, but also the political and religious importance of the struggle on the Continent and its links with tensions at home. The relationship between print and trade was also shown with the appearance of printed lists of London commodity prices. In contrast, printed ballads offered accounts of developments at home. Their cost was lower and their readership greater than those of the news serials. Government unease led to a number of regulatory moves, culminating, as the consequence of a complaint from a Spanish agent, in the prohibition of coranto printing in London by the Privy Council in 1632.

The press was kept under control through a licensing system until the abolition of Star Chamber, a prerogative court, in July 1641, part of the collapse of Charles I's authority and power, led to an explosion of publication. The contested nature of political authority and of the information and regulations produced by political bodies gave greater relative authority to printed news. Serialization was both the means most appropriate to report the Civil War of 1642–6 and also an increasingly important organizing principle within the trade in print.[8] The press fed off the politicization of the 1640s, which greatly enhanced interest in domestic news.

Narrative news was speeded up in the Civil War. The war also saw the production of works directly linked to the competing regimes. Charles I supported the newsbook *Mercurius Aulicus* produced by Sir John Berkenhead from 1643, and this helped ensure a good supply of news. The leading parliamentary competitor was *Mercurius Britannicus*, which was run between 1643 and 1646 by Marchamont Nedham, selling 750–1,000 copies weekly. It belonged to a syndicate of newsbooks owned by the printer Robert White, who had to deal with rival or counterfeit versions of *Britannicus*. Nedham and Berkenhead questioned each other's veracity, news being subsumed to propaganda. This helped polarize public opinion, as the newsbooks of both sides demonized the other and focused on atrocities and sinister schemes. They also exaggerated the difficulties of the opposing side. Thus, for example, parliamentary writers overstated popular hostility to Charles I.[9]

Disenchanted by the growing radicalism of the parliamentary regime, between 1647 and 1649 Nedham switched to produce *Mercurius Pragmaticus*, the foremost Royalist newsbook of the period, but imprisonment and subsequently other problems led him to switch back to produce *Mercurius Politicus*, the most prominent newsbook of the regimes of the 1650s, from the Rump Parliament and Cromwell to the restored

Parliament, before backing the Stuarts again in the shape of Charles II. In 1650, the Rump began to subsidize Nedham. From 1655, his *Mercurius Politicus* and the *Publick Intelligencer* were the only authorized newsbooks. The very fact that there were two weeklies, appearing on different days, indicated what was thought necessary to satisfy the market.[10] In 1649, 1652 and 1655 most of the press had been banned and a licensing system was restored. This did not prevent serial publication, but it reduced the appeal of the end product and inhibited the ability of printed serials to finance a world of commercial print.

The collapse of the Protectorate and Commonwealth in 1658–60 hit regulation, but the licensing system returned after the Restoration of Charles II in 1660. The 1662 'Act for preventing the frequent Abuses in printing seditious, treasonable, and unlicensed Books and Pamphlets, and for regulating of Printing and Printing Presses' was based on the theory that the freedom to print was hazardous to the community and dangerous to its ruler, a threat to faith, loyalty and morality. The goal was control. Printing was strictly limited to the master printers of the Stationers Company of London and the university printers. Only twenty of the former were permitted and vacancies were filled by the authority of the Archbishop of Canterbury and the Bishop of London, who were troubled enough by the dissemination of heterodox opinions not to support a relaxation in the control of printing. Only four founders of type were permitted and vacancies were again filled by the two senior clerics. All master printers and founders were obliged to provide sureties of £300 not to engage in illegal printing. The number of apprentices, journeymen and presses per printer was regulated. The printing of material offensive to the Christian faith, the Church of England, any officer of the government, or any private person was prohibited; and a licensing system was established to enable pre-publication censorship. The Secretaries of State were given authority over publications dealing with 'affairs of state'.

This authority was delegated in 1663 to Sir Roger L'Estrange, who undertook it in return for the profitable patent for the exclusive publication of all newspapers. Existing newsbooks were suppressed to make way for L'Estrange's monopoly, with the publication of the *Oxford Gazette* in November 1665. This became the *London Gazette* (or *Gazette* for short) the following year when the royal court returned to London after the plague and L'Estrange sold his monopoly to Joseph Williamson, as Under Secretary of State. The *Gazette* became a state-directed commercial concern,[11] a good example of the state catching up with private enterprise, for the government needed a means of disseminating news and appointments. The Scottish Privy Council discouraged the printing of news relating to Scotland, and it was not until the parliamentary union of 1707 and the abolition of the Council in 1708 that the situation altered there.

'Published by Authority' as it prominently declared, the bi-weekly *Gazette* was not the sole means of spreading news. Although the trade and advertising newspapers set up after the Fire of London of 1666 contained no political news, this was not the case with the manuscript newsletters. The lack of domestic news in the *Gazette* led readers who wanted political and, in particular, parliamentary news to turn to newsletters. George Larkin's pro-government *Publick Occurrences Truly Stated* reported on 6 March 1688, 'I have set a friend of mine to consult the Letters, and haunt the confiding coffee-houses, where the grave men puff out sedition.' Those who could afford newsletters had access to knowledge denied others who made do with oral reports (including sermons). Thus the character and reliability of news was a class issue.

It was not until the Popish Plot disrupted Charles II's government in 1678 that the *Gazette*'s monopoly in printed news was breached. Public excitement, political commitment and the expiration of the licensing provisions in 1679 led to a sudden proliferation of unlicensed newspapers, the first of which appeared on 3 December 1678. The instability of the monarchy, the dynamism of the expanding print industry, and new and powerful demands for exposition and interpretation interacted to produce a fluid realm of discourse.[12]

By the end of 1679 more papers were being published than at any time since 1649, the year of Charles I's execution, an unwelcome development, and precedent, for the government. The establishment of the Penny Post in 1680 facilitated the transmission of information, and the distribution of publications, helping meet the demand for both at the time of the Popish Plot and the subsequent Exclusion Crisis. A Tory press was founded in response to opposition publications, but Charles II wished not to conduct a propaganda war but to terminate one. The judiciary supported the power of the royal prerogative to control the press, and prosecutions for seditious libel were launched. Chief Justice Scroggs directed that juries were only competent to determine whether the defendants had published the libel; judges alone could decide whether it was seditious, a ruling that greatly limited the role of juries. Certain of government support, officials of the Stationers Company and of the Secretaries of State enforced the law against illegal printers.

Charles II stamped out the Whig newspapers, and in 1685 James II had Parliament revive the Printing Act. Confident of governmental stability and support, the officials of the Stationers Company and the 'Messengers of the Press', officials of the Secretaries of State who searched for evidence of illegal printers, sought to enforce the law. The Company dealt with Richard Baldwin, the Whig publisher of the *Protestant Courant* in 1682.[13]

The ministerial success in stamping out Whig newspapers contrasted with the situation the following century. The press in the 1680s was newer, smaller, confined to London, with a less-developed distributive network and smaller financial resources, and without the loyalties of a long-established readership. Nevertheless, much of the difference can be explained by a contrast in government attitudes. No eighteenth-century ministry sought to suppress the press with the thoroughness and vigour of Charles II and James II. The Civil War, the Popish Plot and the Exclusion Crisis engendered a fear and a desire for action in ministerial circles that had different consequences in terms of press regulation to the situation over the following century and a half: ministries, in common with the political nation, became more accustomed to the expression of various opinions, often antagonistic, in the press.

However, the disruption of the agencies that supervised printing when James was overthrown and replaced in the 'Glorious Revolution' of 1688–9 led to the appearance of new papers, all of them favourable to the new King, William III, who was himself adept at using printed propaganda.[14] On 12 December 1688 alone, three papers were founded. As in earlier periods of crisis, press readership rose. The account book of Sir Robert Walpole's father, another Robert, the Whig MP for Castle Rising, recorded repeated expenditure on (unspecified) 'gazettes'.[15] Nevertheless, once in control, William moved to revive the machinery of press control, attacking unlicensed works. Richard Baldwin found himself in trouble with both Secretaries of State and Parliament in 1690–1, despite his Whig credentials.

In 1695, however, the Licensing (Printing) Act lapsed. It was felt that the existing system for the supervision of printing was inadequate, and plans were drawn up to prepare a new regulatory act. This was killed due to parliamentary divisions and a lack of parliamentary time.[16] Thereafter, despite attempts in 1697, 1698, 1702, 1704 and 1712 to revive a licensing system,[17] the press was free of pre-publication control, although such censorship was imposed on plays in 1737.

It was clear that this was not going to be like previous lapses in the licensing system. Thus, there was a sounder basis for investment. A spate of new titles followed as an aspect of what has been seen as a profit-driven periodicity.[18] The *Flying Post*, *Post Boy*, and *Post Man*, all of which first appeared in 1695, were successful new papers whose layout was based on that of the *Gazette*. Their titles were linked to their frequency: the *Post Boy* was the first tri-weekly. Such papers were published on Tuesdays, Thursdays and Saturdays when the Penny Post left London. At once, this enabled the new papers to meet both metropolitan and provincial demand and to establish their claim to be a national voice. 'King George's news-papers' were read in Moreton in Devon, and on the back of the copy of the *St James's Evening Post* on 1 March 1718 (now in the library of All Souls College, Oxford) is the endorsement 'For Coll: Howe at his house in Great Stoughton, Huntingdonshire by the Kimbolton Bag'.[19]

Newspapers were mostly controlled by their printers who actively sought out profit. The end of the Licensing Act meant the demise of control over the number of printers by the Stationers' Company. The number of printers rapidly increased and many moved out of London, where hitherto very little printing had been permitted. The increase in the number of printers led directly to the foundation of provincial and of London papers. The first successful daily paper, the *Daily Courant*, began publication in March 1702, and the first provincial paper, probably the *Norwich Post*, in 1701.

A political narrative of the development of the press, however, is less than the full account. It is also necessary to look at different attitudes towards the value of news. For example, it has been argued that news and fact became more clearly linked, and were also differentiated from exemplary prose in which morality was seen as defining accuracy.[20]

A new world of printed news had been born. Newspapers were different to other forms of printed news or commentary, such as pamphlets and prints, because they were regular and frequent. They therefore offered a predictable sequence of communication for which the only real counterpart was the weekly sermon. The latter was important, and could serve for both communication and commentary on a wide range of topics, but the newspaper was very much more adaptable in content, format, and audience response. Essay papers, such as the *Review*, *Spectator* and *Tatler*, were very different in their frequency to debate by pamphlet.

This world saw qualitative and rapid quantitative growth and a diversification of type with the foundation of the first dailies and the first provincial papers; the first Sunday newspaper was not to follow until about 1779. There was also a marked growth both in the number of newspapers and in their sales. There were twelve London newspapers by 1712, when the First Stamp Act put several out of business, and about twenty-four English provincial newspapers by 1723. These included the *Newcastle Gazette*, founded in 1716, the *Kentish Post or Canterbury News Letter* (1717), the *Leeds Mercury* (1718), and the *York Mercury* (1719). The first paper in Nottinghamshire, the *Nottingham Post*, appeared in 1710, and in Derbyshire, the *Derby Post-man*, in 1720. The total annual sales in England were about 2.5 million in 1713, about 7.3 million in 1750 and 10.7 million in 1756.

Some towns, such as Bristol, Exeter, Newcastle (in 1711), Norwich and York (1725), acquired more than one title. There was often bitter local competition between the papers. The launching of the *Norwich Post-Man* in 1707 meant that there were three papers in the city, and relations with the already established *Norwich Post* and *Norwich Gazette* were hostile.[21] The *York Gazetteer* declared in 1741 that it was founded 'to correct the weekly poison of the *York Courant*', a comment on the vitality of provincial political partisanship.

Other towns where no paper was founded in the first two decades of expansion acquired one, for example Birmingham (1732), Cambridge, Chester (1721),[22] Coventry (1741), Hull (1739), Leicester (1753), Lewes (1746), Maidstone (1725), Oxford, Sherborne (1737), and Yeovil (1744).

The improvement in distribution networks helped to increase sales and to ensure that the newspaper printer, who stood at the centre of a commercial network, was better placed to sell the other goods, principally books and medicines, that he advertised and sold.

There were great similarities between the newspapers produced after the lapsing of the Licensing Act and at mid-century: the technology of newspaper production and distribution and of the transmission of news and advertisements to the press did not alter. News and advertisements were still produced without the benefit of many illustrations or maps. The most obvious difference was the increase in the physical size of the newspapers and the smaller type produced. Although, as a result of the taxation structure created by the Stamp Acts,[23] the number of pages remained fixed at four, neither the Stamp Act of 1712 nor that of 1725 put a limit on the size of the sheet that bore the tax. The 1712 Act made it possible for papers to register an entire issue as a pamphlet and thus reduce their tax liability. They were printed on a sheet-and-a-half folded into six pages, which was a significant expansion in size. The 1725 Act imposed the half-penny stamp on every half-sheet and thus made the six-page papers too expensive. Proprietors were still able to present increasingly large four-page newspapers as half-sheets, but, as a consequence of the Act, the price of most papers rose to $2d$ and the expansion in the number of titles temporarily stopped. However, the larger size of the half-sheets provided more space. Combined with a reduction in type size over the century as a whole, this led to a rise in the number of columns per page.

The importance of fiscal constraints underlined the nature of the newspaper as a commercial product, a decision that has been traced to Robert Harley, 1st Lord of the Treasury in 1712. He preferred taxation rather than the reimposition of pre-publication censorship, a choice that has been attributed to his understanding of the value of the press as a means of propaganda.[24]

Fiscal constraints were to be a more important control than that of regulation through the courts, but it was also a control the effects of which could be probed and counteracted by entrepreneurs: profitability could be enhanced by gaining more readers or increasing advertising revenues. This, however, was not similarly open to all newspapers. The low-price newspapers, such as *Parker's London News*, were more seriously affected by Stamp Duty, as their readers could not so readily bear higher prices. As a consequence, unstamped newspapers developed in London in the 1730s, several produced from the King's Bench prison by William Rayner. Precise sales figures for such papers do not exist, but the total weekly sale may have been over 50,000. This led in 1743 to legislation and action against street hawkers, the principal method by which such papers were distributed. It was effective and this sector came to an end, although there was an unstamped paper in Exeter in 1755 according to Andrew

Brice. A major unstamped press was not to revive until the following century.

As far as contents were concerned, in essence, the reader in the first half of the eighteenth century was given more of the same although, in addition, there were important developments in new directions. The news was still heavily political, the reports derivative, anonymous and impersonal. There was little role for the 'journalist', which was scarcely surprising as most newspapers were produced by a 'scissors and paste' technique, drawing heavily on other papers, generally, although not always, without due acknowledgement. This reflected a newspaper world that was less sophisticated and less capitalized than that of the late nineteenth century. The difficulty of checking items, given the slow nature of communications in the period, and the role of rumour and conjecture in a semi-closed political society, in which many politicians had a very ambivalent response towards the world of public politics, ensured that many items were inaccurate, unchecked and conjectural. There was little in-depth analysis: events were the focus of attention, and the background was rarely described adequately. Most items were short, without explanation or introduction.

Alongside the trickle-down practice of news that resulted from the 'scissors and paste' technique, there was also another aspect of 'reactive' news construction, namely the extent to which most newspapers relied on contributions from interested readers. The content and source of the material in turn generated responses, helping both to fill the newspaper and to make it more central to its readers as a way to express and debate opinions. The processes by which individual papers selected what to print from what was sent in, and their comments on it, were thus important to their particular character, offering a different form of distinction from that established by the sources of news in the 'scissors and paste' method.

Political impartiality, general utility and the satisfaction of their readers were the general goals pronounced by newspapers, whether new or well-established, provincial or metropolitan; although claims for impartiality frequently disguised pronounced political allegiances. The context was one of the competitive nature and overwhelmingly commercial pressures that shaped the development of the English press. Most newspapers were intended for profit, a truth sometimes obscured by an emphasis on those London papers that were subsidized for political ends. Most subsidized newspapers were short-lived. Although they frequently served as a source for partisan articles for other newspapers, they provide little guidance to the general character of the press, which was commercial.

The struggle to make a profit was complicated by the fiscal demands of government in the shape of Stamp Duty, which made the launching of a new title more of a speculative investment. Competition from other newspapers was more serious. By raising prices, and thus depressing demand, Stamp Duty may have served to create saturation in the market at certain junctures, as indeed did the launching of new newspapers. The *British Observator* and *Common Sense*, on 10 March 1733 and 5 February 1737 respectively, referred to there being too many newspapers.

Thus, particularly at the level of the individual paper, the picture was not necessarily one of a progressively increasing, still less profitable, market. Many proprietors could perceive through the hyperbole and rhetoric of the influence of the press, actual or deserved, the realities of competition or bankruptcy. Many failed.[25] A healthy advertising revenue was crucial for profitability, but its generation depended on a reputation for high sales. Newspapers, especially weeklies, were hit from the 1730s by the rise of the monthly magazine, of which the most famous was the *Gentleman's Magazine*. Magazines seem to have been particularly attractive to female readers, although they were far from restricted to this market. Nevertheless, by mid-century, successful weeklies or tri-weeklies sold about 5,000 copies an issue.

Commercial pressures encouraged a focus on marketing: the limitations of the wooden hand-press provided few opportunities for less expensive production. Marketing could relate to distinctive contents but, in addition, managing demand and negotiating with sales outlets, such as coffee-houses and inns,[26] was very important. Several papers, such as the first number of the *Daily Journal* (24 January 1721), referred to the coffee-houses as deluged by newspapers. Assumptions about the expectations of such outlets helped shape the product. At times, the relationship was more direct as the 'coffee men' exerted pressure. In the late 1720s, they claimed saturation and complained about the cost.[27]

Some London papers, especially the tri-weeklies, sought to generate more sales by exploiting the growth in postal services and the improvement in communications brought by turnpike roads and more regular coach services in order to sell more copies to provincial readers. Provincial newspapers increased their sales by widening their range of circulation and by seeking to monopolize or dominate newspaper sales in this region. Whereas London papers could circulate in the provinces, as part of a system of the distribution of metropolitan news, there was little demand for the opposite process.

Wide distribution circuits were claimed by provincial newspapers. The *Glocester Journal* of 24 April 1725 claimed to be distributed from Llandaff to Trowbridge, Ludlow to Wantage. *Adams' Weekly Courant* (Chester) claimed that its newsmen travelled through nine counties. *Felix Farley's Bristol Journal* of 24 September 1726 claimed a distribution in 'Devizes, Westbury, Sherbourn, Shaston, Taunton, Bridgwater and Bath'. Some claims for wide circulation can be doubted, but the listing of agents offers valuable support. In 1724, the *York Mercury* listed agents in twenty-one different towns. The *Newcastle Courant*'s claim that it was regularly distributed in the Tweed Valley was supported by its naming of agents in Berwick and Tweedmouth in the issue of 2 February 1734. The location of advertisers was also a key, especially where agents were not noted.

In contrast to the London press, provincial papers sought exclusive sway over an area, or at least a sway that was shared as little as possible. A crucial aspect of this was dominance of the advertising market, for, by acquiring all or most of the advertising of an area, it was likely that most of the newspaper readership would follow. The pressure for exclusivity was further enhanced by the expensive nature of rural distribution networks, whose real cost was lessened if they could serve all readers on a particular route. Newspapers were delivered by hand by riders who followed extensive circuits.

As a consequence, papers attacked new and established rivals. The first issue of the *Honest True Briton* noted on 21 February 1724: 'Authors and papers multiplying, give equal uneasiness to one another, like people crowded together in a stage-coach, who perhaps agree in nothing, but going the same road.'

An example is provided by the first Northampton paper, the famous *Northampton Mercury*. It provides the sole evidence of a short-lived rival, the *Northampton Journal*. The *Mercury* for 9 July 1722 carried the following article:

Northampton, July 7

The Readers of this Northampton Mercury are desired to take Notice, That the Printers hereof (R. Raikes and W. Dicey) have not thought fit to alter the Cut in their Title-Page, the Manner of Folding their Paper, nor the Day of Publishing it: But, a Sheep-skin Proprietor having offer'd to the Publick a Sheet and a Half of Waste Paper, embellished with the intended Effigie of her late Majesty Q. Anne, but more like the Wooden Head of the Artist that did it, when stuck upon Tenterhooks, and thrust it into the World under the Name of Northampton Journal, designing to make Use of the Word Northampton, as a Cloak to introduce a Novice into the Custom of some few of our Well-wishers: We therefore take the Opportunity to warn them of the Design, which cannot but be Honourable in Men of Hide-bound Principles, like the new Upstart Author, who, bigotted in himself, and nurtured in his foolish Opinion by others, has lavishly thrown away Money on a Press, more for the Consumption of Paper, than the Benefit he can pretend will accrue to him, or his. The Introduction to his first Parcel of Bum-Fodder shows forth, how much his Design tends to the Publick Good; but now, we would willingly know, Whether he that cannot write his Mother Tongue, especially when standing Candidate for Professor Theory, can, or may expect any Office or Employment in a School of Learning, unless to carry away the Excrements of those young Boys, who, barely prompted by Nature, attain to more knowledge than ever his doting Brain could yet fathom, or the Correction of a Birch Rod drive into his thick and stupid Cranium: For, if we do but peruse the last Half Sheet, published by the Noisy Animal (who, like the Fly on a Wheel, cried out, What a Dust do I raise?) we shall find, that Fifty literal Faults will not excuse the Imposition he has thrust on his Country; and, had not his 20 Correspondents (whom he mentions) in Carter Lane corrected his first sheet for him by confining his Tool of a Compositor to an indefatigable Week's Labour, in taking out Doubles and putting in Omissions, each sentence would have broke the Teeth of a Welshman before he could have uttered them, and have puzzled the nicest Wit of the Age to define their Meaning. Indeed, we are sorry for the Old Doatard, but more for the unhappy Boy of Twenty One that serves him, and is obliged to keep Silence, lest the first Word he speaks should proclaim him a F-l; and then, where will be the Distinction between an Opinionated Master, a Cypher of a Journeyman, and a Good for Nothing Salesman? Who like so many Tantalus's vexed in Hell, are hunting for that Fruit which is their continued Affliction by representing to their Eyes what they cannot obtain, as a Punishment adequate to their Past Folly and Vice.

The following issue of the paper, which appeared on 16 July, warned of another attack:

N.B. Our Readers, we hope, will not think we have forgot to answer the elaborate Epistle published in the Northampton Journal of Saturday last, by Tipling Jack, and his Man Hob; for in our next we shall most faithfully describe the Ignorance of the one, and Insolence of the other; to which will be carefully annexed, A Key to open the Brandy man's Closet Door; Or, A judicious Survey of Pasham's Irish Curiosities, with the common Defect of Literature excepted, and the ignorant Charge of that Author proved to his Disadvantage. All of which would have been inserted in this Mercury, had we had Room.

The attack appeared a week later on the front two pages of the paper.

Gentlemen, etc.
Being willing to fulfil that old English Phrase-: Be sure be as good as your Word, we have inserted a Specimen of the Curiosities contained in Pasham's Northampton Journal of July 7, and also that of the 14th, pursuant to the Notice we gave our Readers in this Mercury of the 16th, viz,
I. The Author of the aforesaid Northampton Journal, says in his Introduction to No. 1. That his Paper will be of general Use, and is designed for the Publick Good: So far we think he is right; for it is fit to wrap up Drugs, and keep Shirts clean; and this is obvious from his

insolent Treatment of most of the ingenious Men that ever engaged in Weekly Performances, whom he ridiculously lampoons with borrowed Wit, (Scandal, I should have said) not considering, that in endeavouring to expose them, he at once discovers their Beauties, and his own Imperfections.

II. As for what this Author says concerning the Reverend and Learned BEN HARRIS tho' there is no danger of this Journal's ever meriting the Pillory, or to die by the Hands of the Executioner, (for it will soon execute itself), yet, as we are credibly informed, a certain Person concerned therein will not have his Deserts, till he has been under the Hands of the latter. However, we shall not trace the Author any farther through his pyrated and dark Encomiums on those whose works, when compared with his, render them worthy of the Laurel, whilst he, the more he writes, lives least regarded, and dies most abhorred; like the noted Romish Historian Lucan, who was so bitter towards every one he spoke of, that he was call'd (as though from Rabies) Rabienus, whose Books being burned, Cassius Severus, a Reader of them, hearing of it, said, Then I ought myself to be burnt, because I have gotten them all by heart.

III. Our new Author's Notion of a Grammatical Style, evidently appears in his Paragraph about Mr Young's being robbed by three Irishmen, Two of which (says he) is taken; then he makes them Two Three; for in Page 4 he tells ye, One Carrick is committed to Newgate for the same Fact: Now you must note, Carrick was one of the Two before spoken of – That's one Curiosity, (as he says) and not to be found in any other Paper.

IV. In another Paragraph he says, This Day there was so many Ounces of Gold have been exported to Holland. – That's another of his Irish Rarieties.

V. In the single Advertisement in the last Page, he placed the Medicine in one Column, and in the Column over against it inserts these Words, the above said Cathartic, etc. but that's nothing, where Diameters are taken Perpendicularly, and so may pass for a Curiosity with the foregoing.

VI. In his Journal of the 14th, he tells us, his Readers shall meet with curious Intelligence not to be found in any other Paper; when the very first Paragraph in that Journal is the same with what was inserted from the St James's Evening Post of July 3, in the 122nd Page of this Mercury dated the 9th. But that's no Curiosity, because he is, as 'tis said, addicted to assert such Falsities.

VII. In the same Page, in a Paragraph dated from the Hague, July 6 he says, The levying of the Hundredth Penny meets with far greater Difficulty; but goes no farther, because he forgot the Reference, and so (as the Irishman said) would not put it in. That's another Curiosity.

VIII. In the 2nd Page of the said Paper is a very modest Paragraph, inserted for the Encouragement of Vice, which relates to the Shaving off from a poor Girl, that which his Compositor wants upon his Chin. IX. In the 2nd Column of the same Page he says, 'tis feared that Circumstances may facilitate the Turks Designs; which every Plough-Boy knows to be both Singular and Plural; so that must needs be a great Curiosity.

X. In the 3rd Page, in a Paragraph from Constantinople, he says; We had a Report, that the King of Persia is dead at Babylon, whether (for Whither) he had retreated after his late Retreat, instead of Defeat. That's an uncommon Curiosity, which none but himself would have made publick, had they any Value for History.

XI. In the Poem he has inserted from a most scandalous Penny Libel, which aims at the Ridiculing no less than the Commanding Officers of His Majesty's Forces encamped in Hyde Park, you'll find these Line, viz,

> But O Great Mars, why should I thus invoke thee?
> I'll cease, least (for lest) Importunities provoke thee.
> And then proceeds,
> Nor let 'em any other Ills sustain,
> That (for Than) what is fighting for thy Cause they gain.

These and the like, are the Curiosities contain'd in that signalized Paper called Northampton Journal, to which we heartily recommend all true Lovers of broken English, bad Irish, worse Welsh, no Sense, but downright Nonsense.

N.B. The Author thereof will, we hope, take this Insertion kindly at our Hands, seeing his Mistake of Literals, which in his last he affirmed was all he was guilty of: In Hopes of his doing that, and giving his Readers an Account of the Money, iron, etc. as he promised in his first, and has confronted in his 2nd by taking no Notice of the Imports and Exports,

We remain, etc.

The attacks in the *Mercury* provide a certain amount of limited information on the *Journal*. It was clearly produced by James Pasham, obviously of Irish descent. The virulence of the attacks on his provenance reflect the strident nationalism that characterized public discussion of the Celtic lands, and was to be seen in such newspaper campaigns as that of the *North Briton* against George III's Scottish favourite, John, 3rd Earl of Bute in 1762–3. Condemnation of the accuracy of other papers and of plagiarism was a commonplace of press discussion and the attacks on the *Journal* are in no way exceptional. Although the ridiculing of senior army officers might appear to characterize the *Journal* as an opposition paper, this does not in fact appear to have been the case. Given concern over

Jacobitism in 1722, it is difficult to believe that the *Mercury* would have neglected to castigate Pasham, an Irishman and therefore susceptible in popular association to accusations of Jacobitism, had there been the slightest hint that the paper had any opposition sympathies, Tory let alone Jacobite. The *Mercury* was solidly Whig in this period.

The conclusion is that the *Journal* was either Whig or apolitical, the latter being a possibility thanks to the relative absence of editorial comment in the newspapers of the period. Thus competition between the two Northampton papers would have been simply commercial and without any political dimension, a situation in no way unique, and in fact to be found on occasions between 1720 and 1750 in other newspaper centres, such as Newcastle, though political rivalry was present in other towns, such as Bristol and Norwich.

It is not clear why the second Northampton paper failed. The most probable reason, although there is no evidence to support this, was an absence of sufficient demand to enable the profitable production of two papers. This suggestion is supported by the failure in succeeding decades to produce a second paper in the town. Evidence for another second paper is not found until 1743 and the evidence for this is tenuous. According to an unsigned article, 'The *Coventry Standard* over Two Centuries', in the *Coventry Standard* of 19 July 1941, a few issues of *Jopson's Coventry Mercury* carried a Northampton imprint in the spring of 1743. However, no copies of these issues are known to survive.

Northampton and its environs could probably only support one paper in the first half of the eighteenth century. This was not surprising. Most of the towns that supported two or more rival papers had large or populous hinterlands. Newcastle papers circulated through the north-east and into Cumbria, North Yorkshire and southern Scotland. Bristol papers were helped by the absence of competition in South Wales. Northampton suffered from nearby centres of active newspaper production, particularly Stamford, Nottingham, Derby, Worcester and Gloucester. In such a situation it was understandable that a well-established paper, such as the *Northampton Mercury*, should have been able to defeat new rivals.

Although excellent work has been produced on surviving records, and the organization and, in some cases, profitability of newspapers has been greatly clarified,[28] it is still difficult to trace the pressures and impact of precarious funding, the range of material, and the demands of readers and advertisers. Possibly the small-scale nature of individual papers, combined with scepticism concerning their impact, was responsible for the relatively limited attention devoted to subsidizing or intimidating newspapers. Such a statement might appear surprising. Some newspapers were subsidized, and much excellent work has been devoted to the relationship between papers and politicians.[29] However, not all politicians were greatly concerned about the press. In addition, it can be suggested that a lack of clarity about the influence of the press increased the sense that it was influential, or that politicians sought to influence the press because it was there, but that their interest did not reflect any informed belief in its efficacy. Such a suggestion can neither be proved nor disproved, but is a possible qualification to the common thesis that political concern with the press arose from a conviction of its importance. Some newspapers indeed expressed scepticism about the influence of the press. The first issue of the *Parrot*, that of 25 September 1728, discussed:

> the Weekly Papers . . . Anybody may observe they are usually marshalled into two parties, plaintiff and defendant . . . one side accuses and aggravates with all the energy of passion and prejudice; the other excuses and palliates with an interested zealous concern. . . . Whatever the affection of these paper combatants may be to their several abettors, yet to the people it's all a sham quarrel; such partialists are never to be credited. Who can believe the clamorous Caleb [*Craftsman*], that is always croaking against a certain Great Man [Walpole], and will not allow him one single virtue.

As a result, the *Parrot* announced that it would be neutral. This did not save it from a fairly rapid demise and from obscurity, but not all such papers shared this fate, and the *Parrot*'s general point, that readers were unconvinced by newspaper wars, may well have been correct for many. The tone of some pro-governmental reporting was scarcely exciting. The *Honest True Briton* of 1 June 1724 declared:

> It must be a very great pleasure, and an entire satisfaction to every honest true Briton, to have observed, how readily and speedily the House of Commons voted and raised the necessary supplies . . . and how easily and quietly all other matters were carried through both sessions. . . . It promises perfect happiness to Great Britain; which is what the bulk of its people have chiefly to covet . . . it importing them very little who are at the head of public affairs, provided the business of the kingdom be duly and carefully attended to . . .

Such a notion of exclusion from politics was not attractive.

Instead, readers of the press were probably interested in politics. In addition, they may have enjoyed seeing figures like Sir Robert Walpole, the leading minister from 1720 to 1742, mocked in the *Craftsman*, although that does not mean that they agreed with what they read, still less that it led them to support the opponents of these ministers. Readers turned to newspapers for what they knew would be in them, and hoped to be interested and entertained accordingly. However, they were far from dependent solely on the press for the formation of their beliefs. Simply to restrict attention to the world of print, it is apparent that newspapers were only one means by which opinion and information were disseminated. Although the press reached what contemporaries considered the 'political nation', most people did not read a newspaper and many who were literate do not appear to have done so. Cost and literacy both acted as prohibitive factors, affecting the total possible readership. Furthermore, it is rarely possible for an industry to exist so that it taps all available demand.

Factors that affected the impact of the press among those who could and/or did consume the product are intangible, not least that of doubt about its value. *Lloyd's Evening Post*, a London tri-weekly, in its issue of 1 January 1762 carried an essay 'On the Authenticity of News', in which the pseudonymous Philalethes claimed:

> There is a vulgar opinion which prevails with the lower class of men, and which Sir Francis Wronghead adopts in the *Journey to London*, that there is little or no credit to be given to newspapers . . . the canaille, or mob, are, like Sir Francis, apt to swim on the surface of things, having but narrow and bounded prospects, and seeing things in a partial light. For certainly it will be granted, even by the meanest capacity, that if there were not ten to one more truths, in the news, than falsehoods, they would never be read; and though, by mistake, design, for want of information, or, what is worse, from wrong information, two or three falsehoods may have crept into a paper, this is no cause whereby to invalidate the truth of the whole; nor would a whole nation flock in crowds to places of intelligence to read the papers if they did not expect, at least, ten truths for one falsehood. To be willingly imposed upon, and to lose their time and money into the bargain, can never be the standard.

A more significant limitation for the mid-century press was its marginality to the bulk of the population. That reflected the failure to develop the inexpensive press. Unstamped newspapers were squeezed out of existence by an Act of Parliament in 1743, while the cut-price London papers of the second quarter of the century disappeared for reasons that are obscure. By mid-century, entrepreneurial printers were less important in the metropolitan press than groups of bookseller-shareholders. The latter were especially attracted by the advertising possibilities and revenues of newspapers, and this has been seen as leading to a period of commercial stability and continuity in titles.[30] The press was largely read by upper- and middle-class consumers, a readership it shared with books and magazines, in contrast to the larger, but less exalted, readership of chapbooks and ballad sheets. This was very important for the development of newspapers over the following century. Attempts to broaden the readership could be made to seem extraneous to the true character, tone or voice of the press. The commercialism that newspapers represented and focused was not that of all the literate members of the community.

The relative absence of local news in papers both underlined their importance as guides to the wider world and intermediaries with it; but also may have lessened the appeal of newspapers to those who were content essentially with the news of their communities. The only local news carried in the single surviving copy of *The Hereford Journal, with the History of the World; Given Gratis,* that of 11 September 1739, related to the price of hops at Hereford and Worcester, the price of grain at Hereford, and the nature of that year's Herefordshire hop harvest. There was no local news in the *Preston Weekly Journal* of 16 January 1740, and the only local news in the *Preston Journal* of 24 September 1742 related to shipping movements at Liverpool. Conversely, advertisements, by their nature, had to be of products or services that could be provided locally.

It is necessary to balance an emphasis on limitations with an understanding and assessment of change and particular character. Expansion was not restricted to England. There were 57 German newspapers published in 1701, 94 in 1750, 126 in 1775, and 186 in 1789. In Europe, the press both increased in circulation and number of titles in countries where it was already established, such as France and the United Provinces (modern Netherlands), and spread to other states. Comparative work is all too rare and is restricted to France and Britain,[31] but it is clear that commercialism was particularly important in the English press, and that advertising played a central role. This reflects a feature that is still essential to the English press: its capitalist or commercial nature, in marked contrast to the official or semi-official newspapers of some other countries.

A similar distinction existed in the eighteenth century. On the Continent, publishing and printing were generally activities taking place in the context of a society and economic system characterized by privileges, privileges to print news or to sell newspapers being crucial. In this context, it is not surprising that most newspapers had an official or semi-official character, a development encouraged by the extent to which there was not an autonomous political world separated from government. Governments were crucial sources of news, understandably so when developments in foreign countries were followed so closely and the nature of censorship regulations ensured that a good relationship between newspapers and the relevant authorities was sought.[32] Thus, for example, the bi-weekly *Mannheimer Zeitung* was both founded in 1767 and transformed into a four-times-a-week paper in 1792 with the backing of the Elector Palatine.

In contrast to most of the Continent and also to the situation in England in the 1660s, the eighteenth-century English press was essentially independent of government and lacked official support. The principal exception to the dominance of commercial factors, the political essay paper, were subsidized newspapers produced for specific political purposes and often without advertisements. Though of political importance, and a source of items for other newspapers, they were frequently (although not invariably) not high-selling papers, and were a feature of the metropolitan press, not its provincial counterpart.

The non-subsidized press depended for its viability on sales and advertisements. It can be discussed in terms both of the notion that England was a commercial society,[33] an approach in which the role of advertisements plays a major role, and with reference to the idea that a political world was being created in which public discussion and consideration between equals was crucial, rather than personal relationships with reciprocal links of obligation, deference and patronage. The press can be linked to commercialization and to the creation of a new civic society. Papers offered a new means for the dissemination of opinion that was not linked to the corporate ritual of urban life, with its heavy stress on group activities, the importance of anniversary celebrations, and the role of religion in defining groups and their values.

Instead of the hierarchical world of different social orders in town and country, newspapers offered a sphere in which all readers were equal. The gaze of the press was not closed to the doings of ordinary folks – for example, the long account in *Berrow's Worcester Journal* of 6 February 1766 of a local race between two naked butchers was scarcely a vision of a society defined by elite politeness – but appropriate behaviour was the ethos actively propagated, as shown in Chapter Five, and material such as this race tended to express distance from such activities, thus reinforcing a sense of separateness between newspaper readers and the lower sort. In addition, many newspapers were surprisingly open to the expression of different opinions. This owed much not only to the fact that many papers sought to maximize sales and advertisements by avoiding excessively partisan stances, but also to the extent that under-capitalized newspapers lacked reporting staffs and required the submission of material to fill some of their columns.

NOTES

1. N. Glaisyer, 'Readers, correspondents and communities: John Houghton's *A Collection for Improvement of Husbandry and Trade* (1692–1703)', in A. Shepard and P. Withington (eds), *Communities in Early Modern England* (Manchester, 2000), pp. 235–51. T. Watt, *Cheap Print and Popular Piety, 1550–1640* (Cambridge, 1991).
2. C. Blagden, 'The Distribution of Almanacks in the Second Half of the Seventeenth Century', *Studies in Bibliography* 11 (1968).
3. S. Sherman, *Telling Time. Clocks, Diaries and English Diurnal Form 1660–1785* (Chicago, 1996); K. Sharpe, *Reading Revolutions. The Politics of Revolution in Early Modern England* (New Haven, 2000).
4. H.R. Hoppe, 'John Wolfe, Printer and Publisher, 1579–1601', *The Library*

4/14 (1933), pp. 241–88; D.B. Woodfield, *Surreptitious Printing in England 1550–1640* (New York, 1973); A. Halasz, *The Marketplace of Print: Pamphlets and the Public Sphere in Early Modern England* (Cambridge, 1997).

5. J. Frank, *The Beginnings of the English Newspaper, 1620–1660* (Cambridge, Mass., 1961); F.S. Siebert, *Freedom of the Press in England 1476–1776: The Rise and Fall of Government Control* (Urbana, 1965); S. Lambert, 'The Printers and the Government, 1604–1637', in R. Myers and M. Harris (eds), *Aspects of Printing from 1600* (Oxford, 1987), pp. 1–29, 'State Control of the Press in Theory and Practice: The Role of the Stationers' Company before 1640', in Myers and Harris (eds), *Censorship and the Control of Print in England and France 1600–1910* (Winchester, 1992), pp. 1–32, and 'Coranto Printing in England: The First Newsbooks', *Journal of Newspaper and Periodical History* 8/1 (1992), 3–19; M. Frearson, 'London Corantos in the 1620s', *Studies in Newspaper and Periodical History* 1 (1993), 3–17, and 'The distribution and readership of London corantos in the 1620s', in Myers and Harris (eds), *Serials and their Readers 1620–1914* (Winchester, 1993), pp. 1–25.

6. A. Walsham, *Providence in Early Modern England* (Oxford, 1999), p. 218.

7. J.L. Lievsay, 'William Barley, Elizabethan Printer and Bookseller', *Studies in Bibliography* 8 (1956).

8. M. Harris, 'Locating the Serial: Some Ideas about the Position of the Serial in Relation to the Eighteenth-century Print Culture', *Studies in Newspaper and Periodical History* (1995), 9.

9. P.W. Thomas, *Sir John Berkenhead 1617–1679* (Oxford, 1969); M. Stoyle, *Loyalty and Locality. Popular Allegiance in Devon during the English Civil War* (Exeter, 1994), p. 32.

10. J. Frank, *Cromwell's Press Agent: A Critical Biography of Marchamont Nedham, 1620–1678* (Lanham, Maryland, 1980); B. Worden, '"Wit in a Roundhead": the dilemma of Marchamont Nedham', in S.D. Amussen and M.A. Kishlansky (eds), *Political Culture and Cultural Politics in Early Modern England* (Manchester, 1995), pp. 301–37.

11. P. Fraser, *The Intelligence of the Secretaries of State and their Monopoly of Licensed News, 1660–1688* (Cambridge, 1956).

12. J. Sutherland, *The Restoration Newspaper and its Development* (Cambridge, 1986); H.M. Weber, *Paper Bullets: Print and Kingship under Charles II* (Lexington, Kentucky, 1996). More generally, T. Harris, *London Crowds in the Reign of Charles II: Propaganda and Politics from the Restoration to the Exclusion Crisis* (Cambridge, 1987).

13. L. Rostenberg, 'Richard and Anne Baldwin, Whig Patriot Publishers', *Papers of the Bibliographical Society of America* 47 (1953), 9; T. Crist, 'Government Control of the Press after the Expiration of the Printing Act in 1679', *Publishing History* 5 (1979), 49–77.

14. L.G. Schwoerer, 'Press and Parliament in the Revolution of 1689', *Historical Journal* 20 (1979), 567, and 'Propaganda in the Revolution of 1688–89', *American Historical Review* 82 (1977), 854–8.

15. BL Add. 74245, e.g. fols. 3, 4, 7.

16. R. Astbury, 'The Renewal of the Licensing Act in 1693 and its Lapse in 1695', *The Library*, 5/33 (1978), 296–322.

17. J.A. Downie, 'The Growth of Government Tolerance of the Press to 1700', in R. Myers and M. Harris (eds), *Development of the English Book Trade, 1700–1899* (Oxford, 1981), pp. 45–50. Relevant pamphlets include, F. Gregory, *A Modest Plea for the Due Regulation of the Press* (1698), D. Defoe, *An Essay on the Regulation of the Press* (1704), and M. Tindal, *Reasons against Restraining the Press* (1704).

18. C.J. Sommerville, *The News Revolution in England. Cultural Dynamics of Daily Information* (Oxford, 1996).

19. *St James's Weekly Journal*, 19 January 1720. For other evidence of the provincial circulation of London papers, *Flying Post*, 4 April 1717; *Weekly Journal*, 30 January 1720; *Mist's Weekly Journal*, 23 April 1726; Accounts of Sir John Swinburne, Northumberland CRO. ZSW 455; Grey Longueville to Thomas Pelham of Stanmer, 28 June 1726, BL Add. 33085; K.S. Dent, 'The Informal Education of the Landed Classes in the Eighteenth Century, with Particular Reference to Reading' (Ph.D. Birmingham, 1974), pp. 147–8.

20. L.J. Davis, *Factual Fictions: The Origins of the English Novel* (New York, 1983), pp. 32–3; M. McKeon, *The Origins of the English Novel 1600–1740* (Baltimore, 1987).

21. *Peter Murray Hill catalogue*, no. 180 (1990), item 36.

22. Though see M.R. Perkin, 'A Note of the Beginnings of Letterpress Printing in Chester', *Factotum* 5 (April 1979), 6.

23. E. Hughes, 'The English Stamp Duties, 1664–1764', *EHR* 56 (1941), 234–64; J. Feather, 'The English Book Trade and the Law 1695–1799', *Publishing History* 12 (1982), 52-4.

24. J.A. Downie, *Robert Harley and the Press* (Cambridge, 1979).

25. R.L. Haig, 'The Last Years of the *Gazetteer*', *The Library*, 5/7 (1952), 242–61.

26. S.C.A. Pincus, '"Coffee Politicians Does Create": Coffeehouses and Restoration Political Culture', *Journal of Modern History* (1995).

27. Anon., *The Case between the Proprietors of News-Papers, and the Subscribing Coffee-men fairly Stated* (1729).

28. M. Harris, *London Newspapers in the Age of Walpole* (1987); K.T. Winkler, 'The Forces of the Market and the London Newspapers in the First Half of the Century', *Journal of Newspaper and Periodical History*, 11 (1988), 22–35, *Handwerk und Markt. Druckerhandwerk, Vertriebswesen und Tagesschrifttum in London 1695–1750* (Stuttgart, 1993).

29. L. Hanson, *Government and the Press 1695–1763* (Oxford, 1936); M. Harris, 'Print and Politics in the Age of Walpole', in Black (ed.), *Britain in the Age of Walpole* (1984), pp. 198–210.

30. M. Harris, 'The Management of the London Newspaper Press during the Eighteenth Century', *Publishing History* 4 (1978), 95–112.

31. S. Botein, J.R. Censer and H. Ritvo, 'The Periodical Press in Eighteenth-century English and French Society: A Cross-cultural Approach', *Comparative Studies in Society and History* 23 (1981), 464–90; B. Harris, *Politics and the*

Rise of the Press. Britain and France, 1620–1800 (1996). R. (Robert) and B. (Bob) Harris are the same person.

32. J.D. Popkin, *News and Politics in the Age of Revolution: Jean Luzac's 'Gazette de Leyde'* (Ithaca, 1989), pp. 36–45.

33. P. Langford, *A Polite and Commercial People: England 1727–1783* (Oxford, 1989). For a particularly observant critical evaluation of recent work, R. Porter, 'The new eighteenth-century social history', in Black (ed.), *Culture and Society in Britain 1660–1800* (Manchester, 1997), pp. 29–50, and, with reference to the press, B. Harris, 'Praising the Middling Sort? Social Identity in Eighteenth-century British Newspapers', in A. Kidd and D. Nicholls (eds), *The Making of the British Middle Class?: Studies of Regional and Cultural Diversity* (Stroud, 1998), pp. 1–18. See also J. Barry and C. Brooks (eds), *The Middling Sort of People: Culture, Society and Politics in England, 1550–1800* (1994) and H.T. Dickinson, *The Politics of the People in Eighteenth-century Britain* (1995). On advertisements, C. Ferdinand, 'Selling it to the Provinces: News and Commerce round Eighteenth-century Salisbury', in Brewer and Porter (eds), *Consumption and the World of Goods* (1993), pp. 393–411.

CHAPTER TWO

Politics to 1750

Are the French very strong at sea in America? and are both the Spaniards and French there distressed for want of provisions? It is long since I have been an unbeliever of the modern histories conveyed to us in sheets of paper to us humble readers, but I have no other intelligence.

John Potter, 1741.[1]

If the direct and indirect influence of newspapers was (and is) probably weaker than has generally been assumed, it is appropriate to ask why governments sought to limit press freedom. From the liberal perspective, this is generally presented in a negative light, because there has been no attempt to grasp the social and political cost of press freedom. Indeed, the modern cult of the 'open society' has further enhanced the already strong nineteenth-century tradition of judging all restrictions on press freedom as wrong, dangerous and anachronistic. Whereas exceptions used to be made in the case of sensitive areas of foreign policy, matters of national security and periods of warfare, the recent history of the American and British press suggests that self-restraint or censorship in these areas is no longer regarded as appropriate by much of the press. Furthermore, the political response to episodes where censorship has been applied suggests that these views are shared by sizeable sections of the political community.

As a result, the views of societies that have sought and seek to apply censorship have been largely ignored. Possibly this reflects a limited understanding of the precariousness of government and the fragility of stability. The assumption that a beneficial democratic consensus can be created and that those who dissent can be persuaded to accept the rules of the political game is a comforting one, and a view that leaves room for the development of an active and unconstrained press. However, it is a view that is outside the past and present experiences of many societies. Frequently the press serves for the creation of dangerous expectations or the expression of hostile views that threaten stability. An obvious example is the publication of material that helps to inculcate hostility and create disorder by defining racial and/or religious and/or linguistic identity. The infringement of privacy can also be an issue, with the 'right to know' in competition with individual reputations.

It is frequently difficult for modern readers to appreciate the rationale behind censorship, or to see it as anything other than a sinister force. This had led to a misunderstanding of past attitudes to the press, and not only to those of successive governments, who were, for example, affected by the consequences of press reporting both of domestic and of international affairs on the views of foreign powers.[2] In addition, a pessimistic interpretation of human nature could lead to a feeling that the press would naturally tend to express dangerous views that were acceptable to, and in turn fortified, negative elements of public opinion. The *Senator*, a pro-government London paper, declared in its issue of 16 February 1728:

> The natural malevolence of mankind, their idleness, their curiosity, their misfortunes, nay even their prosperity, do all most naturally incline them to listen after scandals of all kinds. The abuse of power is undoubtedly of all morsels the most delicious. . . . The author of the *Medley* was a writer of the utmost politeness, and was for that reason little read, and less admired; while the *Examiner* who knew no decency or distinction was the darling of the rabble.

These two papers had competed during the Tory ministry of Robert Harley (1710–14), a period in which a highly charged political environment and a sustained public debate about a number of contentious issues, including foreign policy, the succession and ecclesiastical issues, helped to encourage a vigorous newspaper war. This was located politically as part of the two-party politics under Queen Anne (1702–14), unlike the situation under George I (1714–27) and George II (1727–60), when the Tories were exiled to political oblivion by regal disfavour. Despite earlier Tory support for the renewal of the Licensing Act, the Tory Harley ministry preferred to restrict itself to the introduction of Stamp Duty in 1712. Harley was encouraged by the success of the Tory press, especially Jonathan Swift's *Examiner*. Its leading opponent, Arthur Mainwaring's *Medley*, argued that the Tories were foolish 'to let the *Examiner* deal in descriptions and images', but, as people frequently think in images, they were an effective means of persuasion. The *Examiner*'s strategy marginalized its opponents by stressing the values of homogeneity – a seamless, organic society – and of unanimity of opinion and action, and by presenting itself as above party.[3] The first issue of the *Monitor* reflected, on 22 April 1714, the difficulties created by the competing pressures affecting the discussion of press freedom:

> one of the methods by which the distractions of the present times have been brought to such a height has been the unprecedented liberty of the press, whereby printed pamphlets and daily papers appear in all parts of the nation; in which such provocations are given such indecencies and such expressions as no age can show the like. . . . It is one of the unhappinesses attending a free constitution

that a pernicious liberty cannot be easily restrained, and that no laws can be made to remedy it, but what shall one way or another clash with the general fund of liberty which we all desire to preserve. And therefore this evil is borne to prevent falling into a greater (viz.) that of an arbitrary administration.

Once returned to power under George I, the Whigs sought to use the law to suppress criticism that appeared dangerous. Ministerial papers regularly harped on the malevolent nature of the opposition press. The *Honest True Briton* declared in its first issue, that of 21 February 1724, that the reader:

may depend upon having, in the course of these papers, an impartial, unbiased way of writing, neither courting friends nor making enemies; the placing things in false lights shall be avoided, which seems to have been the great art, and only merit, of *some writers*, with whom (whether they speak of private persons or of public) the character of no man is safe; but scandal and calumny are dealt about like dirt, without regard to things or persons, either sacred or civil.

That was still much the case at the end of the century when papers supportive of the Foxite Whigs were criticized. Commenting on reports of the war against Tipu Sultan of Mysore, which was indeed a difficult struggle for Britain, the *World* claimed on 31 May 1791:

'No news is good news!' But the opposition reverse this totally. When there is no intelligence, they immediately spread abroad 'the spirit of misfortune'. Thus Tippoo Sultan is to cut off Lord Cornwallis.

Such comments could be dismissed as the partisan remarks of particular papers, but they also reflected the experience of eighteenth-century governments. Through their system of postal interception, there was an awareness of attempts by foreign envoys to influence the press, for example the Swedish Count Gyllenborg, who sought in 1716 to stir up opposition to Britain's Baltic policy. When Jacobitism was a significant ideological and political challenge, the expression of Jacobite material in the press was dangerous. This recurred with what was presented as Jacobinism in the 1790s. There were not only opposition elements willing to employ violence to overthrow the government, but also, in a more general sense, opposition activity that lacked guidelines as to what behaviour was legitimate. Furthermore, to complicate the response to opposition activity in the political culture of the age, the position, indeed legitimacy, of opposition was distinctly uncertain, although rather less by the late eighteenth century.

Opposition newspapers also drew attention to what they presented as the harmful impact of inaccurate press reports. During the '45, the Jacobite rebellion of 1745–6, Agricola, writing in *Old England* on 9 November 1745, complained that a failure to take the Jacobite invasion seriously had been one of the major causes of its success. He blamed inaccurate press reports of cowardice, desertion, indiscipline and mutiny among Jacobite forces for a false sense of security, a theme the paper returned to on 22 March 1746.

If it is accepted that there might be a point in censoring the press, that the free expression of news and/or opinion might be regarded as harmful for social and/or political reasons, then it is possible to regard the history of the press in a light that is not the accustomed one. Different societies and governmental systems adopt and have adopted various strategies in dealing with the issue. By avoiding the seductive trap of both dismissing their problems and their solutions out of hand, it is possible to begin a more valuable enquiry, one that proceeds pragmatically by examining the difficulties that faced particular governments in specific circumstances.

A more acute judgement of censorship also requires a different methodology. Unless the purposes that lay behind regulation of the press are appreciated, it is difficult to assess its success. The censorship of the years 1714–60 was inspired by the Jacobite threat and the existence of Jacobite newspapers, although in the late 1720s and 1730s it was powerfully stimulated by the *Craftsman*, an opposition newspaper that was not Jacobite.[4] The situation eased with the collapse of Jacobitism. This had a consequence that is less paradoxical than it might appear. Later controversies over the press in 1763–74 in part reflect the ministerial defence of an established system (if that is not too grand a term) of regulation that was no longer greatly required; or that was already controversial and was now much less easy to defend. The relative success enjoyed by those who pressed then against regulation may have stemmed in part from the lessened stress on defending the system. The perceived need had altered faster than the legal situation.

Aside from that, there was also an increase in scepticism about the direct political impact of the press. Ministerial concern about the press lessened as politicians became more accustomed to newspapers. Papers legally selling in their thousands, carrying informed political comment, advancing party views and containing pieces by eminent politicians, were an innovation to the politicians of the 1690s, whose most recent experience had been the short-lived, often hysterical pieces produced during the Exclusion Crisis. A series of innovations, principally the first daily newspaper, the *Daily Courant* (1702), the first evening paper, the *Evening Post* (1706), both London papers, and, also, the first provincial papers, encouraged a sense of developing possibilities. In 1695, the returns in the general election and the addresses in favour of supply were printed by the newly founded papers.[5]

Some politicians clearly sensed new opportunities,[6] and the medium of print was used with great effect to stir up feelings in a series of issues, such as the Sacheverell case and the conduct of Britain's Dutch allies.[7] Some papers were felt to be worth subsidizing. Politicians and newspapers could, if they wished, attribute changes to the influence of opinion 'out-of-doors', public opinion, the press, whatever best summarized the sense that something outside the world of Whitehall, Westminster and Versailles had an impact on British politics. Some politicians were not active in this sphere, and Godolphin, in particular, was not a great inspirer of printed propaganda, but as one party sponsored a paper another felt it necessary to reply. The personal political role of some writers, such as Steele, and the connections of others, such as Swift, with prominent statesmen may have encouraged greater political commitment to the press. It is, however, unclear how many politicians shared the belief expressed in June 1711 that 'it is possible to scribble these men [the ministry] down'. Queen Anne herself could see opposition literature as evidence simply 'that it was party and faction that was discontented and not the body of the nation'.[8]

As the generation of politicians, such as Addison and Steele, who had been active in the politics of Anne's reign and often written pamphlets, died, they were replaced by others with experience of Whig ministries enjoying substantial parliamentary majorities whose longevity made the opposition press appear as a mere irritant. Serious press conflict was episodic during the Pelham ministry, especially in the early 1750s.

Even so there was still a difference of opinion over press freedom throughout the century, including in the years that preceded the French Revolutionary crisis. On 6 March 1789, the *London Packet* stated:

> The liberty of the press, and freedom of opinion, have ever been esteemed the two grand bulwarks of the British constitution; when however the one is suffered to degenerate into libellous licentiousness, and the other into desperate faction, they become the most dangerous innovations on public peace and security – Yet who are more ready to raise the cry in support of these valuable privileges than those who disgrace them by the grossest abuse? As a pickpocket is always the first to cry *stop thief*!

The threatening context of newspaper criticism for at least part of the period can be considered by assessing the career of a Jacobite journalist, Nathaniel Mist. Such an assessment itself represents a rewriting of newspaper history, for the newspaper that has attracted most scholarly interest for the quarter-century beginning in 1714 is the *Craftsman*, founded by the maverick Tory Lord Bolingbroke and the opposition Whig William Pulteney in 1726, which played a prominent role in the attack upon the Walpolean regime, its ethos, composition and policies, until it was affected by internal disputes and lost direction in the late 1730s. The *London Evening Post*, an opposition 'Patriot' tri-weekly launched in 1727, has also received more attention than Mist's papers.[9]

A concentration on Bolingbroke has led to a misunderstanding of the *Craftsman* and, in particular, a tendency to overrate its influence. There has also been an underrating of the activities and importance of Mist, the leading Tory newspaper figure in the period, and one of considerable interest in the development of the press. He has been the subject of a valuable thesis, but it was never published, and is relatively unknown.[10]

Little is known about Mist's life other than his journalism, a situation that is all too common with eighteenth-century newspaper figures who, unlike Defoe, Johnson, Steele and Swift, lack obvious literary interest. As with many figures, knowledge about his journalism is restricted largely to the papers themselves, brushes with the law, and abuse from other newspapers. In Mist's case, the first have survived well, there was no shortage of the second, and there are some interesting instances of the third.

Mist's first major paper was a weekly, *The Weekly Journal: or, Saturday's Post. With Fresh Advices Foreign and Domestic.* Appearing for the first time on 15 December 1716, as a six-page, small folio paper, with two columns to the page, it cost 1½d, or 18d per quarter, the usual price for a weekly. The paper repeatedly experienced difficulties with the law. In 1717, Mist was tried for printing the details of a trial without permission, and was arrested twice for printing seditious libels. In September 1718, he was arrested, on the complaint of the Russian envoy, for his comment on the death of Peter I's son Alexis, supposedly killed on his father's orders. Mist was questioned later in the year for his attack on British foreign policy. In 1720, Mist criticized the Calvinists in the Palatinate who were being oppressed by their Catholic ruler, but were championed by George I, a policy that aroused little sympathy in Tory circles. Mist's stance led to outrage in Whig circles, William Wake, the Archbishop of Canterbury, receiving a complaint from the excitable Thomas Bray, a London cleric. Bray complained that the *Weekly Journal* and *Post-Boy* were more virulent than Jesuit pamphlets:

> writers, whose newspapers go more throughout the nation than all the others put together. What must the effect be but the poisoning the minds and alienating the affections and damping the prayers and petitions of our clergy, of our gentry, and of all other readers of those papers throughout the kingdom.[11]

Mist was found guilty of reflecting on the persecuted Protestants abroad, and sentenced to stand twice in the pillory, pay a fine, spend three months in prison, and give security for good behaviour for seven years. More trouble, arrests, fines and imprisonment followed in 1723, 1724,

1725 and 1727. In 1724, Mist's wife had a recognizance of £1,400 for-feited for her press activities. However, the paper survived.

The Stamp Act of 1725 led Mist to reduce the size and number of pages, cut out the decorative heading, increase the number of words per page and take a new title, *Mist's Weekly Journal*, beginning the numbering anew. The price increased to 2*d*, as did that of many other newspapers, but Mist fulfilled his promise to his readers that the paper would still be worth purchasing, 'that though it may suffer some diminution in quality of paper, yet it shall be as copious in matter, and as entertaining and useful, in all respects, as at any time since its first publication'.[12]

The first number of the new journal appeared on 1 May and, from the third onwards, Mist began to print his paper in three columns instead of two. *Mist's* lasted for three years before being transmuted into *Fog's Weekly Journal* in 1728. The issue of *Mist's* of 24 August 1728 was an extreme libel on George II. The frequently used device of a Persian Letter (a letter supposedly written by a Persian visitor or, in this case, about Persia) was used to praise the Pretender, 'James III'. The Jacobite envoy in Vienna, Owen O'Rourke, who read it in French, found it 'a smart piece'. On the following day, the Attorney General, Philip Yorke, later 1st Earl of Hardwicke, was ordered to prosecute Mist with the utmost severity.[13] Many of the staff of the paper were arrested, and, although the issue for 31 August appeared, it was followed by only two others: on 14 and 21 September.

The paper was presented to the Grand Jury of Middlesex 'as a false, infamous, scandalous, seditious and treasonable libel', the accusation providing fresh material for the press.[14] The French chargé d'affaires, Chammorel, thought that the use of a Persian Letter would make it difficult to use the law against the paper, as it would be necessary to prove the treasonable nature of the allegory,[15] a difficult task as ministerial legal advisors noted on several occasions.[16] The ministry, however, claimed that the item had been concerted with Jacobite leaders abroad: 'tis assured that the government had discovered that the printing of the treasonable libel in the said journal was a premeditated act, in concert with some disaffected persons abroad'.[17]

Indeed, the previous winter, Mist had fled to France after difficulties over a libel on George I,[18] leaving Edward Bingley, who had acted as a defence witness for the Jacobite Bishop Atterbury, in charge. A govern-ment informant noted that Bingley spent an evening every week with Major Bernardi, a shadowy and suspicious foreigner.[19] Mist, who spent the summer of 1728 consorting with other Jacobite exiles, such as the Duke of Wharton, in Rouen, the town where an attempt was made to print fictional pornographic memoirs of George I's estranged wife, had links with the Jacobite court in Rome. In 1733, Mist was to insert material in the British press on instructions from Rome,[20] and to provide information on events in Britain, including some fine accounts of parliamentary debates.[21]

Moves against newspapers were often held to be of limited effectiveness, serving rather to attract attention to a newspaper and to boost its circulation. A ministerial pamphlet of 1740 noted 'the great success that the most wretched performances, especially upon politics, meet with in this country, if they have the good fortune to be prosecuted'. On the other hand, receiving notice of a trial in 1704, John Tutchin of the *Observator* offered to write no more provided the case was dropped, and was released accordingly on a legal technicality.[22]

In December 1734, Yorke's successor, John Willes, was sent a seditious *Craftsman* by the Duke of Newcastle, Secretary of State for the Southern Department, and asked for his advice upon it. His reply revealed the customary caution of the Walpole ministry in dealing with the press, but he also made an exception that encouraged responses similar to those that *Mist's Weekly Journal* had encountered in 1728:

> prosecutions of this sort ought to be avoided as much as possible. For papers of this kind, if not taken notice of, seldom survive the week, and fall into very few hands; but when a prosecution is commenced everybody is enquiring after them, and they are then read by thousands, who otherwise would never have heard of them. Besides upon trials of this sort, His Majesty's enemies always take an opportunity of spiriting up the mob against the government, and let the success be one way or the other; it always affords a handle for complaint. Where His Majesty's title is called in question, or there are any insinuations in favour of the Pretender, I think that prosecutions are absolutely necessary. In other cases I am humbly of opinion that they should be set on foot as seldom as possible, and always with caution.[23]

By Willes's criteria, the ministry had no choice but to act in 1728. In a clear allegory of Jacobitism, *Mist's* had considered 'the miseries that usurpation had introduced into that unfortunate empire' and described the rightful heir, the Sophi, as possessing 'the greatest character that ever eastern monarch bore'. Praise for the Pretender was common in the 1720s and the enthusiasm that greeted the accession of George II in 1727 was speedily dissipated. However, praise in print in a regularly appearing journal that carried the name of the printer was different from comments in a public house.

In 1728, legal action was limited in its effectiveness. *Mist's* continued, albeit under a different name. Furthermore, although Edward Farley was imprisoned for reprinting the 24 August issue of *Mist's* in his Exeter newspaper, a pardon was granted posthumously in July 1729; he had died in prison in May. Newcastle explained to his colleague as Secretary of State that:

the solicitors employed to prosecute Farley the printer at Exeter, for reprinting Mist's traitorous libel of the 24th of August last, having sent up a slate of that affair, by which it seemed very doubtful whether upon a new trial he could be convicted.[24]

Whatever the limitations of the law for purposes of censorship, the government was still able to harass newspapers. On 14 September 1728, the messengers took *Mist's* from the hawkers in the streets. Stanley's newsletter reported on the same day, 'nobody dares now sell or cry them publicly, so that 'tis believed, it will be entirely suppressed'. A week later, the newsletter reported, 'Mist's Journal came out again this day, but is now become so obnoxious that nobody will sell it publicly, and few or no coffee-houses that will take it in'. The principal London sellers of the newspaper, Mrs Dodd, Mrs Nutt and Mrs Smith, were detained, and the newsletter wrote of 'Mist's Journal, which it is believed, will be entirely suppressed'. Elizabeth Nutt was sent to Newgate, and, an old lady of seventy, she petitioned Newcastle for release on bail. Fearing death, she claimed that the paper had been sold at her shop without her knowing the contents.[25]

On 28 September 1728, the paper reappeared, newly numbered and renamed as *Fog's Weekly Journal*, but it still encountered difficulties: 'Mist's Journal came out this day under the name of Fog's, but people are cautious of selling or buying it as Fog and Mist seem to be synonymous.' Government interference with the dispatch of the paper through the post was alleged.[26] However, these difficulties proved to be of limited effect,[27] an indication of the problems facing a ministry even though it was in control of the judiciary (but not until the Juries Act of 1730 of juries), and with a large parliamentary majority and acting during the recess.

Mist's resilience in tackling earlier legal difficulties, and the problems that the Walpole ministry had already encountered when dealing with hostile papers, such as the *True Briton*, had underlined the difficulty of suppressing a newspaper. It could be denied news and advertisements from ministerial sources and its foreign correspondence and internal distribution through the post could be disrupted, but the most effective course was bribery. In the early 1720s this had been employed to persuade the *London Journal* to abandon the opposition.

The fortunes of *Fog's* reveal the continued vitality of Tory journalism. The paper followed the same political line as *Mist's*, sold at the same price, and adopted the same format, although the printer, John Wolfe, had fled to France. The principal difference was that *Fog's* concentrated far more on politics and printed less of the sometimes whimsical material and of the discursive essays that had characterized *Mist's*. The stark difference in tone and content between *Mist's* and the *Craftsman* was softened. There were fewer pieces comparable to the article on kissing on 28 August 1725, or the description of a hitherto unknown

Greenland sea dog on 13 August 1726. The Jacobite slant, however, continued. On 16 October 1725, *Mist's* carried a long account of Polish politics in the 1690s and 1700s, stressing that the new German ruler, Augustus of Saxony, had been unpopular with the old nobility: the parallel with George I of Hanover was readily apparent. Nine years later, on 12 October 1734, *Fog's* reported on Sicily, recently captured by Spain from the Emperor:

> inhabitants of Sicily . . . complain loudly of their having been harassed and plundered by the Germans for these many years: that the whole wealth of the island was not sufficient to satisfy their voracious appetites; and what added to the impoverishment and misery of the inhabitants was that a very small part of the taxes raised yearly were ever spent in the island; so that all their ready money and other things of value had been transported into Germany.

Fog's and the *Craftsman* were often yoked together when the press was being considered, particularly by ministerial supporters. This possibly reflected a tendency to see them as one, combined with an attempt to discredit the *Craftsman* in the eyes of Whigs by associating it with the undoubted Toryism and Jacobitism of *Fog's*. In 1728, the Sussex estate agent of the Duke of Richmond, a ministerial Whig, complained that the local rural population was being influenced by the two papers. The following year, they were jointly accused of failing to report the ministerial defence of British West Indies trade against Spanish depredations, while in 1731 they were jointly credited with explaining the mysteries of government 'to the Crowd'.[28] On 8 January 1734, the *Corn Cutter's Journal*, a ministerial newspaper using the fictional persona of a cleaver of bunions presented an imaginary conversation in a London chophouse in which the apothecary Mr Pestle read both papers. On 29 April 1732, the first issue of a new London Tory weekly, *The Universal Spy or, The Royal Oak Journal Reviv'd*, referred to 'the great Mr. Mist, the patron of journals' and 'Mr. Craftsman, his creature, dependent and follower', as having improved Mist's 'plan of liberty'.

However, opposition newspapers frequently clashed, for reasons of policy, market or both. In 1721, Mist had leapt to the defence of the Tory, High Church University of Oxford and savaged *Terrae-Filius*, a tri-weekly paper produced by Nicholas Amhurst attacking the university, which had recently expelled him. Amhurst was to go on to edit the *Craftsman*. The *London Journal's* opposition to Walpole in 1721–2 did not prevent bitter attacks because Thomas Gordon, the writer of 'Cato's Letters' in the paper, was a Whig and a Dissenter, whose views on Tories and religious topics offended Mist.[29]

Other disputes appear largely to have reflected newspaper rivalry. Francis Clifton was a Jacobite Catholic, many of whose attitudes, such as his opposition to the Dutch, could have been expected to appeal to Mist.

At the end of 1718, he launched a Tory tri-weekly, the *Oxford Post: or, The Ladies New Tatler*, printed in London, that contained at least one item unfavourable to Mist. Clifton then became the printer of the *Weekly Medley*, a London Tory newspaper, and his relations with Mist became especially poor. On 19 September, Clifton responded to this hostility by attacking Mist for reporting the deaths of those who were either still alive or had never existed and for being lewd, and claimed that the *Weekly Medley* dealt with people of sense, while Mist, in contrast, had 'vast success among the lower class of readers', offered puns, conundrums, double entendres and crime: 'I put down no robbing paragraphs; the stage-coaches have all passed by unmolested and unrifled by my men.'

The following month, Clifton returned to the attack, again condemning Mist's lewdness, adding:

> As to politics, history and giving an account of public transactions . . . you have not a capacity to understand what they mean: You know no further art than reading, and then printing them backwards, from two or three news-letters that are written by men . . . as skilful as yourself. And your foreign accounts of sieges and battles are just as authentic and as important as your domestic fables of assaults upon stage coaches, and skirmishes of highwaymen.

The paper ended in January 1720, pointing an accusatory figure at Mist that provided interesting information on an overly neglected topic, rivalry between papers of a similar political persuasion:

> Such artifices have been used underhand to obstruct the publication of them, that when these papers have been asked for, they have been hid and refused by those persons whose business it was to vend them and others exposed to sale in their room; and large returns have been made by them, when there was a general complaint, that the number printed was too small to satisfy the demands of the town for them. I should be glad to say that professed Whigs only had a hand in endeavouring to hide works from the public, that laid open all the vile aims of Presbyterian and Whiggish principles more at large than has ever yet been done in any treatise now extant; but some who pretend themselves Tories were the men most industrious in procuring the concealment thereof from public eyes partly out of malicious, and partly out of mercenary views.

Readers were urged to transfer their loyalties to another Tory paper, the *Orphan*.[30]

The *Craftsman* and *Fog's* advocated different themes. The former's theme of a Tory-opposition Whig fusion in a new 'Country' party was antithetical to *Fog's* with the latter's hostility to the Whigs and active

defence of the Church of England against Dissenters. The parliament-
arian who best personified Mist's values, the Jacobite William Shippen,
had little time for an alliance with the opposition Whigs and distrusted
Bolingbroke, as indeed did most of the Jacobites of the period. Because
Bolingbroke, his ally Sir William Wyndham, and the *Craftsman* sought to
woo the Tories from Jacobitism into alliance with the opposition Whigs,
their activities and views were more threatening to Jacobite sympathizers,
such as Mist, than those of ministerial papers, such as the *Free-Briton*.

The two papers also served different markets. All Mist's papers, even
Fog's, retained a jaunty, lively tone removed from the cerebral jokes,
earnest and prolix essays, and thoughtful, intellectual and, at times,
rarefied style that characterized the *Craftsman*. Mist's papers were more
removed from the pamphlet style than many other newspapers such as
the *Craftsman*, *Free Briton*, or *Champion*.

This point serves as a reminder of the continuity between different forms
of propaganda that was a feature of the period. If newspapers are abstracted
for study, it must not be forgotten that they often acted as a medium for the
dissemination of verses, pamphlets, magazines, books, sermons, plays,
speeches and poetry, and could as well be influenced by them in method
and tone. Political information and opinion was not a specialized function
of the press, especially in the case of domestic news. Newspapers might
possess an advantage in immediacy, but pamphlets could be printed
speedily. Particularly in the first half of the century, pamphlets were central
to political propaganda, and vigorous pamphlet controversies, with large
numbers of Answers, Confutations, and Replies, established the subject
matter of controversy in particular years. It was only in terms of foreign
news, when there was a mass of fast-changing information to be reported,
that the newspapers were at a distinct advantage.

Furthermore, opinion, rather than events, dominated the political news
of those newspapers that specialized in politics. Instead of 'in depth
reporting', there were discursive essays on general, particularly ideological,
themes. This was a sphere in which newspapers had little advantage over
pamphlets, unless they dispensed with lengthy essays in favour of shorter
items that were often forceful or humorous. Although pamphlets and
newspapers could carry the same information and be read by the same
people, they tended to serve different markets, if only for reasons of cost.
Certain pamphlets enjoyed very large sales, but the average number of
copies printed for a single edition by William Bowyer and William Strahan
in London in the 1760s was 500. Although this figure was not too different
from that of certain low-circulation newspapers, and in particular
subsidized essay-sheets, it represents a lower figure than that of the
envisaged circulation of a successful newspaper. Pamphlets were aimed at a
smaller market and costed accordingly in order to ensure a profit.

In choosing to subsidize newspapers, politicians were therefore opting
for a larger circulation. Subsidized pamphlets were intended for

distribution to a readership that was to a great extent already known and well informed, such as parliamentarians, office-holders, and British and foreign envoys, who, through being largely in London, presented minimal problems of distribution. In contrast, newspapers were designed for a substantially unknown and unquantified readership, whose political awareness, susceptibility and impact could only be guessed.

Mist's papers sold well: 10,750 copies of the issue of 24 August 1728 were printed.[31] On 30 August 1718, the *Weekly Journal* printed a letter comparing its readership favourably with the *Flying Post*:

> Let the Stamp-Office be your register, there let it appear how many readers he may be supposed to have? Whether you do not publish more thousands than he does hundreds, and whether his numbers increase or decline? Let him boast, if he can, how many of this trumpery the world takes off, and let his bookseller show the accounts of his waste paper. How many reams of his laboured slanders have gone to the more useful application of pastry cooks and chandlers?

Mist's Whig rivals did not attack him for being unread. In 1736 Mist returned to London and resumed a more direct role in his newspaper. It did not become a ministerial paper, and there is no evidence that he received any money, but it became neutral. It was suggested in 1740 that dissatisfaction with the unwillingness of his subordinates to remit him money led to his decision to return,[32] but it is equally possible that ill-health played a role: Mist was to die in 1737.

By then *Fog's* was nearly at an end. The newspaper had lost energy by 1736, as indeed had most of the newspapers of the early 1730s, including the *Craftsman*. The ministry decided in 1735 to end three of its newspapers – the *Daily Courant, Free Briton,* and *London Journal* – and unite their talents in a new paper, the *Daily Gazetteer*. No such comprehensive reorganization took place in the opposition press. New papers arose, although far fewer than in the 1710s, and *Common-Sense* and the *Champion* enjoyed considerable success. The *Craftsman* limped on, a shadow of its former self. Mist's last issue of *Fog's* appeared at the end of May 1737. The printer of the paper, John Purser, decided to keep the paper alive. The author, John Kelly, was paid a guinea weekly by Purser for writing the essays in *Fog's*,[33] but the sixth issue led to legal action which, combined with a probable failure to enjoy large sales, led to the end of the paper. Mist's return paralleled Bolingbroke's departure for France in 1735 which reflected his disenchantment with the opposition and his fears of ministerial action.[34] Personal factors were matched by despair with the political situation.

This focus on *Mist's* is a deliberate attempt both to query the standard narrative of newspaper politics, with its emphasis on the *Craftsman,* and to throw light on the ministerial view that government action was necessary. The support in certain newspapers for legitimist, rather than legitimate, opposition was a challenge to the stability as well as the political culture of Whig rule. This point can be underlined by considering the *National Journal; or, the Country Gazette,* a tri-weekly London newspaper launched in March 1746 by George Gordon and of interest as the sole Jacobite paper active in England during the '45. The printer, John Purser, was not marginal to the press world, but had earlier produced the revived *Fog's,* as well as *Common-Sense.* The Pretender had always been hesitant in his approach to propaganda,[35] and a proposal in 1743 that he should subsidize a newspaper to be established by Gordon had come to nothing.[36]

The objectives of the paper appeared in the issues of 23, 25, 27 and 29 March, and indicate what it was believed necessary to promise in a period when relatively few new papers were launched:

> Lest any of our fellow-labourers in this way, should look upon a new paper with the envy of a rival, we take this opportunity to assure them, that we will be upon honour not to incroach upon their province. Let them falsify, palliate and disguise. Let them tell of battles in the clouds, or of complete victories without a battle, they have our free consent; provided always, and be it hereby provided that we have the liberty to relate actions and occurrences fairly and truly as they happened, and that in translating articles from foreign gazettes, we be also allowed to give them to the English reader verbatim, without attention or defalcation, anything in the late and present practice of our contemporaries to the contrary notwithstanding.

The first issue sought to show how the news published in other papers was false. It accordingly commented on one such piece 'an extract of a letter from a foreign minister at Paris' devoted to Russian and French policy. The *National Journal* commented:

> It were to be wished that this foreign minister, or whoever assumes that name, had told us how he came at the knowledge of what M. d'Allion wrote, or Cardinal Tencin said; for no court can keep such things more secret than the court of France does. It may be true that the fate of England will absolutely determine that of Europe, but it is not probable that there is any faction at such an absolute court as that of Russia, and much less that the English faction can gain the ascendant, whilst the Holstein family has any sway at that court.

The issue of 27 March mocked accounts of a reported victory over the Jacobites in the Highlands. The issue of 1 April contained a number of items that cast doubt on the veracity of pro-ministerial accounts and specifically of reports from Scotland unfavourable to the Jacobites. The paper also suggested that Fort William had fallen to the Jacobites. An essay on fiction and falsehood declared:

> Ministers of State are so fond of irony and hyperbole, that they have introduced them into all business. If you impartially examine the memorials, manifestoes, speeches etc. of several years past, you will find they are made up entirely of those two figures. I never read over many newspapers, but I fancy myself at an auction, and it is a pleasure to me to observe that ambition of their authors, in contending to excel each other in the marvellous and improbable; when one of these writers celebrates the valour of a body of troops that never had a shot fired at them, or tells you of an action of a thousand men of a side, wherein the party that had the advantage had five or six hundred killed, a great many more wounded and the rest taken prisoners, I lament that some prize is not appointed for those that excel in this kind of writing, and that such a genius should not be rewarded according to his merit.

The flow of Jacobite propaganda was matched by attacks on critical reports that throw light on techniques that were indeed practised:

> This is one of the Hague letters printed here, and probably first written as well as printed here; but every reader of common sense will observe that it is ridiculous for a common news writer to pretend to give an account of a private conference between three principal ministers of state (8 April); reports of Pitt's speeches in magazines, it is well known, have received their embellishments from the hands of the publisher (1 May).

News of the Jacobite defeat at Culloden reached London on 23 April. The previous day, the paper had commented on a tale of remorse among the lower orders with the reflection 'Among the lower sort of people conscience, we find, has still some effect, but the higher sort murder their mother country without any remorse'. The following issues criticized the violence of the London celebrations over Culloden (26 April) and claimed that Cumberland had refused quarter at the battle (29 April). Subsequent issues maintained the paper's thrust, attacking British foreign policy, Hanover, the Dutch, the accuracy of reports in other papers, government propaganda, and turncoats.

Despite the lack of many advertisements, the *National Journal* cut its price on 13 May from 2*d* to 1½*d*, the usual price for an evening paper, possibly because its sales were good, as it claimed in the issue of 13 May. Four days later, the paper made it clear that it was concerned about the law, when it reported that it had received a letter 'but as the satire rises a little too high, we hope the ingenious author will excuse our inserting it'.

The newspaper continued to publish Jacobite propaganda. On 3 June, a speech by a Presbyterian minister to James II on his granting liberty of conscience in 1687 was printed, followed by a letter on 5 June asking why no wounded had been captured at Culloden. A front-page essay on 7 June discussed the Catiline conspiracy and Britain, making it clear that the Jacobite rising had been headed by some of the country's most old-established nobility and that it had been a reaction to the general indifference to the good of the community. The same issue praised the bravery of Charles Edward and his troops at Culloden and declared that most press reports of the battle were false. An essay on 10 June, sympathetic to James II and James III, suggested that Jacobites would not celebrate the birthday of the latter:

> they will find too much cause, I fear, to give a check to their mirth, when they behold their country, at home, enervated with luxury, involved in an excessive national debt, and in danger of being enslaved by corruption; and abroad, bullied by our enemies, deserted by our allies, and engaged in a foreign expensive war on the Continent, especially since they are so weak as to attribute all these calamities to the exclusion of him, whom they call, the right and lawful king.

The issue of 12 June carried a letter from 'A true modern Whig' defending the killing of the wounded at Culloden, asserting the need to wipe out all the Scots, and calling for the slaughter of all Jacobite women of childbearing age. Tory prejudices were expressed in the issue of 21 June which described the unprovoked murder of an apprentice by his master near Cheadle:

> The following instance of the terrible effects of religion, not under the direction of reason, comes from a gentleman of undoubted credit . . . Joshua Leah hath been for some years a constant and zealous follower of the field-preachers [Methodists], and the only apology that can be made for him, is that he was driven mad by those seducing vagrants, and that he committed the execrable and hellish action in a fit of enthusiastic frenzy.

The *National Journal* provides a good guide to some of the themes of Jacobite propaganda in 1746. Its praise for the Stuarts had to be tempered, but traditional Tory themes, such as hostility to the Dutch, corruption and nonconformists, were well represented, and it was not surprising that the paper ended in early June when the printer was removed to Newgate.[37] This was not the end of Jacobite journalism: the *Mitre and Crown* of 1748–50 was followed by John Baptist Caryll's *True Briton* of 1751–3. There had also been Jacobite voices in the provinces, especially in the *Norwich Gazette* and the *Chester Courant*.[38]

Most press criticism was not Jacobite in sympathy or content,[39] and certainly not during the '45, when the majority of newspapers vigorously attacked the Jacobites, and the press played an important role in creating the illusion that most of the population had sunk their differences in a spontaneous display of loyalty.[40] However, the existence of a Jacobite critique affected the debate over press regulation, and thus had a disproportionate impact. Rather than treating it as marginal, it is necessary to appreciate the degree to which the effective end of Jacobitism in mid-century changed the basic assumptions underlying public debate. The '45 also led to a demand for news that encouraged the foundation of three new provincial newspapers, the *Eton Journal, Sussex Weekly Advertiser* and *York Gazetteer.*

Successive governments also took action against non-Jacobite opposition newspapers, for example the *London Evening Post* in 1755.[41] Such action did not prevent the publication of a range of critical material that surprised foreign commentators. There were particularly savage assaults on the Walpole government during the Excise Crisis in 1733 and over supposed weakness in the face of Spanish treatment of British trade in 1738–9. Much of this material assumed that support for the government was itself worthy of condemnation. In the run-up to the Yorkshire by-election of January 1742, the *York Courant*, the leading newspaper in the region, carried a letter from J.S. of Leeds attacking one of the candidates, Cholmley Turner, for having voted for ministerial measures, including the Convention of the Pardo, an unsuccessful attempt to settle differences with Spain. A week later, anonymous friends of Turner replied claiming that the opposition was using the Convention as 'a cant word, adopted without meaning, and echo'd out amongst the people to influence and abuse them'. Turner won, although Walpole was to resign within a fortnight.[42] Nevertheless, despite a reconstitution of the government, the ministerial Whig 'Old Corps' did not lose power.

The change in government was the occasion for a rare instance of evidence of a complaint being made without recourse to law by private individuals about a newspaper item. Such complaints were probably frequent in what was very much a face-to-face society, but evidence of them is limited. Charles, Lord Mohun, a noted duellist, rewarded John Dyer for his comments with a severe beating. The Duke of Marlborough wrote to Harley in 1706 demanding protection from the *Observator* and threatened that if none was forthcoming he would have the printer's bones broken. In 1707, the printer John Tutchin did indeed die shortly after being attacked. During and after the 1713 election, William Thompson MP raged at Abel Roper for alleging in the *Post Boy* that his property was not such as to come within the terms of the Landed Qualification Act. He demanded a published retraction, threatening supposedly to cut Roper's throat if he did not comply. Five years later, Mist complained about an attempt to intimidate him into retracting an article concerning the indecent behaviour of some women in church. In 1719, 'one Boyer, a French news writer, and author of the Political State, having reflected on the Earl of Dundonald, a gentleman corrected him very severely in a coffee-house, the Frenchman not offering to draw his sword'. In January 1728, the printer of the *London Journal* was beaten up as punishment for an advertisement. This led a correspondent of the *Evening Post* to condemn the attack on Wilkins, adding that 'even in cases of sedition, the government proceeds only according to the known rules of law, and with all possible regards to the liberty of the subject'.[43] An attack in the dark by some hired bullies could be both effective and safe. The frequency and effects of such action are unclear. They belong partly to the world of private action, one in which individuals paid both for puffs and to avoid criticism, and to that of political life, in which hired mobs could be employed for violence and intimidation on occasions such as elections. The *Daily Gazetteer* might suggest on 27 October 1738 that opposition satirists should be 'clubb'd or rather bastinadoed', but governments preferred to use the legal violence of raids by messengers of the press, rather than extra-legal methods.

Algernon Seymour, Earl of Hertford, a prominent placeholder, was asked in 1742 by the new chief minister, Lord Carteret, to surrender his colonelcy of the Royal Horse Guards and to accept the prospect of another regiment. Refusal led to dismissal, and Hertford resigned his other posts. His son-in-law, Sir Hugh Smithson, Tory MP for Middlesex, sought to make political capital, and sent an item to the *Daily Advertiser*. It is noteworthy that Smithson should employ a newspaper for such a purpose, although, with a seat at Tottenham and sitting for Middlesex, he was hardly a typical member of the gentry. The Middlesex electorate was highly politicized and candidates were accustomed to placing items in the London press during elections.

The rationale of the *Daily Advertiser* was advertising revenue, and Smithson's item could be seen as an attempt to politicize its reporting: not only was he presenting his father-in-law in a correct light but also suggesting that the new government was a continuation of that of Walpole, who had had critical army officers dismissed, and should be rejected by the Tories. The traditional world of aristocratic honour interacted with that of public politics and also with the impact of the state. The paper's response indicated the atmosphere of constraint that was the most effective means of influencing the content of the press for the government. In her diary, Frances, Lady Hertford, recorded on 1 March 1742:

> Sir Hugh told me that he had sent a paragraph to the *Daily Advertiser* to say that 'the week before, the Earl of Hertford etc. an old experienced general officer who had served the Crown upwards of thirty four years had been turned out from the command of the Royal Regiment of Horse Guards Blue; upon which he had resigned his

Governments of Minorca and Tinmouth Fort, the Lord Lieutenancy of Sussex, and Custos Rotulorum of Wiltshire'. He was induced to have this inserted by finding that the ministry had industriously spread a report that my lord had resigned his regiment.

Tuesday March the second
When the newspaper came in we found the paragraph which Sir Hugh had directed to be inserted; but the words *turned out* changed to that of resigned. My Lord and Sir Hugh were both very much displeased with this alteration and sent to one of the proprietors to stop its being inserted in the evening papers, and to insist upon their rectifying the mistake in the *Daily Advertiser*, the next morning.

Wednesday March the third
The *Daily Advertiser* came in, without any mention of his name or acknowledgement of a mistake. He then sent once more to ask the meaning of it? and to say he would positively have them set the thing in a true light. The answer they returned was that they dare not insert it no otherwise if he would lay them down five hundred pounds. Upon this Sir Hugh Smithson went himself to a proprietor of the paper to assure him that my Lord would bring them before the House of Lords if they would not retract the falsehood they had published. The man seemed frightened, and said he had done what he could but the printers were afraid to do it. Sir Hugh then asked what they were afraid of, and whether he believed they had received orders to misrepresent My Lord Hertford's case? He answered he must not pretend to make any guesses, but there appeared something uncommon in the obstinacy of the printers upon this occasion, however he would try once more whether he could prevail with them to alter it the next day.

Thursday March the fourth
The *Daily Advertiser* came in again, without the least notice of what my Lord had sent to them; as soon as he was up, he bid me write a note to Mr. Harding (the proprietor whom Sir Hugh had spoken to) to send the printer to him immediately. Which I did, and Harding sent word that the man lived a great way off, but he would bring him in as soon as he could meet with him.

About five in the evening they brought us word that Mr. Harding had brought the printer, they were immediately called in, and my Lord (with a great deal of passion) asked what they meant by inserting a lie in their paper, and then refusing to retract it? The man said he was sorry he had offended him but that they always used the word resigned on those occasions, and were afraid to put it in otherwise. My Lord asked what he was afraid of, and whether he had received orders to the contrary?

To this he made an evasive answer, and said he would own his mistake in the paper the next day if his Lordship would order it so; my Lord said he would give him an order under his hand if he desired it.

The man told him that was unnecessary, he would take his word of honour. Upon which my Lord told him he might also take his honour that if that paragraph was not contradicted he would bring him (and all who had any concern in the paper) upon their knees to the bar of the House of Lords. As the man went out of the room my Lord perceived that he had a sword by his side upon which he asked Harding whether printers wore swords now. He said he was not the printer but Mr. Vanderesch Deputy Master of the Mint, and the original proprietor of the paper.

Friday fifth
The *Daily Advertiser* came in this day with a paragraph to say that the writers 'were misinformed as to my Lord Hertfords having resigned the Blue Regiment, having since been assured from his Lordship that he was removed from the command of it and (we insert this by his Lordship's direction) that he has resigned all his other employments'.[44]

This parenthesis was awkward enough, and clearly inserted for fear of ministerial anger. Hertford's remark about swords was a sign of the ambivalent social position of those involved in newspaper production, while the entire episode is a reminder of the sensitive position of newspapers that are not usually seen as politically prominent.

More generally, the political system constrained the options for legitimate opposition. In its essay of 6 April 1728, the *Craftsman* presented the fictional history of a Persian kingdom as an allegory of British developments. In this account, the rule of the chief minister lasted until royal intervention: 'till the complaints and cries of the people (which were now grown almost universal) reached the court and pierced the ears of a most indulgent Prince'. Neither George I nor George II knew that plot, and the success of the government in the 1734 and 1747 general elections indicated the limitations of opposition campaigns. The capacity of the press to shape the course and nature of political life was less powerful than is generally appreciated.

Yet, at the same time, the press was dependent on public interest in political news and some politicians sought to influence press coverage. In particular, some opposition figures drew attention to criticisms of government in Parliament.[45] On occasion, newspapers also sought to inform electors of the actions of MPs.

Aside from domestic politics, there was strong interest in foreign news, especially, but not only, when Britain was at war. Cheap papers carried nearly as much foreign news as their more expensive counterparts. The headpiece of the *London Farthing Post* depicted four hawkers shouting

'Great News', the second 'From Spain', the third 'From France', and the fourth 'From Holland'. There are numerous suggestions in the London press of foreign news being read by men of unexalted social status. The *English and French Journal* of 12 September 1723 referred to a tobacconist reading press reports about Russo–Swedish relations in a coffee-house. The *St James's Evening Post* of 1 September 1726 reported that 'on Monday night a barber and a porter being discoursing of the present posture of affairs in Europe, at an alehouse in Chancery Lane, they quarrelled . . . the porter stabbed his antagonist . . . so dangerously that his life is despaired of'.

When newspapers sought to advertise their value and to obtain more readers, they often stressed the quality of their foreign news, as in 1728 when the *Post Boy* became a daily.[46] The limited amount of domestic news in many papers was commented upon[47] and, given the relationship between newspapers and their readers, this presumably reflected reader demand as much as the factors affecting the availability of news. The pro-government *London Journal* in its issue of 6 November 1731 referred to 'the close alliance with France, which the writers against the court own to be the chief cause of their papers, and that which gave rise to their numerous productions'. A reader's letter published in the *Newcastle Courant* of 3 March 1733 may have indicated the inclinations of a large cross-section of his fellows when he urged the author to 'by no means let a rhapsody upon the Test Act jostle the Emperor and his dominions out of your comment'.

The press developed and sustained public interest both in foreign affairs and in foreign policy, giving an added depth to political debates in London. Such interest and its link with the culture of print was not new,[48] but its tempo increased with the growth of the press. So also did the interest displayed in peacetime. Thanks to the press, the diaries of a Derbyshire cleric and a Somerset doctor could include references to European affairs,[49] and the political nation became fairly well informed about the wider world and the issues in British foreign policy.

This was especially so in wartime. Edward Owen, printer of the *Gazette*, looked back to the experience of conflict with first Spain and then also France in 1739–48, when in 1757 he commented on the new Stamp Act which led him to put up his prices:

which high price will doubtless diminish the sale, and greatly reduce it, I am certain, in time of peace; for in war time we always keep up a little; for though there is scarce ever anything in it, yet the continual lies that are thrown out by the other papers, keep up the expectations of the people, who are eternally damning the printer for not giving them more news; and some times, when there has been great expectations, they have not only broke the windows, but threatened to pull down the house.[50]

Interest in foreign news was mocked by some writers. The *Plain Dealer* of 13 July 1724 printed a letter from Thomas Tiresom who had gained money by 'selling out my India stock very seasonably upon this melancholy story that is whispered about, so cautiously, condemning the Great Mogull's entering into an alliance against Prince Tockmas, and the Czar of Muscovy'. Other news made him fearful for South Sea stocks. Such items reflected the role of commercial matters in interest in the wider world, but this interest also drew on wider currents of concern and fascination.

If the direct influence of the press was limited, it offered the possibility of pluralism of opinion and public debates that challenged any notion, contemporary or scholarly, of ideological coherence or homogeneity. This point offers a qualification to the argument that the Tory-patriot opposition of the 1730s and 1740s galvanized and directed a national political critique of Whig ascendancy.[51] Instead, it was in the nature of the dynamic relationship between press and public that, just as some publications challenged elite hegemony, government authority, and/or social practices, so many others did not. A relatively unfettered press promoted the diffusion of conservative as well as radical opinions.

NOTES

1. Potter to Sir Robert Wilmot, 25 February 1741, Matlock, Derbyshire Record Office, WH 3429, pp. 272–3.
2. For example S. Burrows, 'Culture and Misperceptions: the Law and the Press in the Outbreak of War in 1803' [with Napoleon], *International History Review* 18 (1996), 793–818.
3. F.H. Ellis (ed.), *Swift vs Mainwaring: The Examiner and The Medley* (Oxford, 1985).
4. P. Hyland, 'Liberty and libel: government and the press during the succession crisis in Britain, 1712–1716', *EHR* 101 (1986), 875–88.
5. H. Horwitz, *Parliament, Policy and Politics in the Reign of William III* (Manchester, 1977), p. 157.
6. Harley to Godolphin, 9 August 1702, L. Hanson, *Government and the Press 1695–1763* (Oxford, 1936), p. 93.
7. D. Coombs, *The Conduct of the Dutch. British Opinion and the Dutch Alliance during the War of the Spanish Succession* (The Hague, 1958).
8. H. Snyder, 'Arthur Maynwaring and the Whig Press, 1710–1712', in P. Haas et al. (eds), *Literatur als Kritik des Lebens* (Heidelberg, 1975), p. 127; P. Roberts (ed.), *Diary of Sir David Hamilton* (Oxford, 1975).
9. The best introduction is S. Varey (ed.), *Lord Bolingbroke: Contributions to the Craftsman* (Oxford, 1982). See also his 'The Craftsman 1726–1752: An Historical and Critical Account' (Ph.D. Cambridge, 1976), and 'The Publication of the late *Craftsman* 1739-40', *The Library*, 5/33, 6/2 (1979–80), 230–3, 220–2. For the *London Evening Post*, G.A. Cranfield, 'The *London Evening Post*,

1727–1744: A Study in the Development of the Political Press', *Historical Journal* 6 (1963) and 'The London Evening Post and the Jew Bill of 1753', ibid, 8 (1966); B. Harris, 'The *London Evening Post* and Mid-eighteenth-century British Politics', *EHR* 110 (1995). For the ministerial press, S. Targett, 'Government and Ideology during the Age of Whig Supremacy: The Political Argument of Walpole's Newspaper Propagandists', *Historical Journal* 37 (1994), 289–318 and '"The Premier Scribbler Himself": Sir Robert Walpole and the Management of Public Opinion', *Studies in Newspaper and Periodical History* (1994), 19–33. For the press as a whole, M. Harris, 'Print and Politics in the Age of Walpole', in Black (ed.), *Britain in the Age of Walpole* (1984), pp. 189–210.

10. A.S. Limouze, 'A Study of Nathaniel Mist's Weekly Journals' (Ph.D. Duke, 1947). See also J.E. Evans and R.B. Lake, 'Publication of the *Censor*', *Notes and Queries* 228 (1983), 38.

11. Bray to Wake, 16 April 1720, Christ Church Oxford, Wake papers, vol. 264.

12. *Mist's Weekly Journal*, 24 April 1725.

13. Vienna, Haus-, Hof-, und Staatsarchiv, England, Varia 8, fol. 212; PRO, SP. 36/8, fol. 74.

14. *Post Boy*, 3 September 1728.

15. AE, CP, Ang, 363, fol. 156.

16. PRO, SP, 36/19, fol. 102, 36/30, fol. 345; Hertford, CRO, Panshanger papers, D/EP, F193, fol. 90.

17. *Ipswich Journal*, 14 September 1728.

18. *Mist's Weekly Journal*, 30 September 1727; *Read's Weekly Journal*, 20 January 1728.

19. PRO, SP, 36/5, fol. 184.

20. RA, 160/85, 168, 143.

21. RA, 159/155.

22. Anon., *An Historical View of the . . . Principles, Characters, Persons etc. of the Political Writers in Great Britain* (1740), p. 13; *Loyal Observator revived; or Gaylard's Journal*, 16 February 1723; PRO, SP, 84/378, fol. 227; on Tutchin, R.B. Patterson, *Robert Harley and the Organization of Political Propaganda* (Ph.D., Virginia, 1974), p. 74. For arrest warrants, [P.C. Webb, ed.], *Copies taken from the Records of the Court of King's Bench at Westminster; The original Office-Books of the Secretaries of State, remaining in the Paper, and Secretaries of State's Offices, or from the Originals under Seal. Of Warrants issued by Secretaries of State, for seizing persons suspected of being guilty of various Crimes, particularly, of being the Authors, Printers and Publishers of Libels, from the Restoration to the present Time* (1763). For an emphasis on the vigour of ministerial repression, J.C.D. Clark, *Samuel Johnson. Literature, Religion and English Cultural Politics from the Restoration to Romanticism* (Cambridge, 1994), pp. 147–9.

23. PRO, SP, 36/33, fol. 147.

24. PRO, SP, 43/79, fols. 102, 109–10.

25. *Farley's Bristol Newspaper*, 21 September 1728, *Ipswich Journal* 21, 28 September 1728; PRO, SP, 36/161, fol. 19.

26. *Original Mercury, York Journal: or Weekly Courant,* 1, 8 October 1728, *Farley's Bristol Newspaper,* 12 October 1728, *Leeds Mercury,* 8 October 1728.

27. AE, CP, Ang., 363, fols. 178, 181.

28. Earl of March, *A Duke and his Friends* (2 vols, 1911) I, 165; *London Journal,* 19 July 1729; Anon., *Sir Robert Brass: or, The Intrigues, Serious and Amorous, of the Knight of the Blazing Star* (1731), p. 14.

29. *Weekly Journal,* 15, 22 April, 13 May, 9 September 1721, 13 October 1722.

30. *Weekly Medley,* 3, 10 October 1718, 23 January 1720.

31. Limouze, '*Mist's Weekly Journal*', p. 13.

32. *Historical View,* pp. 19–20.

33. PRO, SP, 36/41, fols. 206, 240.

34. H.T. Dickinson, *Bolingbroke* (1970), pp. 245–6.

35. P. Chapman, 'Jacobite Political Argument in England, 1714–66' (Ph.D., Cambridge, 1983). For the background, P.K. Monod, *Jacobitism and the English People, 1688–1788* (Cambridge, 1989).

36. M. Harris, *London Newspapers in the Age of Walpole: A Study in the Origins of the Modern English Press* (1987), p. 131.

37. For cautious praise of Charles Edward in Eliza Haywood's journal the *Parrot* (August–October 1746), C. Ingrassia, *Authorship, Commerce, and Gender in Early Eighteenth-century England* (Cambridge, 1998), pp. 122–6.

38. J.B. Williams, 'Henry Crossgrove, Jacobite Journalist and Printer', *The Library,* 3/5 (1914), pp. 206–24; *Manchester Vindicated: Being a Compleat Collection of Papers Published in Defence of that Town, in the 'Chester Courant'* (1749). For a discussion of the extent of Jacobitism in the *London Evening Post,* B. Harris, 'The *London Evening Post*', *EHR* 110 (1995), esp. 1133, 1142–3, 1153–4.

39. R. Harris, *A Patriot Press: National Politics and the London Press in the 1740s* (Oxford, 1993); K.T. Winkler, *Wörterkrieg. Politische Debattenkultur in England 1689–1750* (Stuttgart, 1998).

40. R. Jarvis, *Collected Papers on the Jacobite Risings* (2 vols, Manchester, 1972) II, pp. 3–35; B. Harris, '"A Great Palladium of our Liberties": the British Press and the 'Forty-Five', *Bulletin of the Institute of Historical Research* (1995), 67–87, and 'England's Provincial Newspapers and the Jacobite Rebellion of 1745–1746', *History* 80 (1995), 5–21. On the illusion, p. 16.

41. J. Horden, '"In the Savoy". John Nutt and his Family', *Publishing History* 24 (1988), 18.

42. For rival newspapers and the general election in Newcastle in 1741, W.A. Speck, 'Politics and the Press', in M. Harris and A. Lee (eds), *The Press in English Society from the Seventeenth to Nineteenth Centuries* (1986), pp. 61–3.

43. J. Oldmixon, *History of England* (1730–5), II, 95; HMC, *Bath* I, 105–6; *Weekly Journal,* 11 October 1718, 4 April 1719; *Evening Post,* 3 February 1728; *Weekly Remarks,* 3 March 1715.

44. Frances, Lady Hertford, diary notes, Alnwick Castle, Northumberland papers, vol. 114.

45. C. Jones, 'Opposition in the House of Lords: Public Opinion, Newspapers

and Periodicals 1720–23: Lord Cowper's Campaign of Protests', *Journal of Newspaper and Periodical History* 8 (1992), 51–5.

46. *Post Boy*, 29 August 1728.

47. *Grub Street Journal*, 12 December 1734.

48. See, for example, S.C.A. Pincus, *Protestantism and Patriotism: Ideologies and the Making of English Foreign Policy, 1650–1685* (Cambridge, 1996).

49. V.S. Doe (ed.), *The Diary of James Clegg of Chapel-en-le-Frith 1708–55* I (Derbyshire Record Society, 1978); E. Hobhouse (ed.), *The Diary of a West Country Physician* (1934).

50. Owen to Edward Weston, 'Writer' of the *Gazette*, 26 March 1757, Weston.

51. K. Wilson, *The Sense of the People. Politics, Culture and Imperialism in England, 1715–1785* (Cambridge, 1995), pp. 436–7.

CHAPTER THREE

Balancing the Contents

We are sorry that the great overflow of advertisements this week will, of necessity, oblige us to postpone till next week, such as come late, and are not restricted to the present moment; and in this, we trust, we shall stand excused, as, in justice to our numerous readers, we deem it our indispensable duty to give every material article of general and provincial news that occurs.

Salisbury and Winchester Journal, 29 March 1790

We are obliged to postpone the continuation of the Hints on Geography *and the Extract of Mr. Whittacker's Remarks, on account of the important communication in the third page respecting the insurrection at St. Domingo, and other temporary matter.*

Wheeler's Manchester Chronicle, 18 February 1792

The four-page format of most of the eighteenth-century press, and, more generally, the cost constraint on length encouraged by newspaper taxation, increased the problems of balancing conflicting demands on newspaper space, and this remained an issue as the number of pages increased in the nineteenth century. At times, editors explained this process of selection, but usually such decisions were not discussed or explained, and the pressures affecting content can only be gauged from the surviving copies. These are a source that provide little indication of the ease with which items were obtained, a critical factor at a time when most newspapers could not afford any special reporting facilities. As newspapers grew in the number of words with more columns and smaller print, even when within the four-page format, the potential material that could be included also increased. There were more foreign, colonial, London and provincial papers from which to derive items, a growth in advertisements, the development, albeit seasonal, of regular parliamentary reports, and, thanks partly to the magazines, a greater awareness of the range of non-political news that readers sought and that could be provided.

Papers could not be readily contracted or expanded as modern papers can be, both because of the nature of Stamp Duty, which was linked, however imperfectly, to size, and because the limited capacity of each printing unit would necessitate the provision of additional presses if the paper was to become longer. It was easiest for a weekly to expand its size, especially if the printing press was not being used, as it often was in London, to also print other newspapers, because there was more time to print more copy on the individual press. The *Reading Mercury, and Oxford Gazette* did so in 1771, providing readers with an occasional additional sheet, free and without advertisements, and therefore untaxed, whenever there were sufficient items that were felt to be of interest. Initially episodic, by 1773 these sheets were being numbered as a Miscellany. The *Maidstone Journal* brought out an extra sheet on 19 July 1791 to report on the anti-Priestley riot in Birmingham: 'The following authentic particulars relative to the Riots in Birmingham, having been communicated to us by a neighbouring Clergyman, since the Paper went to Press, this morning, we have thought proper to communicate them to the public, by way of Supplement to the Maidstone Journal'.

In the case of several provincial papers, the amount of information provided was increased by the publication of related magazine-type pamphlets. These benefited from the subscription base, distribution network and printing facilities already provided by the newspaper. These pamphlets or additional sections have received insufficient attention and there is no study of them. In some areas, however, they were clearly important. Thus, both the Sherborne papers published them. The *Sherborne Mercury* was responsible for the *Weekly Miscellany; or Agreeable and Instructive Entertainer*. In December 1782 this was published with the *Mercury* and cost an additional 1*d*, although those who did not buy the *Mercury* had to pay 1½*d*. The *Miscellany* was a twenty-four page magazine, containing anecdotes, essays and poems. The *Dorchester and Sherborne Journal* pointed out on 16 January 1801 that 'the Monthly Magazine' was regularly supplied by its newsmen and agents.

Most editors (and the word should be used without suggesting that this was a distinct function or individual) could not spread the news over more space. Instead, the predominant impression is one of editors uncertain of the balance to strive for, facing criticism, especially when they delayed advertisements in order to insert other material, and tending to conform to the established pattern both of layout and of content. Magazines had an impact on the latter. *Berrow's Worcester Journal* of 9 November 1769 printed an essay commenting on the transformation of newspapers from being 'dry registers of common intelligence' to the 'annals of history, politics and literature' with nearly every paper 'now a magazine'.

In practice there was a contrast between dailies, which tended to be more political in content, and weeklies, which increasingly diversified and became more like magazines. Yet, with the exception of the essay papers that carried no news or advertisements, even papers with a strong political slant had to include other material. There was a continuum of content between the different types of newspapers: 'Deaths, executions, and discoveries of the most shocking, audacious, and unheard of villainies' could be 'read over a whole page in a weekly journal', as much as in a daily.[1] Newspapers declared their determination to serve all markets. The first issue of the *Staffordshire Sentinel* (7 January 1854) announced that it would 'be a paper for all classes – fitted for the politician, the social reformer and the family circle'.

There was also a sense that their very variety helped ensure a value that deserved permanence. News might be ephemeral and transient, but newspapers were of greater significance because of the way they treated the news and because of their other contents. This encouraged an emphasis in many newspapers on the idea that they would serve as records and thus be retained. As products, newspapers should thus be collectibles. Number one of a new series of the *Birmingham Chronicle*, which appeared on 2 January 1823, explained the changes made by the proprietor:

> In its former folio form it appeared only calculated to command a temporary interest; but in the quarto style, which he has now adopted for the commencement of the new series, a permanence will be given to its contents, from the inducement which this convenience of size will offer for preservation throughout the year; while all its various articles will be made easy of reference by a General Index, which will be published at the close of each annual volume. Though the miscellaneous matter that composes a newspaper may be of great fugitive and temporary character, yet there is a great deal in the literary, statistical, local, and entertaining departments, that may be read in after-times with undiminished interest and pleasure; and while its preservation to one class, affords the opportunity of turning over its pages, as a scrap-book of amusement, to another it offers the more important advantages of reference upon local questions, town's meetings, reports of public societies, etc. etc. In addition, the proprietor has to mention that he has provided a new and beautiful type for the Chronicle, with every material for printing it in the best manner.

As neither type nor title of newspaper dictated a specific content, editors were pushed back to their sense of what the readers wanted, a sense sharpened by an awareness of the relatively rapid turnover of titles. There were clearly some serious disputes over the issue of content.[2] However, the scarcity of relevant surviving material makes it difficult to discuss the subject. Whereas business arrangements and financial transactions might be committed to paper and encapsulated in legal documents, the nuances of editorial selection were not thus expressed.

Newspaper authors were aware that they 'were obliged to conform to the prevalency of fashion',[3] but this proved surprisingly constant. Besides much that was essentially news, the press offered its readers the same sort of material found in magazines: songs, poems, verses, stories, anecdotes, and extracts from books and magazines. The serialization of novels and novelettes in periodicals included, for example, Defoe's *Moll Flanders* in the *London Post* in 1722–3 and *A General History of the Pyrates* in the *Original London Post* of 1724.[4] In the *Original Ipswich Journal* of 17 December 1774, a piece on the raising of seedling potatoes and 'A short retrospective view of the first grounds of the present unhappy contention between parliamentary despotism and American jealousy' were accompanied by verses entitled 'The Three Warnings: A Tale', which took up one of the paper's sixteen columns. Less ominous was the three-column description of the Isle of Wight from Sir Richard Worsley's new history of the island, published in the *Hampshire Chronicle* of 15 October 1781. The variety this paper offered its readers is indicated by two items of July 1783: 'Anecdotes of the Bastille', translated from Linguet, 'who was confined there for twenty months' (5 July), and 'Curious and interesting accounts of the wasp from Barbut's Description of Insects, a new work' (19 July). The *Newcastle Courant* offered nearly one column on archaeological excavations under a York by-line (10 July 1742) and one-and-a-quarter columns on 'The impropriety of burning things which are presumed to have a pestilential infection in them, as a means of security from the plague, briefly shown in a letter from a member of the College of Physicians in London' (24 September 1743). Human-interest items included a private baptism of a baby Sarah in Hexham who was discovered to be a boy, with the question asked as to whether the child had to be rebaptized (25 June 1743). A sense of excessive openness on the part of the press to information and opinion and of an absence of necessary scrutiny and authority, comparable to what a modern reader might feel about the claims in the medical advertisements, was captured in a letter by 'Lilliputian' in the *Newcastle Courant* of 24 December 1743:

Your mathematical correspondents grow so numerous of late, that, unless some task be assign'd them, we shall know no end of their debates. It is but too common in those our days for a young student to commence pedant before he thoroughly understands his common arithmetick, and to fancy himself a philosopher as soon as he has gain'd a smattering of Euclid's Elements. To carry on an epistolary correspondence in a private manner, for the sake of instruction, or for finding out the truth, is commendable enough; but to pester the publick with common questions in navigation, which every school boy can solve, is most intolerable. As each of them seems to value himself upon his own abilities, and to think himself more eminent than his fellows, I humbly presume the following will be an infallible method whereby to judge which of them is the best mathematician. There is a collection of ten curious problems in the Gentleman's Diary for the year 1744; now, if any among them be qualified to send you solutions to the four first of these, on or before Candlemas Day next, he will undoubtedly be esteem'd the hero by all the curious part of mankind.

A 'Naturalist's Diary' was a regular feature in the *Birmingham Chronicle* of 1823.

Crime was a major draw in the press, as was humour. Accounts of the actions of criminals not only served to excite readers, but also provided warnings to people fearful of attack, while those who might break the law, either deliberately or inadvertently, could be warned of the consequences. Newspapers clearly thought these warnings of value. A report in the *Leeds Intelligencer* of 28 November 1786 on convictions at Wakefield for false weights and measures was followed by an editorial comment: 'Would it not be right to have the names of these offenders published?' The *Reading Mercury* of 26 October 1778 ended an account of an Andover robbery by announcing, in a different type, 'As the above villains may possibly be lurking in this neighbourhood, these descriptions, if attended to, may be the means of bringing them to justice.' The *Exeter Gazette* of 2 January 1794 reported that 'in consequence of a caution that appeared in the public papers, two men were apprehended at Dorchester the day following'. The *Dorchester and Sherborne Journal* of 19 November 1802 described two murder suspects. The *Taunton Courier* of 12 March 1828 reported:

> Howard, the villain who was lately tried for intending to murder Mr. Mullay, and who has been sentenced to transportation for life, was an active conspirator in one of those gangs of swindlers, under the denomination of London money lenders, against whose artifices we have taken every opportunity of putting our readers on their guard.

Such items allowed the press to claim that it had a public benefit. Thus, the *Glocester Journal* of 6 December 1784 recounted the recent failure of pickpockets and footpads:

> The hint given in our last to set the country people on their guard at the fair held here on Monday was attended with the best effect possible. . . . As often as we receive such useful information, the public may depend on our communicating it; and it may not be improper or unseasonable, at this time, to profess, that the sole object of this paper is, has been, and ever shall be, our own private advantage, in due subservience to the public good.

The press was used extensively by prosecuting associations, and printed advertisements and notices from those seeking criminals were frequently published.[5] An editorial in *Trewman's Exeter Flying Post* of 3 January 1856, calling for the establishment of a county police, noted 'scarcely a week passes without our paper containing the record of numerous thefts, of a more or less aggravated character'.

Interest in a good story seems to have played a large role in the preference for inserting details of crime. The frequency of such items in the foreign news makes this readily apparent. However, most reports were domestic in origin, many written in an exciting manner, especially accounts of attempted jailbreaks and highway robberies. Some papers, such as *Applebee's Original Weekly Journal* in the 1720s, were renowned for their crime reporting, and there was much in the cheap London press of the second quarter of the eighteenth century. Nevertheless, far from being the province of a particular section of the press, interest was general. Papers both reported the activities and punishment of criminals elsewhere in the country, and drew attention to their own reports. Thus the issue of *Trewman's Exeter Flying Post* noted above included, under the heading 'Mysterious Murder', an account from Gateshead. The *Reading Mercury* often contained notices mentioning long accounts on its back page. When Britain was at war, the *Leeds Intelligencer* of 10 April 1781 could still devote nearly two columns to a York murder trial. Even minor crimes were frequently reported; crime tended to share with accidents the local news section of early provincial papers. The lives of villains were frequently discussed, there were regular reports on assizes and executions, and *causes célèbres* were discussed at length. The alleged abduction of Elizabeth Canning in 1753 and the subsequent legal action led to the production of *Canning's Farthing Post*, a two-column, four-page work printed on poor paper that lasted for sixty-five numbers. Four- and-a-half columns of the *Birmingham Chronicle* of 6 November 1823 were devoted to an account of the 'horrible murder of W. Weare Esq.', the 'Gill's Hill murder', near Elstree on 24 October. In addition, the editorial noted:

> The long and minute details of the dreadful crime which fills so large a space of our paper of this day, affords us as little room as inclination for any remarks upon foreign occurrences. The most horrible circumstance in this murder is the condition of life and worldly circumstances of the parties principally accused. Thurtell, the person principally implicated, was a man of good property, and of a very respectable family and connections. . . . Another trait in the evidence brings the affair into a resemblance with those banditti establishments, hitherto peculiar to the Continent, and which have been known to us only as the plots of our melo-dramas. Incredible as it may appear, it has been ascertained from sources leaving no possibility of doubt, that a fraternity existed for the express purpose of robbery and murder.

The following issue (13 November) devoted two entire pages, including four sketches and a map, as well as an editorial:

> We cannot but hail the deep interest which the late horrid murder has excited, to the exclusion of all other subjects, and the general

indignation which it has provoked, as a gratifying proof of the singularity of such horrid deeds in this country, and of the abhorrence in which such human depravity is held by our countrymen . . . we have a sort of domestic treason – a combination of plunderers and robbers amongst the community, unequalled, and not resembled, by anything in the annals of our country. The public voice and public feelings demand that the guilty parties should make a speedy atonement to the law.

Other items were deprived of space. There was no 'Poets Corner' in the paper on 6 or 13 November, while the *Observer* of 7 December gave space to the case rather than to advertisements. The case excited much attention.

Thurtell won much sympathy as a sporting man defrauded by gamesters. Weare was a solicitor who had cheated him at cards. An amateur boxer, Thurtell was a dubious but powerful character. The massive attention devoted by the press showed that it was not only the Sunday press that covered crime extensively. There was also extensive coverage in chapbooks and ballads, including the immortal lines that amused Sir Walter Scott:

> They cut his throat from ear to ear,
> His brains they battered in,
> His name was Mr. William Weare,
> He dwelt in Lyon's Inn.

The response in the press has to be seen in this wider context of interest. Having fostered it, the *Birmingham Chronicle* of 11 December 1823 reported:

our readers will perceive by the account of the proceedings at Hertford, which occupy a considerable space in our paper today, that the trial of the prisoners is postponed until the commencement of next month. Considering the prejudice which has been excited against the prisoners by the numerous publications on this subject with which the country has been inundated, the decision of his lordship has met the approbation of every humane and candid mind; and we sincerely hope that, at the period to which the trial is postponed, all passions and prejudices will be so completely allayed and forgotten, that the unhappy men may receive a fair and impartial trial.

The paper, however, pushed on to provide more details of other trials and crimes, the execution of Pallet at Chelmsford (18 December) and the murder of a Mr Smith at Lewisham (25 December). Thurtell's eventual trial, at Hertford on 6 and 7 January, and his execution there on

9 January, were covered in the issues of 8 and 15 January. The editorial in the last claimed, 'The whole process of these important judicial proceedings, so interesting to the cause of humanity and justice, has been highly honourable to the criminal justice of our country.' The confession of one of Thurtell's accomplices, who had turned King's evidence, followed on 5 and 12 February. More generally, the assizes provided a focus for the reporting of crime and punishment in particular localities. The *Glocester Journal* of 9 April 1836 noted 'our columns are so extensively occupied by assize intelligence that we have been compelled to omit many advertisements and articles of a local nature'.

Most press reports were unsympathetic to criminals, 'this sort of cattle', in the words of one correspondent in the *Northampton Mercury* of 9 July 1739; but highwaymen were sometimes presented as glamorous figures and the cruelty of punishments for minor crimes was condemned. Celebrated pickpockets, such as George Barrington, who was transported to Australia in 1790, were treated as amusing, rather than sinister, figures. *Drewry's Staffordshire Gazette* of 2 August 1827 devoted one of its twenty columns to the calendar of prisoners for trial at the Staffordshire summer assizes, and also provided details of a trial at the Oxford assizes, two attempted break-ins, and a London poisoning. The *Taunton Courier* of 6 February 1828 carried an account from the *Bath Journal* under the heading 'The Murder in Marlborough Buildings, Bath – Confession of the Murderer'. His execution was covered in detail in the issue of 11 June. The *Sherborne Mercury* of 10 January 1837 devoted over a column to an item headlined 'Atrocious Murder in Ratcliff Highway – Examination of the Murderer'. This was followed by another item headlined 'The Edgeware-Road Murder'. Interest in crime encouraged the printing of items from other newspapers. Thus the *Courier*, a London daily evening paper, of 18 September 1832 carried a story headlined 'Shocking Murder' with the *Bolton Chronicle* as the source. Local items were also important. The first issue of Chudleigh's *Weekly Express* reported a case being heard at Exeter under the headline 'Alleged Manslaughter on the High Seas' (11 July 1855).

Accident reports were a variant on crime stories. From the outset, the press had provided details of disasters whether people falling through ice or fires, coaches running off the road or serious falls. For example, the *Sherborne Mercury* of 2 January 1837 reported 'Dreadful effects of the snow at Lewes' – an account of an avalanche that caused several deaths. These traditional-style accidents remained good copy. Thus the *Taunton Courier* of 2 and 9 January 1828 covered recent floods, and the *St James's Chronicle* of 1 April 1845 reported on a serious fire at Doncaster, while the issue of 16 November 1847 covered a shipwreck in which ninety-one lives had been lost. They were joined by others stemming from new developments, particularly in transport but also in industry. Thus, the same paper on 28 June 1845 reported a steamboat accident on the

Thames, and coalpit accidents and explosions were covered, as in the issues of 7 November 1835 and 2 September 1843, and in the *Illustrated London News* of 9 April 1853. The *Morning Chronicle* of 22 August 1807 reported the overturning of the London–York mail coach, the *Illustrated London News* of 19 April 1856 a fire at Vauxhall railway station.

The tone was lightened by the frequent publication of jokes, humorous stories, verses and epigrams. By modern standards the humour was often cruel, with verses directed against cuckolds and excremental jokes both commonplace. Some papers specialized in humour, for example Henry Playford's *Diverting Post* (1704–5), which printed a lot of ribald poetry, and John Henley's *Hyp-Doctor* (1730-41) which had a distinctively knockabout style.

In addition, the elopements and sexual scandals of the great were covered in great detail, helped by the frequently lurid nature of adultery cases in the House of Lords. The discovery of an admiral's wife in a Charing Cross brothel in 1771 was as good copy as Lady Abergavenny's adultery in 1729 and the Countess of Eglinton's in 1788. Robert Trevor wrote from London in 1729:

> Private persons have not escaped the notice and censures of our licentious press; nor can even the grave bury poor Lady Abergavenny's shame, every syllable of whose name, and every particular of whose life are hawked about the streets as articulately as old cloaths etc.[6]

Humorous stories and a ribald style were criticized, and discussion over style was closely linked to debate over content. The lewdness and buffoonery of rivals were frequently condemned, but were believed to help sales. Lady Mary Wortley Montagu instructed her printer to throw in 'a little bawdy' to make her *Nonsense of Common-Sense* sell in 1738.[7]

The argument that opposition newspapers sought to 'democratize' the tone and content of the press and that ministerial papers resisted would be a seductive thesis, but is overly simplistic, both for the eighteenth and for the early nineteenth century. It is true that some opposition figures, such as Mist, Wilkes and Cobbett, sought to broaden the appeal of opposition writing, but the same was also true of certain ministerial publicists, such as Fielding and Henley. In addition, opposition papers did not always seek a popular style. Clifton vaunted the reflective nature of the *Weekly Medley*, while the *Craftsman* rarely emulated the vigorous idioms of Mist's papers, and its leading essays were often philosophical or intricate. The *North Briton*'s discussion of British politics in terms of the history of Lady Wiseacre's family, a device employed already on numerous occasions, was dismissed by the *London Chronicle* of 18 December 1762 as 'an allegory not very intelligible to common readers'. Junius's penultimate letter in the *Public Advertiser* bored his readers and was a serious flop.[8]

Vindictive satire, such as the *Craftsman*'s attacks on Walpole and Junius's on the Duke of Grafton, was readable and interesting, an accessible form of political propaganda, but all too often the opposition used lengthy essays whose tone of high seriousness and moral outrage became repetitive and whose vindictive abuse could not compensate for a general humourlessness. This was true of many of the essays of the *Craftsman*, the *Monitor* and the *North Briton*. The style and content of much of the press was explained by George Colman's remark in the *Gentleman* of 12 July 1775: 'I have even been assured by my friends, that the people of this country will not at present read any article in a newspaper longer than a paragraph.' This was related to the low circulation figures of such essay-papers as the *Review* and the *Briton*; and to the importance from the 1760s of the letter as a form of political comment.

To appreciate the press and the problems of editorial selection, it is necessary to dispense with any idea that closely argued, reasoned discussions of political theory or sophisticated examples of literary analysis represent the goal that newspapers pursued or should have done. J.B. Shipley, for example, commented that the *Weekly Register* of the 1730s 'suffered from a split personality: part miscellaneous, part political'.[9] Such views are questionable. Aside from employing modern critical criteria, they neglect the imperatives which shaped newspaper production. On 11 April 1798, the *Weekly Register* divided the readers of newspapers into seven groups: Interested, Anxious, Curious, Hasty, Idle, Party and Judicious. All could find something in the press, both London and provincial. The variety of material in the newspapers, something not always glimpsed in books devoted to the press and politics, helped to make them an attractive product. Thus, readers of the *Morning Post* on 10 May 1811 could read an account of Lady Warburton's Masquerade under the section heading Fashionable World, as well as war news.

This variety reflected the nature of society, not least areas of expanding commercialization. For example, there was increased reporting of sport from the second half of the eighteenth century. The limited notices and advertisements for horse races, which had dominated the occasional references to sport in the first half of the century, were replaced by lengthy advertisements, sometimes highlighted by illustrations, and by notices for, and results of, a variety of sports. The *Sheffield Advertiser* of 31 August 1792 devoted nearly a column to the results of a local cricket match, while the *Oracle* of 26 July 1796 printed individual scores in a Wiltshire match. The *Newcastle Courant* of 19 July 1788 provided information on the Durham, Hexham, Morpeth and Newcastle races.

In addition, the activities of famous sportsmen, such as the leading pedestrians (speed walkers), were reported. The *World*, which began publication on 1 January 1787, popularized boxing, but the sport was also reported extensively in other papers, for example the *London Chronicle* of 8, 10, 12 and 17 January 1788. Vivid accounts of boxing matches became a feature, particularly with the development of a star system round boxers such as Mendoza. For example, the *Morning Chronicle* of 9 October 1806 and 22 August 1807 offered good reports of matches. The *Morning Post* of 22 May 1811 devoted two-thirds of a column to a round-by-round account of a boxing match between Molineux and Rimmer. Spectacular events, such as the development of ballooning, enjoyed similar prominence. Sports news included correspondence, such as the letter on a new way to score at cricket, printed in the *Reading Mercury* on 21 June 1773, or the controversy over a local match reported in the same paper on 17, 24 and 31 July 1775. Anecdotes and information concerning betting were also printed. Betting was a popular topic in the press for all spheres of life, ranging from matrimony to international politics. With sport, as with much of the press, it was the human interest and therefore it was often the exceptional items that attracted attention.

The greater prominence of sport was reflected in the article headings of papers such as the *Oracle* and the *World* in the 1780s. In addition, specialist periodicals were founded. In 1733 the fortnightly *Historical List of all Horse-Matches Run* appeared, and in 1769, for 4*d* an issue, the *Racing Calendar*, another fortnightly complete with advertisements, could be purchased during the season.

Sport, like crime and cultural activity, was a sphere in which news and advertisements interacted. Indeed the advertisements were news, while sports news was often a form of advertising. Information was important to all these activities, and had not only an economic dimension, but also a wider cultural impact as these activities were increasingly precisely located in time and place and publicly described and commodified. Furthermore, reports led to controversy. For example, Edward Miller, a prominent organist, replied to critical press notices of provincial musicians by publishing a pamphlet, *A Letter to the Country Spectator, in reply to the author of his ninth number* (1792).

Advertising was central to the information culture and economy. The relationship between advertising and the press had its complexities. Items about printed matter and medicines were an important, frequently dominant, feature of the advertisements, for the printers of newspapers often acted as local agents for these in the provinces, while in London many newspapers were owned by booksellers. It is, however, by no means clear how far advertisements of these items were paid for. The biggest advertisement in the *Leeds Mercury* of 11 July 1738 was for Daffy's Elixir, a cure-all sold by the printer, as by many other provincial newspaper printers. It had been made popular through its use by Queen Caroline on her deathbed in 1737. Advertisements in the *Dorchester and Sherborne Journal* of 23 January 1801 announced that Spilsbury's Patent Antiscor-butic Drops, the Cordial Balm of Gilead, and Robberd's Balsamic Elixir could all be obtained from the printer and newsmen. In the issue of *Woolmer's Exeter and Plymouth Gazette* of 23 March 1809, the printer, who was also a bookseller, advertised Dr Anderson's, or, the True Scots pills, Spilsbury's Patent Antiscorbutic Drops, Mrs Vincent's Genuine Gowland's Lotion, the Cordial Cephalic snuff, all of which he sold. Parr's Life Pills was a staple of the 1840s. The rat and mice pill advertised in the *Chelmsford Chronicle* of 6 January 1792 could be purchased from the newsmen who distributed the paper, a normal practice in the provincial press.

The unspecialized nature of many early newspapers in terms of business organization was such that advertisements could serve a useful purpose even if few were printed. The profits on some books and medicines may well have been considerable. Advertising was clearly seen as of value to the local economy. When, for reasons that are unclear, the *Kendal Weekly Mercury* published by the bookseller Thomas Ashburner came to an end in 1749, he produced a flysheet with a proposal for publishing a new weekly, the *Agreeable Miscellany*:

> Since declaring my intention of discontinuing the newspaper, some persons have justly observed that the circulation of advertisements or hand-bills would in some degree be cut off, to remedy which I have, by the advice of several gentlemen etc., determined to publish a weekly paper . . . should this work meet with encouragement . . . the distribution of advertisements, hand-bills etc. will be made very extensive, by being sent along with it to all neighbouring towns, villages, etc. so consequently will be of great advantage in the sale of estates, houses, timber etc. or letting any property.[10]

As the volume of advertising increased it became more important for a paper to ensure that it was in the top tier of advertisers in order to obtain more business. London newspapers had individual advertising profiles, while, from about 1740, three distinct tiers of provincial newspapers, defined by the annual number of advertisements, had emerged.[11] The latter helped to define regional dominance within the urban network. For example, Cumbrian advertisers thought it worthwhile to attract local purchases by advertising in the Newcastle press. The Chester paper, *Adam's Weekly Courant*, carried North Wales and Staffordshire advertisements in 1738. Increasingly, successful provincial papers carried advertisements inserted by London firms, an attempt by London businessmen to penetrate provincial markets via the existing urban provincial hierarchy. This was part of the growing national integration of the press, with provincial papers being regularly obtainable in London.

The importance of advertising was further suggested by the large number of papers, both London and provincial, that included the term advertiser in the title. A primarily political paper such as the *Champion* had a sub-title *Evening Advertiser*. This remained the case in the second half of the century, with new papers such as the *Star and Evening Advertiser* or the *Bristol Gazette and Public Advertiser*. The two largest circulation morning papers in London in 1789 were the *Daily Advertiser*, and the *Gazetteer and New Daily Advertiser*, according to the latter on 10 September. The newspapers of the 1770s and 1780s rarely devoted as large a proportion of their space to political essay material as their counterparts in the first half of the century. In general, advertisements had also displaced political essays from the front page.

Press advertising was an important tool for those seeking to inculcate, elicit or influence consumer demands. Papers were widely available and consulted at coffee-houses and taverns. These were places where commercial transactions took place, and they were particularly important because of the general absence of specialized offices in many commercial, industrial and agricultural businesses and because of the practice of handling most transactions through face-to-face meetings. Advertisements initially were curiosities, but they became a central and dynamic facet of a consumerism built upon making services and certain goods normative for the newspaper-reading public. This was as important as the role of advertisements in making such goods and services 'spectacles'.[12] As the decision to purchase was frequently an aspect of social role and positioning, so the signs and symbols by which these were influenced and sustained were important. Newspaper advertising and comment became more significant in this process with the growth of the press.

The effectiveness of advertisements is a question that cannot be answered. Although without the benefit of market research, the advertisers presumably thought they would obtain a return on their investment. Advertisements were made subject to taxation in 1712, at the rate of 1*s* each, a duty renewed in 1743, and doubled in 1757. In 1789, the duty was set at 3*s*. These increases helped to push up the price charged for advertisements. In 1724, the *Leeds Mercury* and the *York Mercury* charged 2*s* each. In 1712, duty hit advertising in the London press, but, when advertising rates rose in general after the Stamp Act of 1725, although duty on advertisements was not increased, this appears to have had little impact.[13] Possibly some newspapers felt there was reasonable flexibility in the price advertisers would pay, and displaced some of the burden of added Stamp Duty on to them, rather than on to readers, in 1725, while other papers followed the trend in prices. The tax increase in 1757 led many newspapers to raise the price of advertisements to 3*s* 6*d*.

Luxury products, such as coffee, tea, wine, medicines and printed matter, were best able to bear the costs of advertising because the percentage cost of the advertisement was low, the profits in selling the products high and they were branded goods. Commonplace products, such as ordinary foodstuffs, or beer, were rarely advertised. There was less need to encourage consumption of everyday products, individual sales outlets were too small-scale to justify advertising, and the newspaper was not the most effective way of notifying the often rapidly altering availability or price alterations of products that were generally local and frequently sold in markets. However, there was a product range in newspaper advertising: the cheap (½d) tri-weekly *Parker's London News* in 1725 advertised soap, tobacco and cheap brandy, not books or houses. In contrast, the *Newcastle Courant* printed over 1,500 advertisements of property for sale or letting in 1710–30, about a fifth of these in the newspapers.[14] Similarly, services were advertised that were either new to an area or, more commonly, occasional: in effect those of visitors from the outside world and usually products of the metropolitan world and its fashions, for example itinerant doctors, such as the famous oculist John Taylor, or acting companies or lecturers. The *Taunton Courier* of 6 February 1828 reported:

> The irritation and inconvenience occasioned by those excrescences on the foot-corns and bunions – are, we are informed, readily and easily obviated by a new discovery of Mr. Davidson, whose arrival in this town we announced last week, and whose advertisement appears in our first page.

Not all advertisements were for items for sale. Political and economic controversies, such as those of the siting of turnpikes, were often conducted by means of essays, appeals for support, and news items inserted for payment. It is not always easy to determine what was paid for, and whether items from the party supported by the paper were inserted free. On 2 October 1780, the *Reading Mercury* announced, 'An Anti-modern Courtier, A Friend to Liberty etc. and several other pieces are received; but cannot be inserted without the customary compliment attending essays calculated to answer electioneering purposes.'

Advertising was sometimes criticized, particularly for the puffing of worthless products, an accusation that the methods for validating new medicines made particularly apposite. The press lent itself readily to quackery, and, in the *Idler* on 20 January 1759, Dr Johnson condemned irresponsible and inaccurate advertisers. It is indeed possible to find many ridiculous items, especially among the medical advertisements, their claims constituting a system of comprehensive insurance. However, advertisements are a form that did not dictate particular standards and, alongside the continued presence of medical advertisements, their supporting testimonials, and occasional illustrations of, for example, voided stones, can be found an increasing number of advertisements inserted by organizations, many of them official. One of the functions of the *Gazette* was thus extended to most other papers. Two types of material increasingly inserted were notices about criminal activity, by the 1780s a major feature of the advertisements in many newspapers, and information about economic matters, especially lobbying for new projects. Advertisements for societies for agricultural improvements rubbed shoulders with notices from the Quarter Sessions or announcements about local education. In the 1750s, Bristol charitable societies advertised their meetings in the papers, since, as one advertisement noted, this was more efficient and less time-consuming than dispersing printed notices by hand.[15]

Developments in advertising mirrored the general expansion of the press: increases in size and cost and a growing diversification in contents, both in London and in the provinces. In the *Salisbury Journal* the number and diversity of advertisements rose, and services hitherto considered luxuries became marketed more widely. Thus, an established paper meant access to a range of other goods and services.[16] In addition, the standard of presentation improved, with a greater availability of more versatile type, ornaments and engravings, and a finer quality of workmanship.[17]

The benefits offered by advertising were varied, and it helped to increase the value of the press to many groups, whether book advertisers, who paid quite considerable sums, auctioneers,[18] Bradford hatmakers seeking to preserve their monopoly of hat sales from the mercers, or those unaware of the dangers of copper cooking utensils.[19] Newspapers were used to advertise the meetings of joint-stock companies, notices of lottery draws, and appeals for lost property. The relationship between the press and advertising was intimate, and well represented by the fact that so many newspapers were owned by booksellers, and that in 1794 the Licensed Victuallers Association founded the *Morning Advertiser* in order to help their advertising. Fielding founded the *Covent-Garden Journal* in 1752 because of the difficulty of publishing advertisements for his Universal Register Office in the face of a rival Register Office and the hostility of the *Daily Advertiser*.

In 1727, Thomas Robe suggested that the government strike at the opposition press through their advertisements. He envisaged a ministerially-sponsored and inexpensive *Daily Advertiser* with several officials to take in advertisements:

It is evidently true that the certain, excessive profits arising from advertisements are the great support of the proprietors, writers and printers of newspapers and chiefly promote the sale of them. . . . It is further evident that the advertisements, published in the different papers at present is the chief reason with most houses both private and public for their taking in so many. And that in case of a General Advertiser they would gladly decline such a useless expense.[20]

No such arrangement was attempted. The relatively limited authority and weak power of central government could hardly have encouraged any attempt at control. Had there been regulation, it would have been for fiscal reasons. However, spurious they may have seemed, it is difficult to see anyone prohibiting advertisements for Bartlett's Inventions for the Cure of Ruptures. Admonition not regulation was employed. The

Taunton Courier of 2 March 1831 reported under the heading 'London Advertising Money-Lenders':

> One of these blood-suckers has sent us an advertisement, which he requests may be inserted for a series of weeks. We have uniformly resisted the invitation of these fellows to allow our columns to become the vehicles of their depredatory practices, and have reason to know and to rejoice, that in more than one instance we have prevented a serious mischief to unsuspecting individuals. Why some of the London (for all do not allow it) and other papers, tolerate so cruel an imposition upon the needy and credulous is inexplicable.

Advertising was not the sole product of a growing economy. There was also reporting of economic news. In the 1660s, papers were produced in London carrying no political news and simply containing advertisements and news of trade. Papers that were primarily devoted to economic news continued to exist thereafter.

It was not the custom for newspapers to be owned by large companies, though the *British Mercury* of the 1710s was published by the Sun Fire Insurance Company. Other papers had a different genesis. In 1696, Edward Lloyd, a coffee-house keeper, published a tri-weekly *Lloyd's News*, which contained much shipping news, although it ceased the following year as a result of contentious items in the political and religious spheres.[21] In 1781, the *Aurora and Universal Advertiser* was launched with the support of leading London hoteliers.

Other relevant newspapers were *Proctor's Price-Courant*, the *City Intelligencer*, *Robinson's Price-Courant*, and *Whiston's Merchants Weekly Remembrancer*, all published in Anne's reign, the *Weekly Packet, with the Price Courant* founded in 1728, the *Exchange Evening Post* established in 1721, and *Freke's Price of Stocks*, another journal of the 1720s.

Economic matters also played a major role in papers that did not specialize in them. The *Weekly Miscellany for the Improvement of Husbandry, Trade, Arts and Sciences*, a paper that ran for about two decades, was founded in 1720. The *Citizen, or, The Weekly Conversation of a Society of London Merchants on Trade, and other Public Affairs* appeared in 1739.

Shipping and grain were the early staples of economic news in the press. The *Supplement to the Weekly Journal* promised readers in 1716 that it would provide them with information of ships arriving at and leaving London, a service common to many papers. Shipping news, with its accumulation of foreign, provincial and London items, symbolized the role of the press in the circulation of information.[22] Such reports were largely (but not only) found in newspapers produced in ports. Information on inland navigation did not approach the amount of space devoted to the location of canals.

Reports on grain prices were found in most newspapers. The prices invariably mentioned were those at Bear Key, the Bear Quay in London where grain was landed and where a major corn market had been established. These prices and the value of the leading London stocks were carried by many of the newsletters used by early provincial papers as a major source of information. As the eighteenth century progressed more markets tended to be cited and the information given on the grain situation became more diversified and sometimes more fully discussed. On 7 January 1796, the *St James's Chronicle* carried its monthly report on agriculture, a regular feature of the press in the period, but added a qualification in brackets that reflected the association of moralism, reform and legislation:

> We cannot help intimating that we have some hesitation to place anything like implicit faith in the above report. The present high price of corn arises from complicated causes, of which though a real scarcity seems, in some degree, to form a part: yet the evil is undoubtedly increased by private avarice: and we are convinced that absolute legislative restrictions would be far preferable to any palliative recommendations.

By the 1790s London papers which in no way specialized in economic news, such as the *Express* and the *Telegraph*, were providing in every issue nearly a column of information on London markets ranging from the price of butter and hides to that of tallow and sugar. Provincial papers also increasingly provided economic news. By 1774 the *Kentish Gazette* was regularly providing half a column of comparable London material. The 'Market Herald' carried in the *Chelmsford Chronicle* in 1792 gave the London prices of grain, flour, seed, leather, raw hide, meat, tallow, coal, hay, straw, and hops, and the price of wheat in every English county. *Woolmer's Exeter and Plymouth Gazette* of 30 November 1809 provided not only London grain, meat and leather prices, but also Salisbury, Basingstoke, Devizes, Newbury, Andover and Warminster grain prices. The *Sherborne Mercury* in 1837 offered reports on Smithfield as well as the local cattle market. Pressure for such material was noted in the *Dorchester and Sherborne Journal* of 27 November 1801:

> In compliance with the request of many of our readers, and it being our wish to render our journal as extensively useful as possible, we have inserted the current prices of all the leading articles of merchandize, which we mean to continue weekly; and as the greatest care will be taken as to accuracy, we have no doubt it will prove highly interesting to merchants and traders of every description.

Increasingly, space was devoted, both in the news and advertisements sections, to the propaganda of agricultural improvement. New practices were described, pernicious ones discouraged; yields and machinery, weight and enclosure became topics of discussion. Thus, the *Birmingham Herald* of 25 January 1838 offered an account of the Durham breed of cattle from the *Hereford Times*.

New developments in industry and mining were also followed with interest. Particular attention was devoted to details of new machinery. The press provided singularly little criticism of new developments, a marked contrast to the position over agriculture where enclosure and the free market in grain, livestock and wool aroused strong feelings.

In contrast, developments in transportation aroused considerable controversy from the second half of the eighteenth century that were well expressed in the press, partly because of disputes between conflicting interests. These, and similar disputes in such fields as corn exports and pricing policies, suggest the need for a revision of Cranfield's portrayal of the mid-century provincial press as one that was singularly unperturbed by local disputes.[23] The position varied by paper, *Jopson's Coventry Mercury* being less willing to follow majority opinion than *Aris's Birmingham Gazette*, but strongly held opinions over local issues were increasingly noticeable, particularly during the late 1760s.[24]

The as yet restricted development in the editorial comment and local essays of the provincial press of the 1720s and 1730s, and the limited interest of the London press, led to a somewhat episodic coverage of the often bitter prominent labour disputes of the period that affected in particular the West Country cloth industry. Isolated pieces of news were printed with relatively little comment. By the second half of the century, the situation was different. The larger size of newspapers, and the replacement of the front-page essay in nearly all the press and the whole-page essay in most of it by a series of short essays, usually of between one-half and two columns in length, devoted to a variety of topics, permitted a more frequent discussion of local issues.

Major changes, such as turnpiking, bridge building, canal digging and, later, railway construction, provided subjects, writers and reader interest. Canalization schemes in the Thames Valley system led to disputes that were followed in the *Reading Mercury*, while the attempt by York to prevent the construction of a bridge at Selby was controversial. The *Taunton Courier* of 13 February 1828 criticized the Taunton Turnpike Trust for the state of the road between Taunton and Langport. Details of plans for new links provided much copy, for example for the Worcester and Oxford railway in the *Birmingham Herald* of 4 August 1836. A long notice concerning the Bath and Weymouth Railway appeared on the front page of the *Sherborne Mercury* of 2 January 1837, another about the London, Exeter and Falmouth Railway Company on that of 20 February 1837. On 8 February 1838, the *Birmingham Herald* offered an account of a meeting at Worcester of the shareholders of the Severn Navigation Company, while, on 18 January 1847, *Besley's Devonshire Chronicle* devoted two-and-a-half columns and an editorial to a meeting of the proprietors of the Exeter and Crediton Railway, and another two columns to an Extraordinary General Meeting of the South Devon Railway's share-holders. Much space was occupied by the more mundane reproduction of railway timetables. The first number of Chudleigh's *Weekly Express* provided the London–Plymouth timetables (11 July 1855).

The opening of new links and facilities and attendant celebrations provided plenty of copy. The general attitude of the press was that of praise for new links tempered by criticism of schemes deemed inappropriate. The *Staffordshire Advertiser* of 14 October 1848 reported the opening of the Crewe branch of the North Staffordshire Railway 'which will give the district an outlet to Liverpool, Chester and Holyhead as well as for the present to Manchester and the north'. The *St James's Chronicle* of 30 March 1847 provided a lengthy report on the completion of the rail link between London and Paris and discussed the impact of rail travel on the human body. The issue of 26 October 1847 provided details of the opening of the Gloucester and Cheltenham Railway. In reporting improvements to communications, a sense of new opportunities was insistent. Aside from railways, there was also considerable interest in new steamship services.

Many items relating to local and regional improvements were clearly inserted as advertisements, but over some issues the opinions of the printers are clear, while in others their willingness to insert particular items suggests their interest in propounding particular views. Food distribution, especially the supply of urban markets, aroused much controversy. Nevertheless, the active involvement of the provincial press in local disputes came more from printing, often for money, submitted material, than from comments by the printer.

Information and discussion about national economic developments reflected the increased prominence of economic lobbying. Public lobbying in newspapers and pamphlets had been significant in the first half of the century, especially when, as with the Anglo–French commercial negotiations of 1713 and those between Britain and Spain a quarter-century later, they were politically controversial. The (unsuccessful) cause of easier commercial relations with France was championed in 1713–14 by a specially launched tri-weekly, *Mercator: or, Commerce Retrieved*, much of which was the work of Defoe. However, aside from at the time of the South Sea Bubble, when very lengthy reports had been printed, press accounts of the great commercial companies were only occasional. These significant lobbying interests, such as the Bank of England, the East India Company and the Russian Company, preferred to operate largely in private, benefiting from their close links with the ministries of Walpole and Pelham; although there was extensive press discussion of the policies of the latter two towards the National Debt, for example Pelham's debt consolidation programme in 1749.

In the second half of the eighteenth century, there was more press lobbying, as economic interests that had not hitherto appreciated the value or gained access to the press did so, as the close relationship between long-lasting ministries and powerful chartered companies weakened, and as economic issues, particularly trade with America and the position of the East India Company, were pushed to the front of domestic politics.

The press devoted attention to economic lobbying, partly as a result of payments and partly because it was news in its own right. Whether enlarging the dock at Hull, resisting new taxation on tobacco, debating Pitt's Irish trade proposals in 1785 or the Anglo–French commercial treaty of 1786, or proposing parliamentary regulation of the price of sugar, the cause of particular interests received much attention. Thus, for example, under a local by-line, the *Glocester Journal* of 14 February 1791 reported on a Manchester meeting of cotton manufacturers intent on petitioning Parliament against competing Indian products.

Advertisements were an integral part of this economic expansion. Aside from offering items for sale, they also offered units of economic production and exchange: shops, farms, warehouses, industrial sites. Advertisements not only offered services; they also sought them as organizations put out work to tender, such as masonry work for Liverpool pier in 1738 and solitary cells in York Castle in 1789.

This was all part of the flow of information on which the economy depended and which both encouraged and served rising demand. Aside from information on economic conditions, of rumours of alterations in taxation, and of the activities of fraudsters, there were also details of legislation, of meetings of chartered companies, and of those entitled to act in certain functions, such as the brokers of the City of London. The *Glocester Journal* of 28 August 1786 warned against allowing foreigners to discover industrial processes, while the *Salisbury and Winchester Journal* of 8 June 1789 warned its readers, 'Farmers and dealers should be attentive to the new Wool Act. Informers are very busy about the country.' The press was used in 1772 to bolster confidence in the financial system, then afflicted by the crash of several prominent banking houses, although several newspapers spread damaging rumours. Warnings about fraudsters and counterfeit currency, for example in the *Birmingham Chronicle* of 13 May 1824 about counterfeit farthings, were of major importance to particular economic communities. It was also an aspect of the role of the press: good news was designed to drive out or expose the bad.

The press could also be of value in providing information about foreign trade. The dependence of this trade on war and on events, such as the early onset of Baltic ice or the loss of galleons in Caribbean hurricanes, led to a great interest among the mercantile community in news from abroad. The press was well placed to serve this as a result of its drawing on foreign newspapers and also of the access of London papers to information from the private correspondence of leading merchants. Easy to satirize, the evaluation of foreign news for economic information seems to have been common among readers. Newspapers stressed their economic information, and its relative importance increased as a consequence of the greater provision of literary, humorous and social items by the magazines. The advertisements for the *Daily News* in January 1847 included, 'An evening edition under the title of the Express is published every day at four o'clock, containing full reports of the markets of the day.' The *London Evening Post* of 30 March 1762 devoted much of its attempt to publicize its contents to its economic news, offering:

> an exact table of the current price of merchandize . . . an account of the arrival of British ships at, and their departure from, the several ports of the habitable world . . . the several courses of exchange, the prices of gold and silver, of stocks of corn at the Corn Exchange . . . and of other articles of a like nature. All notices given in the *Gazette,* with lists of bankrupts, and such other matters as may be useful to the public.

It was generally accepted that such items were of importance to many readers. In Fanny Burney's novel *Cecilia* (1782), the opinionated, practical man of business Mr Hobson declares, '. . . for as to not letting a lady speak, one might as well tell a man in business not to look at the Daily Advertiser; why, it's morally impossible'.[25]

NOTES

1. *Mist's Weekly Journal,* 14 May 1726.
2. R. Bataille, 'Arthur Young and the *Universal Magazine* of 1762', *The Library,* 6/6 (1984), 284–5.
3. *Cirencester Flying Post,* 5 April 1742.
4. R.M. Wiles, *Serial Publication in England before 1750* (Cambridge, 1957); R.D. Mayo, *The English Novel in the Magazines, 1740 to 1815* (Evanston, 1962); J.L. Wood, 'Defoe Serialized', *Factotum,* 19 (1984), 21–3.
5. P. King, 'Prosecution Associations and their Impact in Eighteenth-century Essex', in D. Hay and F.G. Snyder (eds), *Policing and Prosecution in Britain, 1750–1850* (Oxford, 1989), pp. 171–207, and 'Newspaper reporting, prosecution practice and perceptions of urban crime – the Colchester crime wave of 1765', *Continuity and Change,* 2 (1987), 423–54. Newspapers have been used extensively by those writing on crime, for example B.J. Davey, *Rural Crime in the Eighteenth Century. North Lincolnshire, 1740–80* (Hull, 1994).
6. Trevor to Stephen Poyntz, 21 December 1729, BL, Althorp MSS E3.
7. *Nonsense of Common-Sense,* 17 January 1738.
8. J. Cannon (ed.), *The Letters of Junius* (Oxford, 1978), p. 320.
9. J.B. Shipley, 'James Ralph: Pretender to Genius' (Ph.D. Columbia, 1963), p. 298.
10. Flysheet, 8 April 1749, Kendal Library.
11. R.B. Walker, 'Advertising in London Newspapers, 1650–1750', *Business History*

15 (1973), 120, 123; G.A. Cranfield, *The Development of the Provincial Newspaper, 1700–1760* (Oxford, 1962), p. 210. See also I. Asquith, 'Advertising and the Press in the late Eighteenth and Early Nineteenth Centuries: James Perry and the Morning Chronicle 1790–1821', *Historical Journal* 18 (1975); T. Nevett, 'Advertising and Editorial Integrity in the Nineteenth Century', in M. Harris and A. Lee (eds), *The Press in English Society from the Seventeenth to the Nineteenth Centuries* (1986), pp. 149–67; C. Ferdinand, 'Selling to the Provinces: News and Commerce round Eighteenth-century Salisbury', in J. Brewer and R. Porter (eds), *Consumption and the World of Goods* (1993), pp. 393–411; and A. Brooks and B. Haworth, *It Paid to Advertise: A Look at Newspaper Advertisements – From Early Pre-Victorian Newspapers* (Bury, 1993).

12. T. Richards, *The Commodity Culture of Victorian England: Advertising and Spectacle, 1851–1914* (1991).

13. J. Feather, 'The English Book Trade and the Law', *Publishing History* 12 (1982), 52; Walker, 'Advertising', *Business History*, p. 119; Cranfield, *Provincial Newspaper*, p. 225.

14. Walker, 'Advertising', pp. 120–1; A. Green, 'The Property Market in the Press: Houses in Early Eighteenth-century Newcastle upon Tyne Newspapers', unpublished paper.

15. Ex. Inf. Jonathan Barry.

16. Ferdinand, *Benjamin Collins and the Provincial Newspaper Trade in the Eighteenth Century* (Oxford, 1997).

17. J. Raven, 'Serial advertisement in eighteenth-century Britain and Ireland', in Myers and Harris (eds), *Serials and Their Readers* (Winchester, 1993), p. 113.

18. R.J. Goulden, 'Edmund Baker and Jasper Sprange', *Factotum* 38 (1994), 19, re *Sussex Weekly Advertiser* 1762–73.

19. *York Courant*, 17 March 1747; *London Chronicle*, 17 January 1788.

20. Robe's proposal, Cambridge, University Library, Cholmondely (Houghton) Manuscripts, papers 75/1a.

21. F. Martin, *The History of Lloyd's* (1876), pp. 65–76; C. Wright and C.E. Fayle, *A History of Lloyd's* (1928), pp. 21–4; J. McCusker and C. Gravesteijn, *The Beginnings of Commercial and Financial Journalism* (Amsterdam, 1991).

22. M. Harris, 'Shipwrecks in print; representations of maritime disaster in the late seventeenth century', in Myers and Harris (eds), *Journeys through the Market. Travel, Travellers and the Book Trade* (Folkestone, 1999), pp. 40–54.

23. Cranfield, *Provincial Newspaper*, p. 257.

24. J. Money, *Experience and Identity. Birmingham and the West Midlands 1760–1800* (Manchester, 1977), pp. 54-6.

25. F. Burney, *Cecilia* (1904 edn), p. 857.

CHAPTER FOUR

Continuity and Change 1750–1833

It is this desire for quick and incessant intercourse that has arisen in this kingdom within the last half a century, that has tended so much to increase our power as a nation. . . . The grand lever in all these astonishing inventions, has been the Press; for while with our steam engines we smile at the winds and disregard the operation of the tides, with the press we surpass the power of Archemides; for we actually lift the universe – not the material world, certainly, but the world of thought – of mind – of conception! And by this power we shall be enabled, eventually, to overcome all the obstacles which prevent the great family of mankind from uniting cordially in the bonds of affection and brotherhood.

North Devon Journal, first issue, 2 July 1824

If the emphasis in English newspaper history is to be placed on the extent of change, then the late eighteenth and early nineteenth centuries, a period closing in 1833 with the first reduction in taxation, can be seen as one in which developments were essentially within existing forms, rather than transforming in character; it was mostly a case of more of the same. This is apparent whether production, distribution, ownership, content, or types of papers are considered. There was change, not least in the growing weight and respectability of the press, and it will be considered in the following discussion, but it was less fundamental than in 1680–1750 or 1833–1900. Why that should be is an important question, although it is obviously necessary at the outset to make it clear that there is no intention of adopting a teleological approach in which development to the present situation is assumed to have been inevitable and, in some respect, desirable, and, therefore, in which past episodes can be judged in accordance with the extent to which change was welcomed and furthered. To argue that the mid-nineteenth century marks the moment when the press became a mass phenomenon is not, however, to deny that change was important and substantial between the later eighteenth century and 1833.

The years 1750–1833 might seem to be obviously a period of change in Britain. It is one that is usually regarded as the age of Industrial Revolution, of economic transformation, technological birth, and the unleashing of power in the service of a new human order. In such a context, the retention for long of familiar methods of printing and paper production might seem anachronistic; as also might the generally small-scale nature of newspaper production, in terms of print runs, size and differentiation of labour force, and size and equipment of premises. There was no rush to follow *The Times* in introducing the steam-press.

And yet, this view of the Industrial Revolution is one that has been qualified by recent research, much of which has emphasized the slower rate of industrialization, the role of adaptation and innovation within the workshop form of manufacturing, the extent to which radical change was for long restricted to a few sectors, principally cotton textiles, and the limited use elsewhere of steam power and factory production. Instead, workshops remained central, as in Birmingham, while manual skills were still crucial to much industrial activity.[1] In such a context, the newspaper press does not appear as unduly conservative in its techniques.

It is clear, however, that the newspaper press was not at the cutting edge of industrial change, in either organizational or technological terms. This reflected the nature of the market and the capitalization of newspapers. The newspaper market of the eighteenth and nineteenth centuries is generally presented in optimistic terms, steadily greater sales indicating a buoyant commercial context. The total sale of stamped papers in million copies rose as follows:

1713	2.5	1780	14.0
1750	7.3	1835	31.0
1760	9.4	1837	48.0
1765	9.7	1851	85.0
1775	12.6		

These increases did not, however, mean guaranteed profitability. There was no licence to print money, for the lapsing of the Licensing Act in 1695 led to a situation in which anybody could start a newspaper. In the eighteenth century nearly all newspapers, at least initially, were part of a general printing business. The *Penny London Post, or The Morning Advertiser* of 6 January 1749 was not alone in carrying an advertisement by the printer for printing hand bills or shop bills. It was therefore relatively simple for printers to test a market by setting up a newspaper and, if it failed, they could concentrate on their other activities.

This lack of specialization reflected the absence of any need for specific equipment or trained staff for newspaper production (although, thanks to the law, there was a need for a supply of stamped paper), and therefore the relatively limited investment required when founding a paper. This suggests that the potential market was fairly well explored, particularly in London, where there was a large number of printers. A saturated market ensured a competitive atmosphere and a large number of failures. Newspaper rivalry was an economic imperative that ignored political affiliations. *The Times* complained about the *True-Briton's* speedier access to government-supplied foreign news in the 1790s. Whatever their politics, newspapers competed for advertisements, other than the essay-sheets, such as the *Gray's Inn Journal, Monitor, Briton* and *North Briton*, which did not print any. Thus for newspapers, in competition for advertisements and readers, rivalry was natural.

The absence of a system of privilege akin to that practised in most Continental countries, permitted a growth in the number of titles. In 1760, London had four dailies and five or six tri-weeklies. A decade later, at least five dailies, eight tri-weeklies and four weeklies were published there; in 1783, nine dailies and ten bi- or tri-weeklies, by 1790, thirteen morning, one evening, seven tri-weekly and two bi-weekly papers. By early 1792, the number of dailies had risen to fourteen and, by the end of that year, sixteen. In 1811, the total of papers in all categories published in London was fifty-two, a number swelled by Sunday newspapers, the first of which, the *British Gazette and Sunday Monitor*, was started in about 1779. The average sales of Sunday papers rose considerably in the early nineteenth century, in large part thanks to their popular format. The number of Scottish, Irish and English provincial papers also rose markedly.

Growing sales were therefore chased by more titles, and, although the sales of some individual titles rose markedly, those of many titles did not. This reduced the capital resources available for investment in new work processes and technology, and also the need for such investment: most newspapers in 1830 were expected to do what they had done sixty and, indeed, a hundred years earlier. It is not, therefore, surprising that the first newspaper to embrace the new technology was *The Times* because, in having the largest sales, it had both need and capital for technological change. In 1814, the paper began to use Koenig's steam-press, which allowed the production of 1,000 impressions an hour, as opposed to the 250 an hour from an unmechanized hand-press. The machinery was secretly prepared to prevent the opposition of the workers, who had already mounted a strike in 1810. On 29 November 1814, *The Times* announced 'the greatest improvement connected with printing since the discovery of the art itself'.

The new machinery allowed *The Times* to go to press later and thus contain more recent news than its competitors, a crucial advantage for a London daily, though less so for a provincial weekly, and also to dispense with duplicate composition on the larger number of presses required before the rate of production was thus increased. This cut the wage bill. The essentially 'commercial' nature of the change was, however, shown by the extent to which the appearance and content of the paper were not altered. Koenig's press was followed in 1827 by that of Augustus Applegath which produced 4,000 impressions an hour.

There was no rush elsewhere to introduce steam-presses. Instead, the Stanhope press, introduced from 1800 and, with its use of an iron frame, permitting a clearer impression but no faster a rate of production, sufficed. The type was on an iron bed, or carriage, that was moved into and out of the press by human effort. It was not until the 1820s that some titles began to follow *The Times*, for example the *Morning Herald* in 1822 and the *Manchester Courier* in 1825. As the possibilities of profitable technological change became more apparent and newspaper sales shot up from 1835, the rate of change increased. The *Manchester Guardian* had been founded in 1821, and had acquired a steam-press in 1828, but it was in 1838 that Jeremiah Garnett devised new methods of feeding the presses of the paper so that 1,500 impressions an hour could be produced.[2] The first issue of the *Wiltshire County Mirror* (10 February 1852) announced that it coincided 'with the first introduction into Salisbury of Printing by Steam . . . printed . . . by one of Napier's double-feeding machines, propelled by steam'. In response, the *Salisbury Journal* immediately adopted steam-printing.[3] The more prominent *Bristol Mercury* had acquired its Napier machine in 1836, and the *Halifax Guardian* in 1841. This led to the enlargement of the latter from four to eight pages.

Despite the efforts of John Walter, who, in 1785, founded the *Daily Universal Register* in order to publicize logography, there were no significant developments in typesetting until the 1880s, though mechanized papermaking, which became commercially viable in 1807, led to the steam-powered production of plentiful quantities of inexpensive paper. More rapid printing contributed to an increase in the size of newspapers, many of which by the 1830s were eight pages long, each with six columns. *The Times* also led the way in having a larger staff: printers, compositors and writing staff. Other papers followed, although not at the same rate.

The parameters of distribution techniques did not alter until the creation of a national railway network in the mid-nineteenth century. Prior to that, human and horse-power remained crucial, both in the local distribution patterns of all papers and in the national distribution of a number of London titles. The national distribution of London newspapers depended on the mail service, initially horse-mail and then the mail-coach. Improvements in the road system and in the provision of Post Office services ensured that distribution by the traditional methods became more rapid and reliable. Initially distributed through the Post Office, largely by means of the franking privilege of the Clerks of the Road, who distributed newspapers in return for payment, the system changed when franking was replaced by free postage for newspapers.[4] Furthermore, improvements in communications speeded up the movement of information and of goods, the latter a boon for advertisers. *Jackson's Oxford Journal* reported on 19 June 1773:

> The difference in the number of stage coaches, etc. travelling on the Western road, within these few years, is not a little remarkable. About ten years ago there only passed through Salisbury in the course of a week, to and from London and Exeter, six stage coaches. . . . At present there constantly pass, between the above places, in the same space of time, 24 stage coaches . . . and 28 stage chaises.

Newspapers frequently carried advertisements for new coach services and this became more common as traffic and competition increased. Thus, for example, the *Birmingham Commercial Herald* of 30 January 1804 carried long advertisements for competing services, while the *Birmingham Chronicle* of 9 January 1823 carried an item from the *Sheffield Independent* about a new coach service between the two cities. In the *Taunton Courier* of 23 January 1828 there was an advertisement for a tri-weekly coach service from Taunton to Bath, connecting there for London. The paper commented:

> As we have ourselves experienced the advantages of the improved communication which has been effected between London and this town and neighbourhood, by the establishment of regular traders from Bridgwater, we feel much pleasure in calling the attention of our readers to the advertisement in this day's paper. A regular and cheap communication with the markets of the metropolis being equally important to the manufacturer and agriculturist, for the disposal of their produce, as it is to the tradesman and shopkeeper, for the purchase of their stock, we trust, and indeed feel confident, that the public will support an undertaking which has been begun and is now carried on with so much spirit.

Speedier and more frequent transport links created the potential for more frequently appearing provincial newspapers, as the flow of copy to them increased. However, the economic basis for provincial bi-weeklies, let alone dailies, did not yet exist: the Canterbury-based *Kentish Gazette* was unusual in being a bi-weekly. As a result, better communications instead accentuated the appearance of more frequent newspapers in the provinces by increasing the speed and frequency of the distribution of the London press. In addition, well before the railway and the telegraph, newspapers contributed to, and sought to benefit from, a sense of news as a crucial aspect of a speeded up and increasingly linked world. This was commodified by reference to accessibility to speedy news as a reason for the purchase of particular titles.

The London tri-weeklies, for which country sales were particularly important, were not alone in benefiting from better communications. It was not only London papers that used the mail. The first number of the *Newark Herald and Nottinghamshire and Lincolnshire General Advertiser*

(5 October 1791) was keen to assert its national range and local circulation, clearly offering itself as an intermediary between nation and locality:

> Being published early in the morning, it will be dispatched by the South Mail of that day, to London, and all the intermediate market towns; and by the North Mail, and by-posts, at two o'clock, it will be forwarded to a number of key cities, including Newcastle, Hull, Leeds, York, Liverpool, and Birmingham. In addition, in the following villages in the counties of Nottingham and Lincoln, it will be regularly published every Wednesday, free of expense, by distributors employed for that purpose; and any orders given to them will be punctually executed.

Ninety-five places were listed.

Distribution networks did not change radically until an integrated and comprehensive railway network had been created. This was later than is sometimes appreciated. Though the Stockton and Darlington railway was opened in 1825 and the Liverpool to Manchester in 1830, a national network was only really in place by mid-century, the main line system was not completed until the early 1870s, and many local and branch lines were built thereafter. In 1852, there was still no link between London and Cornwall; that to Norwich had only opened in 1845. Suffolk, predominantly rural, was fairly slow in acquiring rail links. The railway only reached Ipswich and Bury St Edmunds in 1846, Newmarket in 1848.

Furthermore, a national press did not have to wait for the coming of the railways; as the earlier country distribution of London newspapers showed. In January 1775, John Campbell wrote from his seat at Stackpole Court in Pembrokeshire to his grandson John, then in London, 'I read in the Public Advertiser of Tuesday the 3rd inst. that you had lost at Drury Lane playhouse a fine enamelled gold watch with your crest cypher and motto on the back.'[5]

The content of the press, both London and provincial, changed relatively little in the second half of the eighteenth century, though more in the following half-century. This reflected the combination of only limited changes in the market and an essentially constant news-gathering system, especially in so far as the general absence of reporters was concerned. Indeed there were great similarities between the newspapers published after the lapse of the Licensing Act in 1695 and those that appeared a century later. News was still usually produced without the benefit of illustrations or maps. The lack of novelty was far from surprising. Alongside a fascination with new or newly popular forms and devices, whether umbrellas or turnpikes, balloons or steam engines, magazines or foreign travel, there were important elements of continuity. Neither the social nor the political system changed as greatly as they were to do in the last three-quarters of the nineteenth century.

In addition, both in 1695 and a century later, Britain was at war with France. The press was dominated by the conflict and by its ramifications, for its impact was general. War and international affairs did not only affect statesmen and coffee-house politicians; the merchant scanning for information about privateers, the farmer eager to know the effects of hostilities on the corn trade, and those with family members in the armed forces, shared their concern, and the press obliged. 'The New Year's Present of the Men who carry The Dorchester and Sherborne Journal, and Taunton and Somersetshire Herald, for the Year 1799', a flysheet commenting on the news of the last year and asking for a tip, stated

> Much blood, 'tis true, still stains his pages,
> But this must be, where battle rages . . .[6]

A memorandum of 1765 on the Stamp Duties noted that newspaper sales were affected more by the public's demand for news than by the taxation regime: the 1757 increase of duty had not cut sales, but the end of the Seven Years War (1756–63) had:

> the vent of them depending much less upon the price than upon the circumstances of the times exciting more or less curiosity. The highest duty . . . before the year 1756 was £17,999 14s 4d . . . during the whole war it was never less than £21,624 16s but last year it fell to £19,030 4s 10d from whence it may be presumed that during a peace this branch of the Stamp Duties will fall short of the sum above-mentioned.[7]

This portrayal of a peacetime limit on sales was to be proved inaccurate over the following decade, though it was true that war and international crisis both increased public interest in the news and made it easier to fill the columns of the press. In consequence, the newspapers were to be faced with a more difficult situation after 1815 for, thereafter, until 1914, Britain only engaged in one European conflict, the short-lived Crimean War, and, in reporting distant colonial conflicts, it was impossible to rely on foreign newspapers for information and necessary to use expensive telegraphy.

The most obvious difference between the press of the 1690s and that of the 1790s, and still more the 1830s, was the increase in the physical size of the newspapers and their use of smaller type. The double column folio half-sheets of the late seventeenth and early eighteenth centuries were replaced by larger and more densely printed papers. Most papers increased their size and number of columns in the early eighteenth century. The *York Courant* of 13 March 1739 noted that there was not enough space to print the advertisements and announced that the printer 'designs next month to print the Courant in a much larger size, by which means it will contain more than any newspaper extant', a reference to the competitive relationship that guided issues of size and cost.

Restricted for tax reasons to four pages, papers increased their number of columns in the second half of the century. The *Leeds Intelligencer* switched to four columns in early 1767, *Berrow's Worcester Journal* made the change at the beginning of 1770, and the *Newcastle Courant* in 1775. In the spring of 1792, the *Chelmsford Chronicle* increased both the size of the paper on which it was printed and the number of columns per page, from three to four. Readers were promised that these increases would lead to an improvement in content. The *Bristol Chronicle, or Universal Mercantile Register* was launched in January 1760 as an eight-page, two-column per page weekly but, on 27 December 1760, the paper announced that it would appear 'next year in three columns, after the manner of the London and British Chronicles, as we apprehend it will thereby contain a greater quantity of news than either of the other papers. We have, after much trouble and expense, established as extensive a correspondence for it as any in this city.' On 11 July 1761, the paper announced that 'the proprietor . . . being advised . . . to alter the form . . . on account of making the advertisements inserted here more conspicuous' had decided that from the following issue it should appear in 'four folio pages and four columns in the page . . . in which form it will contain as much intelligence as at present, and rather more'. *Berrow's Worcester Journal* of 4 January 1770 declared that it would be able to publish 'a still greater variety of useful and interesting matter'. On 1 February 1774, the *Middlesex Journal* was enlarged 'in order to give a circumstantial account of the debates in both Houses of Parliament'.

In practice, news was still predominantly political, the reports derivative, anonymous and impersonal. Events, rumours and manifestos were printed, not interviews. Most items were short and without explanation or introduction, and for domestic news there was a relative absence of pieces providing background information.

There were, however, shifts, so that, to compare three peacetime decades, the press of the 1780s, and even more the 1820s, was different to that of the 1720s. There were more advertisements by the 1780s and even more by the 1820s, and they occupied both a larger and a more prominent proportion of the papers. In place of many newspapers striving to emulate essay-sheets by devoting their entire first page to an essay, most papers gave the first page over to advertisements. Political news was no longer so dominated by the affairs of the Continent. Instead, colonial news, and that from the newly independent United States of America, were discussed, while, from the early 1770s, there were, during the session, regular and lengthy reports of parliamentary debates. There was more non-political news, particularly items devoted to social habits and fashions. Literary, particularly theatrical, news had become a regular feature, and there were more items of commercial information. The activities of criminals were still a popular topic, and in the first half of the nineteenth century were to become more so as they became the central subject of the Sunday newspapers. Sporting news, virtually absent in the 1720s, was regularly carried by the 1780s. Provincial newspapers provided accounts of local races.[8]

These are but one example of the greater quantity of local news carried in the provincial press. The increase in the number of words per paper meant that there could be more local news, even though political news remained dominated by metropolitan sources of information, and the exciting events of the period. The American War and the French Revolution were best covered from this perspective. The liberalization of parliamentary reporting at the beginning of the 1770s further increased the importance of items about London, as did the greater interest in the fashionable world that was reflected not just in items about fashion or London society, but also in those about the theatre or books.

Some early printers held strong political views, but, in so far as their papers revealed this, it was generally in terms of the London papers that they selected as sources for their items, though a study of the Bristol press has concluded that it does not vindicate the common contention that the eighteenth-century provincial press was simply a 'scissors-and-paste' affair, put together by professional printers with purely commercial interests and devoid of local content and ideological significance. Instead, it has been argued that in Bristol the pressure to establish alternative channels of news and opinion owed more to ideological than financial considerations, that the customary claim to impartiality was a device designed to enable partisan groups to lay claim to a common set of values, and that much reporting was designed to strike a particular political resonance.[9] This argument can also be advanced for other towns where rival newspapers contributed to and reflected a divided political world, such as Norwich. Partisanship was less pronounced in some other papers, a reminder of the danger of treating all provincial papers as if they were similar.

Most provincial newspapers existed to disseminate news of the wider world, rather than to focus local political sensibilities and elicit opinion, though the two were not incompatible, and the situation changed, especially from the 1790s. The provincial press did not contain much local news, for its readers could be assumed to know that through oral report. Instead they purchased and read newspapers because these provided regular access to the affairs of the wider world.

The foundation of London Sundays ensured that there were more types of papers at the close of the eighteenth century than there had been earlier; but, otherwise, the division between provincial weeklies and London dailies, bi- or tri-weeklies and weeklies remained the case. On the other hand, the unstamped London press had been extinguished in the early 1740s, while the London cheap press, penny tri-weeklies, disappeared a decade later. As a result, the press consisted of a variety of products at similar prices and in similar forms. The Second Stamp Act of 1725 had not prohibited the production of papers of more than four sheets. It simply made them more expensive. The basic physical appearance of newspapers set in 1725 was to last, though, in the 1750s, a variation was made with the appearance of tri-weekly 'chronicles', such as the long-lasting *London Chronicle,* in eight smaller pages.

There was also an unwillingness to deviate from the price charged by other papers of the same type. The essential stability of the form established in 1725, which was not to be broken until the following century, was a testimony to the role of commercial considerations and to the inherent conservatism of the newspaper world as much as to the determining constraints of taxation. Although 'stop press' sections developed on back pages, the inability of most newspapers to respond to particular upsurges in news by printing longer issues is instructive, as is the failure to print longer tri-weeklies and weeklies despite the general increase in available material. Given the money spent on magazines, which were more expensive, it is difficult to believe that a market did not exist for weekly newspapers combining the news with magazine-type articles and costing more than most papers because they were longer.

Longer papers, however, might have jeopardized the ratio of advertisements to length that was so crucial to profitability. The combination of larger pages (the Second Stamp Act failed to define a standard size for a single sheet of paper, enabling printers to treat increasingly large four-page papers as half-sheets), more columns and smaller type still allowed more material to be printed. The pressure was increasingly on columns and type, because the Stamp Act of 1757 closed the sheet-size loophole. It imposed a duty of $1d$ on all papers, whether printed on a whole sheet or half a sheet.

Irrespective of tax, however, the cost of paper acted as an important restraint on size. Before the introduction of wood-pulp and esparto grass as cheaper and readily available sources in the nineteenth century, paper was expensive. This discouraged speculative printing as, although unused copies could be recycled as waste paper, this increased costs. Although the cost of paper was a less important restraint than taxation, it also served to encourage the technique of cramming.

Bell's Weekly Messenger, a recently launched Sunday, responded on 12 June 1796 to reader complaints about the size of the print by commenting: 'we are enabled to afford more interesting information than is contained in any other *two newspapers*'. Such an expansion posed the question of layout, but the general increase in size was not automatically accompanied, in either the London or the non-metropolitan press, by an improvement in the organization of the news and in the layout of the paper. The absence of pictures meant that there were no captions to guide the reader, while, unlike some magazines, there were no tables of contents.

By the 1790s the position had improved, with some titles, the *Argus*, *Evening Mail*, *Oracle*, *Star and Sun*, employing reasonable headlining. This was accompanied in some papers by a system of sub-headlines that helped to define the organization of the news. This often followed the traditional pattern by which items appeared by post or under the source of the report. In the *Oracle* of 14 November 1791, the sub-heading 'Insurrection in St Domingo' appeared under the Paris heading, 'India News' under London. Most papers by the 1790s resorted to leading and the use of rules across the columns to differentiate between major items, though *Bell's Weekly Messenger* of 1 May 1796 disapproved:

> It has of late been the custom in newspapers to distinguish the most prominent articles by leaving greater space than usual between the lines, which is called giving them lead. The proprietor of the *Messenger*, however, wishing to afford his readers as much inform-ation and amusement as possible, means to put as little lead as may be, in his paper. He trusts that their taste and discrimination will enable them to find out of themselves which is the most interesting part of his Miscellany.

This unsystematic 'cram it in' attitude also affected the organization and layout of advertisements in the press. Nevertheless, the once largely amorphous mass of news was increasingly differentiated and organized into new categories, the introduction of which enabled newspapers to appear to be providing new types of news and to stress aspects of their coverage that they felt were especially good or distinctive. On 11 June 1789, the *Oracle* printed a speech to Congress by George Washington under the heading 'United States', followed by the claim that

> these original, authentic, and important papers, thus early communicated to the Public by means of the Oracle *alone*, will show the extended sources of intelligence which are peculiar to this print. The New World is now opening scenes and subjects for great political speculation, wherein the interests of Europe may be deeply concerned. . . . It shall be the object of the Oracle to report the rising consequence of the American states, whenever circumstances may challenge the attention of statesmen, or the contemplation of a politician. We have assurances of constant communication with persons high in confidence, and of the most unimpeachable integrity.

On 1 July 1795, 'The Field of Mars' first appeared as a headline in the *Oracle*, and its explanatory notice stressed the mutually reinforcing relationship of a specific readership and good advertising potential; a facet of the attempt by all papers to boost their appeal to crucial advertis-ing revenue by increasing their readership:

Under this head, all communications respecting military affairs will be arranged in future. Gentlemen of the army are requested to favour the Oracle with every information which they may think beneficial to the service. Such articles, as well as any others of an interesting nature, will be most respectfully attended to. From the extensive sale which this paper has now established in military circles, all advertisements respecting the army will be read with advantage. They will be received by the agents at the different camps, who are appointed to distribute this paper, or at the Oracle's office.

Many newspapers increasingly offered a distinct editorial. Lucyle Werkmeister suggested that the spurious *Star* in 1789 was the first paper to present a well-developed editorial. She discerned a definite shift between the expression of opinion in short paragraphs or letters from real or invented correspondents, and the example of the spurious *Star* which offered a daily commentary for which it took the credit itself, located in the central column of the third page, where it would attract the most attention. Werkmeister exaggerated the contrast between the short paragraphs of earlier papers and those of the spurious *Star*, but it is clear that in the 1790s most London papers had clearly defined editorial sections. Provincial papers essentially continued their practice of making comments in the local section of their news, though some, such as the radical *Manchester Herald* (1792–3), published clear editorials. The credit for first publishing editorial articles in the provincial press has been given to two Unitarian reformers of the period, Benjamin Flower of the *Cambridge Intelligencer* and Joseph Gales of the *Sheffield Register*,[10] though, as with the London press, it is difficult to define an editorial. It is noteworthy that some provincial papers were as advanced as their metropolitan counterparts.

Many features of the press changed during the last years of the eighteenth century, ranging from improved distribution to larger staff, which permitted greater differentiation in function, from the foundation of more Sunday papers to the increase in the country section of London newspapers, with many papers, such as *Bell's Weekly Messenger*, making provincial news a regular feature. Alongside these developments, continuity can also be stressed, the natural result of the technological constraints of assembling the news and producing a paper and the consequence of the conservative nature of a newspaper world in which well-tried methods that produced successful results were maintained by men whose conception of the potentialities of print was based on experience.

The papers of the 1790s, lacking a corps of journalists, still actively encouraged correspondents to send in items, as did their nineteenth-century successors. John Harland, the *Manchester Guardian*'s first full-time reporter, was an uncommon figure in the provincial press of the 1830s.[11] On 1 June 1789, the first issue of the *Oracle* asked 'Ye Moralists, ye Poets, Historians, Philosophers, and Politicians! Ye Artists and Men of Commerce, send therefore your communications hither.' Nine days later, the paper was able to comment on sixteen contributions, three of which were rejected for 'venom', one for libel and one for blasphemy. The *Birmingham Commercial Herald* of 3 January 1818 asked for essays on agriculture, botany and horticulture, while the *Birmingham Chronicle* of 16 January 1823 thanked its Coventry correspondent for his account of the recent sessions.

Numerous contributions were not the sole reason why newspapers faced the same problems of selection that had confronted their predecessors. The limited size of the paper created the essential problem, but it was exacerbated by the lifting of restrictions upon the reporting of parliamentary news, the growth of economic, theatrical, sporting and provincial news, and Britain's war with France for most of the period 1793–1815. Newspapers frequently referred to having to choose what material to insert. The *Courier* of 6 January 1795 noted 'We have received a great number of letters, and of Dutch, German, and French papers, of which the extreme length of the debate in the House of Commons prevents us at present from entering into detail.'

Reporting the war created problems for the press similar to those in earlier conflicts with France. The use of foreign correspondents was very rare. Most foreign news came from traditional sources, the foreign press and the British government. Rather than seeking the news themselves, newspapers continued to be derivative, competing for primacy in government information or struggling to obtain copies of the French papers as speedily as possible. Newspapers remained dependent on the Continental mails, with concomitant problems of delayed information and uncertain news.

Similar problems concerning the speed and verification of news also affected the non-metropolitan press. There was no sign in 1820 of the changes that were to follow the widespread introduction of such innovations as the railway and telegraphy. Competing papers continued to stress the speed with which they obtained the London news and this was transmitted by familiar methods. Rebutting the claims of a rival to publish fresher news, the *Sheffield Advertiser* of 7 September 1787 declared:

> This paper is published about 8 o'clock in the morning of every Friday, and contains the most important intelligence from all the London and other papers, and the last post from the Wednesday evening London papers . . . which arrive at Sheffield late on Thursday night.

Although there was no problem in filling newspapers with material, it was still relatively difficult for both the London and the non-metropolitan press to fill their columns with unique items of news. The need to obtain news from other publications encouraged the reprinting of items on a large scale and this was particularly marked in the case of tri-weeklies and weeklies, less so for morning dailies. This limited the development of particular styles for individual papers. It was not common practice to rewrite borrowed items, and a consistency of style was not the goal of most of the press, with the important exception of the essay-papers. The *Weekly Register* of 11 April 1798 commented,

> As the Weekly Register will not be a mere selection, *servilely copied*, as is the usual manner from the public prints; but contain a great variety of original articles, and the whole be entirely recomposed, it is hoped it may preserve a consistency, both of style and fact, not very usual in a newspaper, and be found worth the inspection even of gentlemen who are in the habit of perusing the daily papers.

Significant changes have been discerned at the end of the eighteenth and the beginning of the next century. It has been suggested that the growth in the advertising revenue of certain leading London papers enabled them to become independent of political sponsorship, and was the most important factor in enabling the press to emerge as the fourth estate of the realm. Attention has been focused on the development of higher editorial standards, the rise of the Sundays, the growing challenge to the metropolitan dominance of advertising, the expression of radical opinion in the provincial press and the beginning of 'the age of the provinces'.[12]

These shifts are certainly more significant than any detected in the mid-eighteenth century, and yet caution is necessary in evaluating and dating the concept of a major discontinuity. A 'tendency to accept established news values uncritically', stemming from long professional experience, noted of Victorian journalists,[13] was also true of their predecessors. Most papers remained similar, though that is partly a matter of perception. Distinctive features stressed by papers in the past that may appear of scant significance to the modern reader may have impressed contemporaries. Papers that appear very similar today had widely varying fortunes.

Much of the similarity was, however, inevitable given the limited resources in terms of staff and access to individual sources of news that particular papers possessed. Though the number of staff employed by successful London papers rose in the late eighteenth century, the increase was limited. In the early 1780s, no printing house employed more than one parliamentary reporter. Foreign correspondents were exceptional figures. It was only in the 1810s and 1820s that the increasing financial resources of the major newspapers began to be used for a significant expansion of the regular reporting staffs.[14] Given this situation, it was difficult for newspapers to develop individual strengths.

An appreciation of the essentially conservative nature of the London press, in terms of the organization and contents of newspapers, helps to place in perspective the customary view of the provincial press as merely derivative. Provincial papers indeed retained many traditional features at the close of the eighteenth century. Despite the increase in the number of post days, the news was still customarily grouped in the papers of the 1780s in three sections, corresponding to different posts, with little, if any, cross-referencing. Most eighteenth-century comments on popular readership of the press and discussion of politics related to London, where the impact of print, in its varied forms, was more sustained and socially more far-reaching. Correspondingly the press was developed and differentiated there, with daily, tri-weekly, Sunday and financial newspapers. Provincial centres could not support such forms, but it would be unsatisfactory to approach their press simply from the point of view of a poor imitation of a metropolitan trendsetter. The absence of a provincial daily press should not be seen in terms of failure, but rather as a response to the nature of market and news opportunities. Furthermore, the provincial press was growing rapidly.

Many of the articles in the press were well calculated for the placards that were developed in the first quarter of the nineteenth century to highlight particular items. This use of large typeface advertising extended the visual impact of newspapers. The placards were fixed to mail-coaches and put up around newspaper offices. Crimes had always been a staple. The Sunday papers took up this interest and made it the basis of their success. At least eighteen Sundays were published in London in 1812 and some, such as the *Weekly Dispatch* founded in 1801, were great successes. The Sundays were to enjoy a burst of expansion in the 1840s after the lowering of stamp duties, with the foundation of *Lloyd's Weekly London Newspaper* (1842), later shortened to *Lloyd's Weekly News*, the *News of the World* (1843), the *Weekly Times* (1847) and *Reynolds's Weekly Newspaper* (1850), all of which were very successful in employing the formula developed earlier in the century, and coining the high murder rate of a society that was changing rapidly.

The Sundays benefited from the high cost of taking a more regular newspaper, from the increasing definition of Sunday as leisure time in the more regulated urban environment and economic system that was developing, and from their clear association with more accessible and exciting news. They represented a particular facet of a widespread phenomenon of the early nineteenth-century press: the growth, across the whole range of periodicals, of specialization. This reflected a more developed society, the desire and ability of those who controlled and composed the world of printing and publishing to create and respond to opportunities, and the increasing sense in sphere after sphere that it was necessary, or at least desirable, to have a periodical to note changes, discuss options and activities, and act as a focus, a means of coherence, as was done, for example, by the *Ecclesiastical Gazette* (1838–1900), the trade paper of the Church of England.

The press searched for new markets, as with the *Children's Companion* (1824–1932), and offered a way to display and fortify solidarity. This was to lead for example to a number of army and school newspapers. The *Lower Bank Gazette* (1837–41), produced at a small boarding school near Preston, ran to over sixty issues, composed and printed by the boys themselves. The articles ranged from school news and classroom trivia to the reprinting of early verse by Tennyson and others. Original verses and essays also appeared, along with serious addresses from the headmaster. Both tone and content were very different from the penny dreadfuls produced for boys in the 1840s.

The increase in religious periodical publication was a noteworthy aspect of this differentiation. Two papers of the 1730s, William Webster's Anglican *Weekly Miscellany* and Samuel Chandler's Dissenting *Old Whig*, had essays commonly devoted to religious topics, but, in addition, there were periodicals that were more dedicated in content and approach. A series of Calvinistic Methodist journals were published between 1740 and 1745 under successive titles: the *Christian's Amusement*, the *Weekly History*, and *An Account of the Progress of the Gospel*. Other papers were brought out by friends of George Whitefield. William McCulloch produced in 1742 the *Glasgow-Weekly-History Relating to the Late Progress of the Gospel at Home and Abroad*, sold only to subscribers at ½d. The *Christian Monthly History* (1743–4) was produced at Edinburgh. In 1750–1, John Gillies, a leading Glaswegian evangelical minister, issued a weekly sermon, an *Exhortation to the Inhabitants of South Parish of Glasgow*. The Methodist *Arminian Magazine* began publication in 1778.

The London weekly *Man* (1755), an essay-paper offering Christianity and morality, rather than advertisements and news, ended with the year: 'For the future it is thought more advisable to continue the design of these papers in pocket-volumes, occasionally, than in single sheets', a reminder of the fluidity of the medium of print and its responsive nature to market conditions. The variety of the world of print was indicated in the late 1780s, for, alongside new 'West-End' papers, such as the *World*, whose morality was limited to that of its subject-matter, fashionable society, a new monthly, the *Family Magazine; or a Repository of Religious Instruction and Rational Amusement – Designed to counteract the pernicious tendency of immoral books*, was launched in 1788. The following decades were to see a tremendous growth in the religious periodical and newspaper press, with, for example, the foundation of the *Evangelical Magazine* (1793), and of a whole series of periodicals linked to different sects. The number of religious newspapers rose markedly from the late 1820s.[15] With their confessions, often lurid tales of sin, redemption and retribution, pious deaths and element of the supernatural, many religious papers were accessible, providing a readily grasped content, an exciting series of individual morality tales that paralleled crime literature. In the nineteenth century, non-Protestant and non-Christian newspapers appeared, for example the *Catholic Standard* and the *Jewish Chronicle*.

The presence of religious periodicals did not mean that other newspapers did not publish such items; nor did it mean that important religious figures could not secure the insertion of material favourable to their cause in sympathetic newspapers. The *Westminster Journal* of 25 September 1773 commented on:

> the large number of letters which we lately published, the subject predestination, or the searching into the secret decrees of the omnipotent God. This one was sure he was right, and that other was sure he was right. This brought texts of scripture to prove he could not err, and that to convince his readers that he was on the indubitable side of the question. And what did all this amount to, more than to demonstrate that the thoughts of men are vain.

Locational differentiation, the foundation of new titles in towns that had hitherto lacked their own paper (and the same with partisan newspapers), can be seen on an imperial as well as a British scale; indeed the former indicated the extent to which an active press was one of the aspects of British civilization in this period. The first English provincial newspaper was probably the *Norwich Post* in 1701, while the first Scottish newspaper, the *Edinburgh Gazette*, appeared briefly in 1680 and reappeared in the 1690s. English serials were shipped across the Atlantic, but, as early as 1704, Boston, Massachusetts, had the *Boston News Letter*, the first regular newspaper published by authority in the Thirteen Colonies, though in 1690 an unlicensed, and swiftly suppressed, paper, *Public Occurences Foreign and Domestic*, had been published. The colonial press was to be a buoyant aspect of the eighteenth-century British press, in part dependent on it for printers and machinery and, increasingly, exchanging information.[16]

With their large population of white settlers and their wealth, the North American colonies soon provided copy for British newspapers, although the extent of this coverage should not be exaggerated. In 1735, the *London Journal* carried colonial items under a heading 'News from the Plantations', announcing on 23 August that 'the British Colonies are of so much importance to the trade and commerce of Great Britain that we shall continue . . . to make a separate article'. 'Plantation News' was a heading employed in a number of papers, including the *Newcastle Courant* and the *Penny London Morning Advertiser* in the 1740s.

Increased colonial news reflected not only greater interest in the colonies, which can also be seen in the magazines,[17] but also the growing ease of providing such news, due in particular to the development of a colonial press. This provided a regular source for items of colonial news, reducing the significance of information provided by personal letters. It thus corresponded in its effect to the improvement in the network of British provincial newspapers. By the 1780s, items were regularly appearing in British newspapers with acknowledgement to papers such as the *Calcutta Gazette*. Interest in empire became even stronger the following century.[18] The linked interest in empire and trade also had a political impact, helping to create an image of national identity that was focused on maritime and imperial themes.[19]

In the West Indies, newspapers began on Jamaica with the *Weekly Jamaica Courant* (1718), and the number of towns supporting a paper increased with the *St Jago Intelligencer* (1756), the *Cornwall Chronicle* from Montego Bay (1773), and the foundation of newspapers at Savanna-la-Mer (1788) and Falmouth (1791). Other colonies acquired their first papers later in the century: the *Barbados Gazette* (1738), the *St Christopher Gazette* (1747), the *Antigua Gazette* (1748), the *Royal Grenada Gazette* (1765), the *Bermuda Gazette* (1784), and the *Bahama Gazette* (1784). British occupation of other colonies was followed speedily by the launching of papers: the *St Lucia Gazette* (1780), the *Royal Essequebo and Demerary Gazette* (1796) in Guyana, the *Trinidad Weekly Courant* (1800), and the *Cape Town Gazette, and African Advertiser* (1800). The *Ceylon Government Gazette* was first issued in 1802.[20]

As in Britain, the early nineteenth century saw the foundation of newspapers in towns hitherto lacking them, the *Honduras Gazette and Commercial Advertiser* (1826) in Belize, the *Turks' Island Gazette and Commercial Reporter* (1845), and the first Trinidad paper published outside Port-of-Spain, the *San Fernando Gazette* (1850); as well as of competing titles in existing centres, for example the *Barbados Mercury* (1762), *Royal Gazette and Bahama Advertiser* (1802), *Royal Gazette* (Bermuda, 1809) and *Bermudian* (1819). Pronounced rivalries developed, for example the *St George's Chronicle and New Grenada Gazette* (1789) with the *Grenada Free Press* (1826). There was a measure of differentiation. Papers aimed at the emancipated slaves began to appear, though the Jamaican *West Indian* (1838) proved short-lived, possibly as a result of limited advertising and heavy postal charges.[21] In contrast, Lieutenant Hugh Pearce Pearson, sending news home of the Indian Mutiny, told his parents, 'the *Friend of India . . .* is a paper you can rely upon as containing the puckah news and is the *Times* of India'.[22]

The British also established an English-language press in their 'informal empire', the regions they dominated commercially. By 1835, for example, the *British Packet and Argentine News* was an established weekly in Buenos Aires, with a strong mercantile emphasis. The movement of foreign ships was regularly reported, together with the current prices of such commodities as skins, wool and salt. Expatriate communities elsewhere developed their own newspapers, while the emergence of English as the *lingua franca* of business was further to assist the market for English-language periodicals outside the British empire.

The independence, self-confidence and proclaimed sense of mission of the press was enhanced by its growth. Increased circulation and the rising volume of advertisements represented, despite the duty they carried, a source of financial independence. In 1793, the profit on the *Morning Chronicle* was £6,000. Such profits were too large to be jeopardized by selling political support, and no ministry would have been prepared to pay the £40,000 that the *Morning Chronicle* was sold for in 1821.[23]

This process culminated with the rise of *The Times* to pre-eminence among British newspapers. It already had the largest sale by 1801, though, at less than 3,000, this was little more than the *Morning Advertiser* and *Morning Herald*. In contrast, the *Leeds Mercury* sold an average of 700–800 a week.[24] By 1821 *The Times* sold an average of 7,000 copies per day, its nearest rival, the *Morning Chronicle*, 3,100. Though sales of *The Times* declined in the early 1830s, they revived thereafter, and exceeded those of its next three metropolitan rivals in 1840 and the next five in 1850.[25] A paper whose opinions could not be bought, *The Times*, had rather to be influenced by careful and sensitive management, not least by providing access to information, especially in the field of foreign policy.[26] There was no equivalent of the deprivation of revenue from official notices employed by the governors of Caribbean colonies to discipline the press.

The voice of confidence can be glimpsed in a complaint received by Henry Addington, the Prime Minister, in 1802. His correspondent was John Heriot, the conductor of the *Sun* and the *True Briton*, both pro-ministerial newspapers:

> This forenoon a gentleman from the Treasury (Mr. Unwin) called upon me with a message from Mr. Vansittart [Joint Secretary of the Treasury] to inform me that if such paragraphs as that in the True Briton of today appear in it, I can no longer receive the protection of government . . . it must be as far from your ideas that I, or any man, should be *threatened* into a support of government, as it is inconsistent with my feelings to receive such a threat with apathy and submission.

Addington, in reply, pointed out the problems caused by press criticism of foreign powers, but adopted an emollient tone.[27] For their part, the Whigs had a strained relationship with the press, including the Foxite *Morning Chronicle*, whose editor, James Perry, stressed his independence from party leaders. None of the Whig leaders had much leverage over the press, and Brougham and Lord Grey complained that Perry put circulation and advertising revenue before his commitment to the party.

The growing independence of the press was linked to a clearer sense of its own purpose that reflected a political world in which public opinion was felt to have a more pronounced and acceptable role. There was not, however, a public for which different papers competed, but rather several, each represented by a different style of political consciousness.

William Mackinnon, elected in 1830 as a Tory MP, offered, in his *On the Rise, Progress and Present State of Public Opinion in Great Britain and Other Parts of the World* (1828), a socially specific definition of public opinion:

> Public opinion may be said to be, that sentiment on any given subject which is entertained by the best informed, most intelligent, and most moral persons in the community, which is gradually spread and adopted by nearly all persons of any education or proper feeling in a civilized state. It may be also said, that this feeling exists in a community, and becomes powerful in proportion as information, moral principle, intelligence, and facility of communication are to be found. As most of these requisites are to be found in the middle class of society as well as the upper, it follows that the power of public opinion depends in a great measure on the proportion that the upper and middle class of society bear to the lower, or on the quantity of intelligence and wealth that exists in the community.[28]

Mackinnon offered no support for the modern tendency to treat public opinion as an essentially democratic political phenomenon. There was a moral dimension to politics or rather public consciousness, one in which terms such as obligation and obedience acquired meaning, and the press helped to define and express it. However, the popular moral dimension or dimensions explored by scholars through concepts such as the moral economy of the crowd found only a limited echo in the late eighteenth-century press. Instead, a more socially specific moral resonance was struck by the press, one more in keeping with a medium whose circulation and social range was restricted in comparison to that of genuinely popular written forms: almanacs and chapbooks. That would not have disturbed advertisers offering high-value goods and services, which required advertising and justified the cost in a world where most goods and services were not advertised other than orally; nor writers calling for the moralizing of a supposedly dissolute populace.

The call for moral policing and improvement that grew so markedly in the last quarter of the eighteenth century could be ascribed to growing social pressures in the industrializing parts of the country, for newspapers such as the *Leeds Intelligencer*, *Leeds Mercury* and *Sheffield Advertiser* criticized such popular pastimes as bull-baiting, cock-fighting, drunkenness and profanity. Alternative values were ignored; the virtuous had to unite to convert or compel the reprobate and the culture of print was to advance the cause. Such comments were not restricted to industrializing regions and can instead be seen as an aspect of widespread secular evangelicalism that complemented the religious variety.

A moral critique could have political and social consequences that were not directed against the establishment, as with the piece in the *Birmingham Chronicle* of 10 April 1823 that pressed for the abolition of the

Game Laws which were presented as a cause of injustice and hardship, but with no accompanying social critique. The first half of the nineteenth century witnessed a shift, however, in that an anti-establishment critique became more powerful, largely as a consequence of the fusion of the moral economy of the middling orders with specific political causes. This critique was of a certain type: opposed to privileges, but not calling for social redistribution.

The growing population of early nineteenth-century Britain (excluding Ireland: 1801, 10.5 million; 1831, 16.3; 1851, 20.8), and rising literacy levels that in part reflected an increased desire on the part of the working class for literacy, ensured that the market for printed material was steadily increasing. The response as far as the press was concerned can be seen in two lights. Per capita readership of newspapers did not rise until from the later 1830s and the proportion of literates purchasing newspapers was low: 2–4 per cent of the 'lower working classes' in 1840,[29] although, at a higher level, there is evidence of artisan reading clubs from the 1770s and, even more, the 1790s. Accounts which emphasize the scale and scope of newspaper readership in the eighteenth century tend to be heavily focused on London. The total circulation of the *Exeter Gazette* in 1793 was about 1,000, while the *Western Times* by the 1840s had a circulation of about 3,000, although newspapers were read by more people than bought them. These were not high figures for newspapers that circulated widely in the south-west. Furthermore, copies sold as a percentage of households was low: for *Flindell's Western Luminary* in 1815 little more than 2 per cent in the areas of highest sale.[30]

The social location of the newspaper-reading public was restricted not only by the specific 'taxes on knowledge', and the consequent cost of papers, but also by the general social context. In this, both illiteracy and poverty were important, but, within the parameters set by these constraints, it is important to stress the element of reader choice. Newspapers were of less interest than almanacs and chapbooks, and the development in the early nineteenth century of an extensive readership for the sensational, represented by stories in the Sunday press, provides a strong indication of what the press as a whole lacked in terms of public interest the previous century. Lurid accounts of crime were provided more fully by the early nineteenth-century Sundays than by eighteenth-century newspapers.

Even a constant share of a rapidly growing population ensured that the total circulation of newspapers was rising rapidly. Again, both change and continuity can be stressed. There was more of the same, but that itself represented an important change, a source of greater aggregate revenue and profit. The 'sameness' should not anyway be exaggerated, as the press was also more varied by the second quarter of the nineteenth century than it had been fifty years earlier.

The newspaper became an accepted means for the pursuance of disputes, possibly contributing to a more peaceful and a more public

means of conducting political, social, economic and religious disagree-
ments. And yet accessibility or democratization are not the same as
democracy; publicity did not entail the public nature of all politics. It is
necessary not to exaggerate the impact of the press in the period
1750–1833, as well as to stress the often limited information that survives
for discussing both the internal history of the press and its impact.
Furthermore, rather than a unified campaigning force, the press was
(and is) a medium, not a message. It is important to emphasize the
different views that were presented. In addition, caution is required
before changes in different spheres are combined to produce a common
chronology and pattern of development. The press was not isolated from
society, but neither was there any simple pattern of change, any clear and
consistent causality. Growth, in the number of titles and in combined
sales, was considerable, and there was quite significant continuous
change in the press but, compared to the changes that were to come later
in the nineteenth century, 1750–1833 was the period of British press
history in which it is most appropriate to stress continuity.

NOTES

1. N.F.R. Crafts, *British Economic Growth during the Industrial Revolution* (Oxford, 1985). Among the large number of attempts to take the debate forward and advance a post-revisionist view, P. Hudson, *The Industrial Revolution* (1992) and R. Price, *British Society 1680–1880* (Cambridge, 1999), pp. 17–51.
2. *C.P. Scott 1846–1932. The Making of the 'Manchester Guardian'* (Manchester, 1946), p. 23.
3. H. Richardson, 'Wiltshire Newspapers – Past and Present', *Wiltshire Archaeological and Natural History Magazine* 41 (1922), 493.
4. W. Albert, *The Turnpike Road System in England, 1663–1840* (1972); B. Austen, 'The Impact of the Mail Coach on Public Coach Services in England and Wales, 1784–1840', *Journal of Transport History*, 3/2 (1981); J. Greenwood, *Newspapers and the Post Office, 1635–1834* (Reigate, 1971).
5. Carmarthen, Dyfed CRO, Cawdor papers, box 138.
6. BL, L23c4(45).
7. BL, Add. 38338, fol. 128.
8. For example, *Leeds Intelligencer*, 8 July 1766; *Berrow's Worcester Journal*, 4 September 1766; *Reading Mercury*, 28 September 1767, 29 August, 26 September 1768; *Newcastle Courant*, 26 April 1788.
9. J. Barry, 'The press and the politics of culture in Bristol 1660–1775', in J. Black and J. Gregory (eds), *Culture, Politics and Society in Britain 1660–1800* (Manchester, 1991), pp. 62, 70.
10. L. Werkmeister, *The London Daily Press 1772–1792* (Lincoln, Nebraska, 1963) p. 255; D. Read, *Press and People, 1790–1850. Opinion in Three English Cities* (1961), pp. 69, 71; D. Liddle, 'Who Invented the "Leading Article"?:

reconstructing the history and prehistory of a Victorian newspaper genre', *Media History* 5 (1999), pp. 5–18.

11. D. Read, 'John Harland: The Father of Provincial Reporting', *Manchester Review* 8 (1958), 205–12.

12. I. Asquith, 'Advertising and the Press in the Late Eighteenth and Early Nineteenth Centuries: James Perry and the *Morning Chronicle*, 1790–1821', *Historical Journal* 18 (1975), 721; I.R. Christie, *Myth and Reality in Late-eighteenth Century British Politics and Other Papers* (1970), pp. 311–58; H.R. Fox-Bourne, *English Newspapers. Chapters in the History of Journalism* (2 vols, 1887), I, 289; Looney, 'Advertising and Society', p. 278; Feather, *Provincial Book Trade*, p. 124.

13. L. Brown, *Victorian News and Newspapers* (Oxford, 1985), p. 100.

14. Christie, *Myth and Reality*, p. 322.

15. L. Billington, 'The Religious Periodical and Newspaper Press, 1770–1870', in M. Harris and A. Lee (eds), *The Press in English Society from the Seventeenth to Nineteenth Centuries* (1986), pp. 113–32; J.L. Altholz, *The Religious Press in Britain, 1760–1900* (New York, 1989); F.E. Mineka, *The Dissidence of Dissent: The Monthly Repository, 1806–1838* (Chapel Hill, 1944); E.S. Turner, *Unholy Pursuits. The Wayward Parsons of Grub Street* (Lewes, 1998).

16. C. Nelson, 'American readership of early British serials', in Myers and Harris (eds), *Serials and their Readers* (Winchester, 1993), pp. 27–44; C.E. Clark, 'The Newspapers of Provincial America', *Proceedings of the American Antiquarian Society* 100 (1990), 367–89, *The Public Prints. The Newspaper in Anglo-American Culture* (Oxford, 1994), and 'Boston and the Nurturing of Newspapers: Dimensions of the Cradle, 1690–1741', *New England Quarterly* 64 (1991), 243–71; S. O'Brien, 'Eighteenth-century Publishing Networks in the First Years of Transatlantic Evangelicalism', in M. Noll, D.W. Bebbington and G.A. Rawlyk (eds), *Evangelicalism. Comparative Studies of Popular Protestantism in North America, the British Isles and Beyond, 1700–1990* (Oxford, 1994).

17. K. Wilson, *The Sense of the People. Politics, Culture and Imperialism in England, 1715–1785* (Cambridge, 1995), p. 76. For a sensible note of caution, B. Harris, '"American Idols": Empire, War and the Middling Ranks in Mid-eighteenth-century Britain', *Past and Present* 150 (1996), 123–5.

18. E.M. Palmegiano, *The British Empire in the Victorian Press, 1832–1867. A Bibliography* (1987).

19. K. Wilson, *The Sense of the People*, pp. 38–40; P. Lawson, '"Arts and Empire Equally Extend": Tradition, Prejudice and Assumption in the Eighteenth-century Press Coverage of Empire', in Lawson, *A Taste for Empire and Glory: Studies in British Overseas Expansion, 1660–1800* (Aldershot, 1997), pp. 119–46.

20. G.W. Shaw, 'Printing by the British in Sri Lanka at the end of the Eighteenth Century', *Factotum*, 32 (1990), 21–3.

21. R. Cave, 'Printing in Nineteenth-century Belize', *Library Quarterly* 46 (1976), 20–37, 'The First *Trinidad Guardian*', *Publishing History* 3 (1978), 61–6, 'Early Printing and the Book Trade in the West Indies', *Library Quarterly* 48 (1978), 163–92, 'West Indian Printing', in *Encyclopedia of Library and Information*

Science 33 (1982), '"To instruct and enlighten the Negro", the *West Indian* (1838) and its failure', *Journal of Newspaper and Periodical History* 1 (1984), 12–28.

22. Pearson to his parents, 19 July 1857, BL, India Office, MSS Eur C 231, p. 57.

23. Christie, *Myth and Reality*, pp. 345, 358.

24. D. Fraser, 'Edward Baines', in P. Hollis (ed.), *Pressure from Without in Early Victorian England* (1974), p. 185.

25. *Annual Register* (1822), pp. 350–2; A.P. Wadsworth, 'Newspaper Circulations, 1800–1854', *Manchester Statistical Society* (March 1955), 8–9.

26. T. Morley, '"The arcana of that great machine": Politicians and *The Times* in the late 1840s', *History* 73 (1988), 38–54.

27. Heriot to Addington, 10 August 1802, reply 12 August, Exeter, Devon CRO, 152M/C 1802 0Z 126–7.

28. Mackinnon, *Rise*, p. 15.

29. D.F. Mitch, *The Rise of Popular Literacy in Victorian England. The Influence of Private Choice and Public Policy* (Philadelphia, 1992). See also M. Dalziel, *Popular Fiction 100 Years Ago: an Unexplored Tract of Literary History* (1957); L. James, *Fiction for the Working Man 1830–1850. A Study of the Literature Produced for the Working Classes in Early Victorian Urban England* (1963); M. Vicinus, *The Industrial Muse. A Study of Nineteenth Century British Working Class Literature* (1974); V. Neuberg, *Popular Literature. A History and Guide from the Beginning of Printing to the Year 1897* (1977); J.O. Jordan and R.L. Patten (eds), *Literature in the Marketplace. Nineteenth-century Publishing and Reading Practices* (Cambridge, 1995).

30. Maxted, *Newspaper Readership in South-west England: An Analysis of the Flindell's Western Luminary Subscription List of 1815* (Exeter, 1996), and 'Printing', in Kain and Ravenhill (eds), *Atlas*, p. 244.

CHAPTER FIVE

'Improvement':
The Social Politics of Morality

Yesterday there was a great disturbance here, occasioned by the market people asking 8d and some 9d a pound for butter, and refusing to take 6d, whereupon the populace seized several baskets, and sold out the butter at six pence per pound. But notwithstanding the great confusion there was for about two hours, we do not hear of any personal hurt being done. And we are very glad to observe likewise, that it does not seem to be at all the intent of the poor to plunder the property of others; – that they only desire (for their ready money) to be supplied with a price agreable to the well-known plenty with which the divine goodness has been pleased to bless us this season. This, their reasonable remonstrance, it is hoped, will be duly considered by those who usually supply this market with provisions; and who, we are persuaded, will not meet with the least abuse, either in their property or persons.

Berrow's Worcester Journal, 25 September 1766

Progress is the great animating principle of being. The world, time, our country have advanced and are advancing.

The Western Luminary, 2 January 1855

With most reporting, there were accounts of events but little in the way of lengthy or serious commentary. Analysis was provided largely by partisan anonymous or pseudonymous contributions that tended to make moral points. The extent to which newspapers favoured a programme of social improvement can be related to the manner in which politics was generally discussed. There was little difference between upbraiding food hoarders, as the cause of riots, and declaiming against drunkenness or slavery: political discussion, thought and reflection were not divorced from their ethical context. The resulting social politics was very much that of a moral politeness, to which both information and opinion contributed.

This morality drew on the major cultural themes of the middling orders in this period, especially Christian conduct, polite behaviour, and moral improvement, and was important to the shaping of that body of society,[1] and, by exclusion, of the rest as well. The shaping of the middling orders in terms of a set of practices and opinions required their agreement, and thus entailed the striking of resonances to elicit a process of identification. An emphasis on the importance for the entire community of the values of the middling orders also helped focus attention on the press. A sense of what was appropriate, and thus respectable, was inculcated through print. This was more markedly so in the early nineteenth century, but can also be seen throughout the eighteenth. In part this reflected the success of creating a common code of behaviour for what was termed 'polite' society, one that spanned town and countryside. On the completion of its first year of publication, the achievements of the tri-weekly *Tatler* (1709–11) were summarized by one of its major contributors, Joseph Addison:

> I took upon me the title and dignity of Censor of Great Britain, reserving to myself all such perquisites, profits, and emoluments as should arise out of the discharge of the said office. These in truth have not been inconsiderable . . . I have made a narrow search into the nature of the old Roman Censors, whom I must always regard, not only as my predecessors, but as my patterns in this great employment . . . the duty of the Roman Censor was twofold. The first part of it consisted of making frequent reviews of the people. . . . In compliance with this part of the office, I have taken many curious surveys of this great city. . . . The second part of the Roman Censor's office was to look into the manners of the people, and to check any growing luxury, whether in diet, dress, or building. This duty likewise I have endeavoured to discharge.

The association of humour with such ends was continuous, but they were not defined by humour. *Punch*, founded in 1841, was 'a critic of neglectful society',[2] that campaigned, for example, against capital punishment and the filthy state of the Thames.

In Henry Fielding's *Covent-Garden Journal* (1752) many of the essays were devoted to the cause of good behaviour both against specific abuses, such as gambling, adultery, and an interest in pornography, and against the general problem of selfish and improper conduct. Much of the satire was directed at the abuses of the polite world. 'People of Fashion' were criticized for their behaviour and their attitudes and presented as dangerous role-models for tradesmen.[3] This approach was far from novel. A frequent theme in the press of the first half of the century was social criticism of the upper orders for betraying national values by, for example, their preference for foreign fashions. In newspapers such as *Mist's Weekly Journal* this had clear political allusions, but in the *Covent-Garden Journal* it reflected a politically unspecific sense of social tension, arising in large part from the uneasy neighbourhood of the City and the West End.[4] Such social criticism can be seen throughout this period. Under the heading 'The Lord Lieutenant and the North Devon Railway',

Trewman's Exeter Flying Post of 3 January 1856 reported at length a clash between the mores of aristocratic society and the notion of public responsibility:

> Express trains will not do the bidding of Lords Lieutenant. Railways are not managed as were coaches; – the times of arrival and departure, as advertised, are kept as regularly as possible; and a railway superintendent would as soon think of keeping a train back to accommodate a peer of the realm as he would of ending off a train too soon to baulk a director. Lord Fortescue, however, seems to think that in his case exceptions ought to be made to the rule which governs all railway companies. It was his misfortune to be in the down express from Bristol last Saturday afternoon week, which did not happen to reach Taunton until till after the time it was due at Exeter. The North Devon train is advertised to leave the station at 3.30, – half an hour after the arrival of the express. The superintendent having ascertained by telegraph that the express was much behind its time, started the North Devon train at 3.45.

Fortescue complained about the failure to delay the latter, despite the large number of passengers on it. The paper asked, 'Does Lord Fortescue mean to say that these should have been detained an hour and a half to suit his Lordship's convenience?'

It would be misleading, however, to underrate the potential political bite of social commentary and criticism, and wrong to draw a sharp distinction between politics and morality. Thus, for example, comments on the state of public morals could be seen as a comment on the Church, and therefore governmental ecclesiastical policies. More generally, opposition critiques were often presented in moral terms.[5] Thus, Mist's dedication of the volume of his collected miscellany which appeared in 1727 claimed:

> the whole aim and design of the following papers has been to censure and correct those monstrous vices and corruptions which have of late so openly showed themselves in all public affairs, as well as to ridicule the little follies and impertinences of fops, coquets, prudes, pedants, and coxcombs of all sorts.

The zest for repeating information that was such a feature of newspapers offered repeated lessons. Many had no obvious moral or political point, other than contributing to a general culture of improvement. The *Salisbury and Winchester Journal* of 5 January 1789 offered an instance of the attempted systematization of knowledge:

> An ingenious correspondent observes that it has been asserted for time immemorial, that a certain oak tree near Cadnam in the New

Forest never fails to bear and put forth leaves of a considerable size early in the morning of Old Christmas Day, multitudes of which are gathered by the people of the neighbourhood, and the remainder wither at the time of the sun's rising, the tree becoming leafless as before. He therefore wishes that some persons of credit and abilities near the spot will examine with due circumspection into the truth of this report, which has also been corroborated by some of our most respectable historians, and that they will favour the public with the result of their enquiries, through the channel of this paper.

The queries of correspondents were a fruitful source of information. On 16 August 1790 the paper offered cures for a viper's bite:

Several respectable correspondents have favoured us with answers to the enquiry in our last by R.P. respecting the most effectual cure for the bite of this noxious animal, all of which concur in recommending the oil of olives, or common salad oil, warmed and rubbed into the wound, as infallible. The fat of vipers, extracted by frying it, is also said to be a cure equally certain. Some of these letters from medical gentlemen, in which the subject is scientifically treated, will be inserted in the next *County Magazine* to which will be added authentic proof of cures, extracted from the transactions of the Philosophical Society.

Such an interchange between the newspaper and the *Western County Magazine* was helped by their common ownership by Benjamin Collins. Vipers were not the sole problem in Hampshire. On 27 September 1790, the paper reported, 'A correspondent, about to lay flooring in a house newly built, asks how he may best prevent rats harbouring between the joists? We will thank the intelligent to inform him by a line to the printer.' The state of property continued to be a concern of readers. The *Birmingham Herald* of 25 January 1838 reprinted an account from the *Quarterly Journal of Agriculture* on how to deal with dry rot. Fields and lawns also had to be defended; the *Dorchester and Sherborne Journal* of 23 July 1802 printed an account of how to kill moles. The exposed state of man was more vividly underlined by an item in the *Salisbury and Winchester Journal* of 25 October 1790:

Last week died in a state of canine madness Miss Tomkins near Exeter. What is very remarkable, this young lady had never been bit, but received her death, it is thought, from permitting a dog to run about the house after being bit by a mad dog. This should be a caution to many unthinking people, who suffer such dogs to run about the house, never considering that the poison remains on the coat of the animal, and by the means is communicated to their clothes etc.

A regulated society was the answer, suggested an item on 20 December 1790:

> A correspondent of Frome informs us that in consequence of several persons of that town having been bitten by a mad dog, the parishioners, at a vestry, entered into a resolution of relieving no pauper who should keep a dog. A laudable example for other parishes to follow!

Mad dogs were also an issue in the *Birmingham Chronicle* of 31 July 1823, with an item that referred to a report in the *Sheffield Mercury*, and in the *Sherborne Mercury* of 9 January 1837. Dogs were linked to regulation in the *Taunton Courier* of 2 January 1828: 'We have been requested to draw the attention of those in whom the duty consists of abating the nuisance, to the number of dogs that are continually prowling about this town.' The call for action in the paper on 27 August 1828 was very different: 'More explicit directions than those now afforded on the finger-posts, on the new and beautiful mail-coach road, from Minehead to Taunton are very desirable. Much perplexity occurs to the traveller in several instances.'

Other local items were more pointed, intended to criticize or persuade, and often related to local rivalries in ways that are now frequently obscure. The state of local amenities was a frequent topic of comment, the *Salisbury and Winchester Journal* of 5 January 1789 noting that

> Whilst the cities of London and Westminster, and many other cities, towns, and villages in this kingdom, suffer infinite inconvenience for want of their usual supply of water, Salisbury is happy in abundance. Whilst the inhabitants of other cities have cause to dread the ravage of fire in a more than tenfold usual degree from the scarcity of its opposite element, we have nothing to apprehend in that score. We have also fire engines in plenty, and of excellent constitution. It is to be hoped they are in excellent repair, for should they be unhappily wanted, and from disuse be then found useless, what must be the feelings of even a spectator to behold the devouring flames raging uncontrolled, and reducing those who are now happy in affluence of sufficiency, to distress and penury! IF THE ENGINES ARE NOT IN COMPLETE REFRAIN NOT AN HOUR SHOULD BE LOST IN REPAIRING THEM – THE NEGLECT OF A DAY MIGHT LAY THIS CITY IN ASHES!!!

A quarterly inspection of Taunton's fire engines was suggested in the *Taunton Courier* of 9 February 1831. Under the Derby by-line, *Drewry's Derby Mercury* of 8 October 1773 claimed that 'The frequency of all kinds of felonies is complained of by all degrees of people, and some counties have (in order to lighten the burden from an individual) laudably formed associations for apprehending and prosecuting all offenders within their several districts', and urged that the same be done in Derbyshire. The *Middlesex Journal* of 21 October 1783 complained about the number of prostitutes on the streets of London and their shocking obscenities, and proposed that they should be taxed and restricted to certain streets. A complaint in the *General Advertiser and Morning Intelligencer* of 16 August 1777 about the drunkenness of a coach driver on the Brightelmstone stage coach began:

> It is with the utmost pleasure that you give admittance, in your sensible and impartial paper, to every complaint that affects the public. It ought, and you have most judiciously made it the business of your paper, to hold up in exposure whatever is rendered obnoxious or hurtful by crime or malice.

Publicity was seen as of value, as for example in the report in the *Dorchester and Sherborne Journal* of 26 February 1801 on the punishment of Frome shopkeepers who used false weights: 'we wish so laudable a step was taken in other towns, and that the names of such iniquitous miscreants were held up to public execration'.

Newspapers tended to be keen supporters of local associations. They were validated by their purpose, and their reactivity to problems in some cases served in the press as an implicit or even explicit contrast to corporate associations that were often seen as self-serving. An editorial in the *Birmingham Commercial Herald* of 16 January 1804 supported the local plan for an association 'to protect the property of the honest and industrious' laid out in an advertisement for a 'society for preventing, detecting and punishing fraudulent bankrupts, swindlers etc.' The *Sherborne Mercury* of 23 January 1837 praised the associations formed in different parts of Somerset 'for the purpose of enforcing good order and sobriety in the houses licensed to sell beer and cider'. They were presented as hitting drunkenness and thus crime. Chudleigh's *Weekly Express* provided on 11 July 1855 an account of the annual local treat of the National Schools, adding 'we must record our conviction of the great benefit the Chudleigh National Schools have been to the town and neighbourhood. The children of our poorer brethren here receive a sound religious and moral education.'

The *Birmingham Chronicle* of 11 March 1824 was far more critical of a long-established local corporate body, and emphasized accountability and information, with the press playing a central role in both. Under the headline 'The Free Grammar School of Birmingham' the paper declared:

> A considerable interest having been excited in the town relative to an intended application to Parliament for enlarging the objects and appropriating the funds of this noble and invaluable institution, and

several correspondents having addressed letters to our journal on the supposed intentions and objects of the governors, we have been at some pains and expense to procure correct and entire copies of the charters and documents of its original foundation and present government. We now place them collectively before our readers, certain that publicity is the best guarantee of integrity in public trusts, and that the executive management of the school can have no objection to a free statement of their powers and the objects of the trust. The governors of this and every similar institution are selected from the inhabitants at large, for their probity and public experience, as the representatives of the aggregate body interested in the objects of the trust; and they cannot or should not have any sinister interest or end separate from the general body from whom they are selected. Some deference is also due to public opinion: this institution is the property and use of the inhabitants of Birmingham; and we are sure that the governors of the school would not wish to act covertly; would not take the responsibility of directing the funds or changing the situation and site of the school, without the knowledge or without the entire approval of the town at large . . . we shall proceed to the historical account of the foundation of the school, and the several characters, orders, and decrees for its government.

On 13 May the paper called for an annual statement of receipts and expenditure.

Whatever the irritation with individual practices, there was little sign of any widespread press rejection of hierarchical norms. The possibility of radically different arrangements was discussed very rarely. An anonymous essay, 'Thoughts on Levelling, with an Account of the insurrection of Wat Tyler', published in the *Bristol Journal* of 5 April 1777, declared that:

A consciousness of primitive equality is strongly impressed on the heart of every man; and a desire of recovering their original consequence, joined to the pressure of present inconveniences, has at different times roused the populace of every nation to arms.

The *Hampshire Chronicle* of 9 January 1779 carried a letter from a local correspondent adopting the pseudonym Vox Populi. He proposed to substitute taxes on hunting, hunting horses, coach horses, racehorses, and Jews, for those on the necessaries of life, urged a prohibition on the wearing of jewellery and called both for the abolition of salaries for major posts and for financial contributions from the peerage.

Such bold suggestions were rare prior to the crisis of the 1790s, and newspapers campaigned for moral improvement, rather than radical political reform. This accords with work on the electoral system which argues that the 'need' or desire for reform was limited and that electoral politics, although lively, were centred on specific grievances, rather than on any fundamental disaffection.[6]

The version of British history offered by the press, especially praise for the Glorious Revolution of 1688, which became stronger after the mid-century defeat of Jacobitism and atomization of Toryism, was not one that encouraged a total rejection of the established political system. Thus, the centenary in 1788 of the Glorious Revolution provided an opportunity for a restatement of the value of that episode in which calls for specific reforms could be related to the public myth. A local item printed in the *Leeds Mercury* on 11 November 1788 urged the abolition of the slave trade and praised the events of 1688:

> In order to know the true value of that glorious and important event, which has just been commemorated throughout this island, we should contrast our present state with what it would inevitably have been, had not that triumphant change produced by the Revolution been effected. Bigotry and superstition, despotism and tyranny, would, lone ere this, have defaced this fair flourishing isle, and have so contracted and damped the noble and emulous spirit of Britons, that they would, compared with what they now are, scarce have seemed like men. . . . Instead of that free communication we now enjoy, we must have conversed by nods and shrugs, with doubtful and ambiguous looks.

A disinclination to call for significant change was accompanied by a hostility towards those who did. Thus, in the 1790s papers tended to disapprove of demonstrating workers and of artisanal opposition to new machinery. The *Salisbury and Winchester Journal* of 3 May 1790 reported the dispersal of what was presented as a mob near Pewsey threatening to cause devastation unless wages were raised:

> We are happy to find that the bad example of these reprobate fellows, and not real necessity, was the sole cause of these tumultuous proceedings. We are further told that many of the farmers of that part of the country have very humanely supplied their labourers with wheat at 6 shillings per bushel, and that with equal humanity and good policy, they have now agreed to a temporary increase in the wages of those who have large families. May these laudable examples be everywhere followed! The present sufferings of the labouring poor deserve commiseration; and we hope that some effectual and lawful means will be found to relieve them; but we can by no means approve of those riotous proceedings amongst them; – they are contrary to the laws, and subversive of the good government established in society for the mutual advantage of the whole, and for the immediate protection and redress of every individual.

On 7 June 1790, the paper added:

> It is much to be lamented that the lower orders of manufacturers betray on every occasion such a propensity to fly in the faces of their employers, whenever any improvements are attempted in the manufactures of this country. For unless we adopt the same improvements which are adopted on the Continent, other countries will undersell us at market, and of course our manufactures will be inevitably ruined.

Those this issue termed 'deluded and infatuated' as yet lacked a voice in the press. The *Salisbury and Winchester Journal* of 23 May 1791, commenting on a recent riot at Bradford-on-Avon, Wiltshire, stated: 'Eighteen or twenty years experience in Yorkshire has shown that all machinery in manufactures does not lessen, but increases the ability and means of employing the poor.' Similarly, on 18 July 1791, an article about the lack of workers in the cotton industry, and the consequent rise in prices, drew forth the comment: 'the above account strongly favours the opinion, that the introduction of machines for the abridgments of labour, tends ultimately rather to increase than diminish the employment of the industrious poor'. The *Dorchester and Sherborne Journal* was unsympathetic to workers using violence during disputes in the Wiltshire cloth industry, describing them as 'banditti' in 6 August 1802 and calling for action against them on 11 March 1803.

Newspapers were also critical of attempts to raise wages. The *Birmingham Chronicle* of 13 February 1823 pressed the need for 'a good understanding between the manufacturers and the workmen' to restrain wages so that export markets were not lost. The next issue, a week later, returned to the theme: 'taking into consideration the present low price of provisions, the workmen should rest satisfied with moderate wages'. The paper also included an attack on the radical William Cobbett, a theme returned to on 27 February. The issue of 27 May 1824 added:

> We have ever regarded the Combination Laws as one of the most fruitful sources of discontent and discord between the body of workmen of all descriptions and their employers; and we feel confident, that, if they are removed, so as to permit masters and workmen to arrange the price of labour as they do the price of other commodities, without the interference of the magistrate, it would be done with comparative ease, and without any serious breach of the peace.[7]

A somewhat unsympathetic attitude to the 'idle poor' was suggested by an item in the *Salisbury and Winchester Journal* of 19 January 1789:

A correspondent asks if it would not be more consistent if those men who daily receive the bounty of the inhabitants etc. of this city, from the Council Chamber, were to employ their waste time in cleaning the Marketplace of ice, snow, and filth, than to lounge it away with folded arms in Blue Boar Row? Aye, but this is dirty work, my gentle masters.

Such views are unsurprising, given the social location of the press, which indeed was removed from the bulk of the population. The frequent attacks on popular superstitions, drunkenness and a range of activities that were held to characterize a distressingly wide section of the population, such as profanity and cruelty to animals, does not suggest that the press was asserting values shared by all. The *Cumberland Paquet* of 20 November 1792 attacked cock-fighting as 'barbarous'. *Woolmer's Exeter and Plymouth Gazette* of 5 January 1809 printed a critical account of 'gross superstition'. In the *Birmingham Chronicle* of 19 June 1823, 'Mercator' attacked the profanity of 'the lewd rabble which daily infest a gateway fronting the Bull-ring'. A letter in the *Taunton Courier* of 16 January 1828 condemned drunkenness in the streets and obscenity to women, referring to 'the morals of that portion of its population which is commonly called the lower class, but among which, in other places, (and I would fain hope in this) may be found men much respected for information, such as, till lately, was expected from the educated classes only', and also to 'the extreme laxity of morals now pervading the bulk of the lower class'. The issue of 19 March 1828 commented on the conviction of three prostitutes:

By the praiseworthy efforts of some respectable individuals, the inhabitants of this town are likely to be protected, for the future, from the audacious profligacy which has so flagrantly been exhibited in our streets. The insults and revolting behaviour of the most vicious of the lower classes, especially of the females, have been for some time past of a nature to demand some corrective interference, and the present example, which our Guildhall report supplies, will, it is hoped, operate as a timely warning among those who are only to be restrained from daring infamy, by the severities of public justice.

This was a socially specific moral resonance, appropriate for a medium with restricted circulation. This would not have disturbed writers calling for the moralizing of a supposedly dissolute population, subscribers to good causes wishing to see their names, causes and prejudices recorded for posterity, or advertisers offering high-value goods and services that required advertising in a world where most were not advertised other than orally. The *British Chronicle or Pugh's Hereford Journal* of 15 July 1779 published a letter attacking 'wakes or feasts' as 'little else than nurseries of vice', both on religious grounds and because:

The morality of the people is a circumstance inseparably connected with the welfare and happiness of society. Throw down the barriers of religion, law, order, and decency, and then see what will be the discharge of the relative duties of life. Can he who is grown hardy enough to fly in the face of his God be supposed to retain any reverence for a master? Can he who is accustomed to give a loose to unbridled licentiousness, at times when he is under the most solemn obligations to a grave and peaceable demeanour, be expected to behave with modesty and sobriety at other seasons? Or, can he possibly have any veneration for the laws, who has been suffered to trample, uncontrolled, upon those which guard the most sacred concerns? . . . the profligacy and insolence of the lower class are risen to a very alarming pitch; and, if they do not meet with a timely check, bid fair to terminate in anarchy, ruin, and misery. Such is the reward of irreligion, and a suspension of the laws enacted for the support of morality.

The press reflected the interests and views of the middling orders. The paternalist nature of the views and notices published in the press, with their frequent stress on charitable acts by the fortunate, is readily apparent. Paternalism grounded in moral behaviour and religious attitudes rather than economic dominance was the justification of the social policy required for the well-ordered society that was presented by the press as a necessary moral goal. The contents of newspapers was part of a polite, sociable sphere, just as their presence in coffee-houses and other meeting places was part of the furniture of this sphere. Newspapers were more part of polite culture than of its popular counterpart, although it would be misleading to contrast the two sharply.

This paternalism was to influence legislative programmes in the early nineteenth century and their discussion in the press. The *Leeds Mercury*, for example, explicitly pressed the values of the 'middle class', opposed universal suffrage, supported factory legislation for children, but not adults, and defined reform in a way that enhanced order and capitalism.[8] Christian welfare rather than egalitarianism was advanced, although it could lead in different political directions. The *Birmingham Commercial Herald* of 3 January 1818 declared

We have beheld the sufferings of the labouring classes, destitute of employment, met by the Christian liberality of their wealthier neighbours; we have seen resistance to constitutional authorities quelled by the timely interference of legal power.

The paper called for patience over the economy, a remedy in line with its editorializing about 'a righteous Providence' (3 January 1814) and 'the Supreme Disposer of events' (2 January 1815) and referred to 'the triumph and domination of order and law over the madness and misery of popular tumult'. The *Western Luminary* of 5 June 1855 declared:

> Tributes to humanity are necessarily co-existent with the progress of civilization. A deaf ear cannot be turned to the one while the other is applauded and helped forward as a duty binding upon us. The cupidity of man has been robbed, in some degree, of those injurious powers and baneful terrors which were beginning to clothe the genius of trade in the garments of an inexorable and grinding tyrant. The Factory Act set limits to the demands of the mill-owner upon the strength and endurance of young people; the statute abolishing the use of children in the abhorrent practice of climbing, in the process of cleansing, chimneys; and the salutary provision interdicting the employment of females in coal mines; – all these prove that the instincts of humanity are not only alive in us, but have been aroused and actively exerted in vindication of our character as considerate and civilized beings. A constantly-excessive and unnatural claim upon humble, and dependent, and helpless labour – terribly over-taxed by sordid avarice – still growing in power and desire of getting by reason of acquired wealth – calls loudly for the interference of a people who, above all others, feel it a duty to succour the oppressed, and pride themselves upon a ready and liberal redress of grievances and suffering, particularly when the weak and the innocent put themselves forward as the objects of our commiseration. We have been led to these few cursory remarks by the introduction of the Needle-women's Bill.

To suggest that the press was at best a limited guide to the opinions of the public (public opinions rather than public opinion), does not mean that it was without consequence. Much of its importance was negative: for example, the provincial press did not serve to foster feelings of regional identity. There were occasional items, especially at election time, in which preference was voiced for local individuals or interests, but, in general, a striking feature of the provincial press was its absence of a distinctive sense of place and of accompanying hostility, towards either London or other regions. This offers a parallel to the general 'enlightened' character of most of the European press: provincialism and parochialism clearly being dismissed alongside popular superstition. The English provincial press helped to create a national awareness of public politics, so that issues resonated through the political community. Equally, newspaper agitation suggests as much a sense of desperate prodding of apathetic opinion and hostile interests as it does any control of priorities for debate and action by a broad, united and mobilized middle class. In part, the attack on the slave trade[9] can be seen in this light.

National awareness of public politics may have been less important than the role of the provincial press in spreading interest in issues that were not so obviously partisan. However, the challenge of assessing the social impact of the press is greater. For the political impact, the issues are clear even though the methodology may not be. The extent and nature of political news can be established, judicial and governmental records of censorship exist, and an examination of correspondence offers some guidance on the extent to which newspapers were considered. The situation is very different in the case of social issues. The didactic and educational nature of the press was expressed in a letter from J.W. of Bradford, published in the *Leeds Mercury* of 21 November 1775, that began:

> When any public alteration is to be made, or a new law proposed the nature and use thereof ought to be explained, in order to inform the judgements of such as will of course be affected thereby; so that every person for himself may determine how far he ought to assist in obtaining or opposing the same. The intended application for an Act to establish a Court of Requests, for an easy and speedy method of recovery of debts under forty shillings, within a few parishes round this town, is now become a general topic of conversation.

Newspapers played a major role in disseminating and sustaining fashions among those who possessed the interest, knowledge and funds to pursue fashions, but were otherwise removed from the world of the metropolis. Fashions entailed not only clothes, on which items appeared in newspapers, but also opinions and ideas, fads and hobbies. There was a growing appetite for fashions in this wider sense in the middle class, and this appetite was facilitated by their growing wealth. The provincial press helped to keep these people informed, to ensure that the metropolitan world did not appear remote, and, in this respect, news and advertisements performed a complementary function. If this does not amount to a suggestion that the press performed a similar role for the whole of society, this reflects both the extent to which the newspapers were socially circumscribed and hesitation about endorsing the notion of a vertically integrated society in which ideas and practices were readily disseminated down the social hierarchy. At the same time, the widely held notion of the newspaper writer as taking the role of instructor and guide to the reader[10] presupposed that didacticism was as central to the function of press comment as this comment was to journalism. The role of the writer was not limited to that of a reporter. Such a point reminds us of shifting understandings of goals and thus notions of good practice that are different to those which are prevalent today.

NOTES

1. On this process see A. Briggs, 'Middle-class Consciousness in English Politics, 1780–1846', *Past and Present* 9 (1956); P.J. Corfield, 'Class by Name and Number in Eighteenth Century Britain', *History* 72 (1987), 38–61; D. Wahrman, *Imagining the Middle Class. The Political Representation of Class in Britain, c. 1780–1840* (Cambridge, 1995). For literature, reading and gender, J. Pearson, *Women's Reading in Britain 1750–1835. A Dangerous Recreation* (Cambridge, 1999). On the *Tatler*, see D.F. Bond (ed.), *The Tatler* (Oxford, 1987).

2. R.D. Altick, *Punch: The Lively Youth of a British Institution, 1841–1851* (Columbus, Ohio, 1997), p. 186.

3. H. Fielding, *The Covent-Garden Journal*, edited by B.A. Goldgar (Oxford, 1988).

4. For this aspect of Fielding, see, more generally, W.A. Speck, *Literature and Society in Eighteenth-century England. Ideology, Politics and Culture, 1680–1820* (1998), pp. 107–11.

5. P. Harling, *The Waning of 'Old Corruption': The Politics of Economical Reform in Britain, 1779–1846* (Oxford, 1996).

6. F. O'Gorman, *Voters, Patrons and Parties: the Unreformed Electorate of Hanoverian England, 1734–1832* (Oxford, 1989).

7. For a modern discussion, M. Milne, 'Strikes and Strike-breaking in North-east England, 1815–44: The Attitude of the Local Press' and J.V. Corrigan, 'Strikes and the Press in the North-east, 1815–44: A Note', *International Review of Social History* 22 (1977), 226-40, 23 (1978), 376–81.

8. D. Fraser, 'Edward Baines', in P. Hollis (ed.), *Pressure from Without in Early Victorian England* (1974), pp. 184–7.

9. J.R. Oldfield, 'The London Committee and mobilization of public opinion against the slave trade', *Historical Journal* 5 (1992), 331–43.

10. D. Liddle, 'Salesmen, Sportsmen, Mentors: Anonymity and Mid-Victorian Theories of Journalism', *Victorian Studies* (1997), 33, and 'Mentor and Sibyl: Journalism and the End(s) of Apprenticeship in George Eliot', *Victorians Institute Journal* 26 (1998), 8.

CHAPTER SIX

The Development of the
Provincial Press

In 1805, Thomas Flindell, who had founded Cornwall's paper, the *Cornwall Gazette and Falmouth Packet* in 1801, was involved in a legal dispute with his former partners. His defence of his position throws light on the problems that provincial papers encountered, as well as on the difficulty of confronting a well-established paper, in this case the *Sherborne Mercury*, which circulated widely in Cornwall. The *Cornwall Gazette* had failed, only to be re-established at Truro in 1803 as the *Royal Cornwall Gazette*. Flindell wrote of his former partners:

> they now cavil at particular articles of charge – my occasional journies collecting money, which were necessarily very frequent from the inadequacy of our floating capital to answer the prompt demands for stamps, advertising duty, labour etc. but these journies had the additional object of extending our advertising connexions, obtaining orders, etc. it being frequently necessary to *court* connexions by civilities and expense, and advertising connexions were actually obtained in many instances by these means – Another charge they now object to is that of £6 per week for editing, printing, etc. after the paper was enlarged to the size of the Sherborne paper, since the first agreement was only for £3 10s a week, but the paper . . . was very small when begun – we soon, however, found that it was impossible to establish our paper, it being too small for a weekly paper, and that the Sherborne contained much more matter at the same price . . . anyone who had an idea of the labour and expense requisite in establishing a newspaper in opposition to such old-established papers as I had to contend with in a remote and narrow part of the country, with no previous connexion or patronage . . . must consider the sum of £320 as a mere flea-bite; and, my success has since proved that had they but duly nursed the paper in its infancy, the returns before this period would have recovered the whole sum sunk, and double that sum at the back of it – But what better could be expected from 3 inn-keepers, a shop-keeper, and a custom-house clerk![1]

Despite these problems, the number of provincial papers rose, from about 24 in 1723 to 32 in 1753, 35 in 1760, 50 in 1782, over 100 in 1808, 150 by

1830 and over 230 by 1851, a numerical increase that was far greater than that in the London press, and that was obtained despite the increased provincial circulation of London papers. This success enhanced the possibilities for profit and increasingly social mobility offered by newspaper ownership.[2] The provincial expansion was due both to the increase in the number of towns with papers and to more towns having more than one. Newspapers ceased to be, as many originally had been, a means to use spare printing capacity and to probe market opportunities, and became, instead, more central to the activities of the concerns producing them. Towns and areas that had hitherto lacked a successful paper obtained one, though there were difficulties. The failure of the *Darlington Pamphlet* (1772–3) ensured that the needs of Teesside continued to be met by the Leeds, Newcastle and York press. No other paper was launched at Darlington until the *Darlington and Stockton Times* appeared in 1847. Similarly, after the *Union Journal: or, Halifax Advertiser* (1759–*c.* 1763) ceased publication, Halifax had no paper until the *Halifax Journal* of 1801–11.

In Cumbria, in contrast, the *Cumberland Pacquet or Ware's Whitehaven Advertiser*, launched in 1774, was successful. Given the failure of the *Kendal Courant* (1731–6), *Kendal Weekly Mercury* (1735–47) and *Whitehaven Weekly Courant* (1736–43), this suggests that the situation in Cumbria had become propitious for the development of a successful newspaper, though the next to be founded, the *Cumberland Chronicle and Whitehaven Public Advertiser*, only lasted from 1776 to 1779. It was the period 1798–1818 that really saw the development of a numerous and competitive Cumbrian press, with the foundation of the *Carlisle Journal* (1798), the *Westmorland Advertiser and Kendal Chronicle* (1811), the *Patriot* (1815) and the *Westmorland Gazette* (1818), all of which lasted into the twentieth century, only the *Carlisle Chronicle* (1807–11) meeting with a speedy demise. Similarly, the number of Liverpool papers rose markedly between 1812 and the late 1820s. The first newspapers in Wales were founded in the 1800s: Swansea's *The Cambrian* in 1804 and Bangor's *North Wales Chronicle* in 1808. Hereford was like Cumbria. The *Hereford Journal* (1739) was short-lived, but the *British Chronicle, or Pugh's Hereford Journal*, launched in 1770, lasted into the twentieth century, and was joined by the *Hereford Independent* (1824–8) and the *Hereford Times* (1832–twenty-first century). The first newspaper in Staffordshire, the *Wolverhampton Chronicle and Staffordshire Advertiser* (1789–93) was short-lived, possibly because of the competition of the nearby *Birmingham Gazette*, but the Stafford-based *Staffordshire Advertiser* followed in 1795.[3]

Distribution was crucial to the profitability of provincial newspapers. In contrast to papers serving the London market, provincial newspapers generally carried details about their agents and area of circulation. These served to advertise the scope of the papers to potential advertisers, both local and metropolitan, and were of some importance in encouraging readership across what was often a wide area. Thus, the *Chelmsford*

Chronicle in 1764 named agents, 'where letters, articles of intelligence, advertisements, etc. are received', at Harwich, Dedham, Colchester, Brentwood, and Braintree; the last two were booksellers: these often served as agents. In addition, the Peele coffee-house, on Fleet Street, and the George at Epping were listed. That agents were named is of some consequence, for suspicion frequently attaches to long lists of places where unnamed agents supposedly existed. A decade later, the *Original Ipswich Journal* revealed a regional reach when it named agents at Bury St Edmunds, Colchester, Cambridge, Norwich, Yarmouth, Harleston, Halesworth, Beccles, Chelmsford, Sudbury, Woodbridge and Needham Market. A degree of organization is suggested by the comment that 'all letters from Cambridge, Newmarket, Thetford, etc. directed to be left' with Mr Green, the bookseller in Bury, 'before Thursday evening, will be in time for that week's paper'. It was presumably by means of these agents, where 'advertisements and articles of intelligence are taken in', that the paper was able to devote one column of its sixteen to local news, mostly accidents, deaths, and robberies, under the by-lines of Ipswich, Harwich, Bury, Cambridge, Norwich, Colchester and Chelmsford.

In January 1779, the *Hampshire Chronicle; or, Portsmouth, Winchester and Southampton Gazette*, recently launched in Southampton, offered a list of far-flung named agents where 'advertisements, articles of intelligence, etc. for this paper are taken in'. These were again indicative of a regional reach: Winchester, Portsmouth, Bath, Gosport, Newport, Cowes, Titchfield, Bristol, Poole, Andover, Farnham, Reading, Romsey, Lymington, Petersfield, Chichester, Havant, and Alton, and at seven London coffee-houses. The same month, the *British Chronicle or Pugh's Hereford Journal* named agents by whom advertisements were taken in and 'this journal is regularly distributed in their respective neighbourhoods' in London, Bath, Bristol, Gloucester, Worcester, Tewkesbury, Ledbury, Bromyard, Shrewsbury, Ludlow, Leominster, Kington, Builth, Aberystwyth, Cardigan, Lampeter, Haverfordwest, Pembroke, Narberth, Tenby, Swansea, Neath, Cowbridge, Pontypool, Monmouth, Abergavenny, The Hay, Brecon, Landovery and Carmarthen.

There are indications that the network of agents of individual newspapers became more dense and comprehensive as the century progressed, with obvious consequences for the system as a whole. For advertising reasons, agents in London and other major towns were of great importance: they were the point of access to the world of national commerce and thus extra-regional advertisements. Often these agents were a great distance from the newspaper's place of publication. Arrangements between newspapers could also be important for transmitting news items and advertisements. Thus local networks of circulation were integrated into national networks of information, for both news and advertisements, while the postal system offered an increasingly sophisticated system of circulation for non-local sales. In

January 1786, Thomas Wood's *Shrewsbury Chronicle and Wood's Shropshire, Montgomeryshire, Denbighshire, Merionethshire etc. General Advertiser* carried at the beginning the notice: 'This paper is circulated with great expedition thro' the above counties, also thro' part of Cheshire, Staffordshire, Worcestershire, Radnorshire, Cardiganshire, Flintshire, Carnarvonshire, and Anglesea, and to greater distance by the general post'. Wood's paper also announced that advertisements were 'taken in by the different booksellers within the circuit of this paper', at seven locations in London (six of them coffee-houses, including the Salopian), and by the printers of the 'Birmingham, Manchester, Chester, Derby, Worcester, Glocester, Bristol, Bath, Whitehaven, Newcastle, Liverpool, Ipswich, Oxford, Cambridge, Reading, Nottingham, Leicester, Lewes etc. newspapers'. In addition, the newspaper could be 'sent by post frank'd to any part of Great Britain at 15 shilling per year'.

These details of circulation and distribution are an important reminder of the extent to which most provincial papers were not local papers in the modern sense; indeed were not to develop in such a direction until after the mid-nineteenth century. It was only some of the major provincial centres that had newspapers that circulated mainly in the immediate vicinity. This was true of the Bristol and Leeds press, for both cities offered a buoyant local market, while nearby towns, Gloucester and York, had newspapers that sold more widely in the hinterland (though Bristol papers did sell in South Wales). Elsewhere, towns of publication simply did not offer a large enough market. Thus, the provincial press had to be regional, not local, for commercial and advertising reasons, and this process was helped by the limited nature of local news and the role instead of the provincial press as regional vehicles of national and international news. The linking of town names in newspaper titles such as the *Leicester and Nottingham Journal* (1755) reflected the regional character of much of the provincial press. The *Bury and Norwich Post; or, Suffolk, Norfolk, and Essex Advertiser* named agents for taking in advertisements and news items, and for sales, in fifty East Anglian towns in February 1787. The network was clearly expanding: the issue of 21 February 1787 announced a new agent in Beccles. The *Salisbury and Winchester Journal and General Advertiser of Wilts, Hants, Dorset and Somerset* declared that from 23 February 1789, 'this paper is published every Sunday and Monday through the extensive counties of Wilts, Hants, Dorset, Somerset, and part of Berks; particularly in the following cities and towns, and also in all the intermediate villages – To each place is annexed the name of some respectable bookseller, or other correspondent, by whom all books, stationary, medicines, perfumes, etc. are sold, and advertisements and intelligence taken in, and duly forwarded.' Agents were named in fifty-eight towns besides London. The notice continued,

This paper is also forwarded by the post to the houses of many of the principal nobility and gentry in London and the country; also to the

several coffee-houses in London, Bath, Bristol, Exeter, etc. Gentlemen living out of the circuit, may have this paper franked by the
post, at 16s per annum.

The *Chelmsford Chronicle* provides some indication of the expansion and
increasing sophistication of newspaper networks. In place of the six
agents outside Chelmsford of 1764 (as well as the sole London agents),
the paper in 1792 listed six London agencies (three of them coffee-
houses and two booksellers), and another twenty agents outside
Chelmsford. The paper's network had both expanded geographically and
become denser, and this was true of newspapers all over the country.
Launched on 20 October 1774, the *Cumberland Pacquet or Ware's
Whitehaven Advertiser* offered a greater number of agents on 10 November
1774, and on 13 April 1775 added the announcement 'this paper is now
circulated through every parish, village, township in the county of
Cumberland; several parts of Westmorland and Lancashire; the western
part of Scotland and the Isle of Man', then on 27 July 1775 noted:

A newscarrier with this paper to Ravenglass, Bootle, Broughton,
Ulverstone, Dalton, Hawkeshead, and Cartmell, began the last week;
those subscribers who can be more readily supplied by this
distribution, than by the method hitherto practised, are requested to
signify the same.

The *Wolverton Chronicle and Staffordshire Advertiser* named agents in twenty-
one Midlands towns and London in 1792, and noted that advertisements
and other items would also be taken in 'by the printers of all the country
papers'. In 1795 the *Portsmouth Gazette, and Weekly Advertiser* named
twenty-eight agents on and near the south coast. On 2 January 1801, the
Dorchester and Sherborne Journal listed agents in twenty-seven towns,
including three in Cornwall. By 1818, the rival and Whiggish *Sherborne
Mercury* had over eighty agents.[4] To encourage distribution, the *Taunton
Courier* in the late 1820s and early 1830s was offered to 'innkeepers and
publicans' for 5½d, while everyone else was charged 1d more.

The development of newspapers in the Home Counties had been
limited by the ready accessibility of London papers. Some of these were
designed to tap nearby markets. The *Country Oracle and Weekly Review*, for
example, in its issue of 25 April 1741, offered Basingstoke, Newbury,
Reading and Salisbury grain prices as well as those in London. It also took
in advertisements at Abingdon, Aylesbury, Farnham, Guildford,
Marlborough, Newbury, Oxford, Reading and Salisbury. The *County
Chronicle and Weekly Advertiser, for Essex, Herts, Kent, Surrey, Middlesex, and
Berks. All parts of Bedford, Bucks, Cambridge, Hants, Huntingdon, Northampton,
Oxon, Suffolk and Sussex. And particularly for the Two Universities of Oxford and
Cambridge* was produced in London explicitly for the provincial market,

the issue of 6 November 1798 devoting eleven of its twenty columns to advertisements and notices. In addition, most London papers, especially the tri-weeklies, appear to have circulated in the south-east. The *General Advertiser, and Morning Intelligencer* of 16 August 1777 announced,

> For a considerable time past it has been sent express, and circulated at the same price and the same day that it is published in London, by agents purposedly fixed, in the towns of Bath, Bristol, Portsmouth, Gosport, Oxford, Birmingham, Cambridge, Southampton, Isle of Wight, Winchester, Brightelmstone etc. and great numbers are daily sold in all these places. This is the first time that a daily newspaper printed in London, has met with so extensive a circulation . . . will be extended . . . advertisements, news taken in at all places above.

Dependence on London decreased in the early nineteenth century as titles were launched in the Home Counties, including the *Buckingham-shire, Bedfordshire and Hertfordshire, Huntingdonshire, Bedfordshire, Cambridge-shire and Isle of Ely Mercury* (1828), and the *County Press for Hertfordshire, Bedfordshire, Buckinghamshire, Essex, Cambridgeshire and Middlesex* (1834). Although Canterbury and Maidstone were already newspaper centres, the first paper published in Dover, the *Cinque Ports Herald*, appeared in 1825. However, the first Bedford newspaper did not follow until twelve years later. Prior to that, aside from London papers, the county was within the scope of the *Northampton Mercury*, which was launched in 1720, and, from 1815, the *Cambridge Oracle*.

As newspaper consumption increased, however, the system by which the provincial press in large part acted to relay London news adapted. The growth of the provincial press helped to increase non-metropolitan sources of information, and the use of other newspaper printers as advertising agents fostered links between provincial newspapers. Increasingly they were cited as sources in other papers. For example, the *Birmingham Commercial Herald* of 30 January 1804 based its report on damage in Gloucester in a recent gale on the *Gloucester Herald*, while the *Chester Chronicle* provided an item on local volunteers. The issue of 3 January 1814 cited the *Bristol Journal* in its discussion of relations with France and the need for a clear victory and a firm peace. The *Birmingham Chronicle* of 28 August 1823 referred to the *Bath Chronicle*, the *Salisbury Journal* and the *Dublin Evening Post*. The issue of 31 July made clear that the paper took 'the Paris journals direct'.

The impact of the growing and developing provincial newspaper network is open to discussion. In my book *The English Press in the Eighteenth Century* (1987), I stressed the limitations of newspaper growth and impact, especially political impact, and in general that viewpoint is to be adopted as a corrective to interpretations that exaggerate the role of the press and of the often nebulous concept of public opinion. Most of the claims made on behalf of public opinion relate to national politics and are based primarily on unrepresentative urban opinion in a largely rural society. Although rural literacy was measurably lower than its urban counterpart, the extensive rural distribution systems of newspapers indicate the importance of the rural readership. In so far as they specify the press claims on behalf of public opinion tend to focus on the London press, but the situation in London is not the best guide to that elsewhere. In addition, in the metropolis, because of the diversity of opinions advanced, the press was most obviously a medium, rather than a message. Furthermore, in the field of national politics, there was obvious resistance to accepting dictation from 'public opinion', even though sympathetic opinions were eagerly elicited.

In the provinces, urban oligarchies were not going to welcome dictation, but in the case of many of the provincial newspapers, certainly before the 1790s, there was no extensive agenda for political debate and action equivalent to that advanced in *some* London newspapers, more especially those that have received a lot of scholarly attention. Instead, many provincial papers had more modest goals and their political impact should, on the whole, be seen in the dissemination of information and opinion, mostly derived from the London press, and the creation of a medium, rather than in the propagation of distinctive views.

Nevertheless, it is worth noting the extent to which cities in which there was more than one newspaper, for example Exeter, Newcastle and Norwich, had a more politicized press and, more generally, the degree to which some provincial newspapers were willing to carry their own comment not only on local but also on national politics. Some of the comment by-lined as from the place of publication in fact derived from the London press, but it is worth noting the degree to which a local by-line was regarded as valuable, while most of such items in fact derived from local sources. Thus the *Leeds Intelligencer* of 6 July 1784 attacked Pitt's fiscal plans and linked them to the political weight of the East India Company:

The new window tax is the most alarming that ever was imposed in the country – God knows to what extent it may hereafter be carried – at present it will be found to be cruelly oppressive, particularly upon tradesmen, farmers, manufacturers, etc. who use little or no tea – are no smugglers themselves, nor are benefited thereby. It is meant to be a sop for the East India Company, who will avail themselves of the monopoly, and who are known to have above sixty members in the House in their immediate interest, and at the absolute command of the ministerial junto. The cheapness of tea is insidiously held out as a lure to catch the unthinking vulgar; when behold, in lieu of this tax, another ten times more burdensome is to be substituted: the former is a tax upon luxury, and at our own choice – the latter is laid upon one of the greatest blessings of life, unless, as in some parts of Scotland, we suffer the light of Heaven to come in only at the chimney-tops.

The quantity of local news published in the provincial press increased in the second half of the eighteenth century, though it took a while before political items became common. The *Chelmsford Chronicle* of 14 September 1764 offered its readers only half a column of local news out of its total of sixteen. This included the results of the Brentwood races and news of accidents, crimes, deaths, and the militia. None of the local news was political, though the paper did reprint anti-ministerial pieces from the *St James's Chronicle* and the *Monitor*. Fifteen years later, the *Hampshire Chronicle*, based in Southampton, regularly had a column on Portsmouth and news of ship movements there. The paper adopted a line that was clearly critical of the ministry of Lord North. In its edition of 9 January 1779, it observed,

A correspondent, who has read the proclamation of a general fast, observes, that fasting and praying one day, and at the same time employing those wicked ministers, whose counsels have brought ruin on these once flourishing kingdoms, appears little better to him than a solemn mockery of Heaven.

More common were the crimes and deaths that accounted for most of the local news in the *Norfolk Chronicle* of 11 June 1785, which filled just over one column of the sixteen in the paper (fifty-six advertisements and notices filled nine). The paper did, though, carry an account of a parliamentary speech by William Windham, one of Norwich's MPs, designed to underline the shared views of member and constituents in opposition to the proposal for a shop tax.

Nevertheless, increasingly, alongside the births, deaths, and accidents that had been the staple (but not the only) items of local news in the first decades of the century, there was a discussion, variously partisan or balanced, informed or otherwise, both of issues of local importance and of local perspectives on national matters. There was a dynamic relationship between the growing local political coverage of the provincial press and the increasing sophistication and public dimension of provincial politics. Provincial papers were used to express provincial opinions, and to advertise and record the events, such as meetings, petitions and demonstrations, that constituted the crucial process by which such opinions could be articulated and developed in order to produce an impact, both locally and nationally. An obvious example in the 'moral' sphere was the cause of anti-slavery which occupied much space in the late 1780s and early 1790s, and was indeed the great issue in the *Newcastle Courant* in the spring of 1792.

The previous year, the Ochakov crisis, a confrontation with Russia that seemed likely to lead to war, led to serious criticism of the Pitt ministry. Unlike previous comparable foreign policy episodes, for example the controversies over Spanish depredations in 1738–9 and over the terms of peace with the Bourbons in 1762–3, when provincial expressions of opinion had substantially responded to initiatives from London and there had been scant attempt to elicit provincial support elsewhere, in 1791 the provincial press was used to spread a message of concern. The resolutions of a critical meeting in Manchester, reported at length in the *Newcastle Courant* of 30 April 1791, included 'That the foregoing resolutions be published in some of the London, and in the Manchester, Liverpool, Birmingham, Leeds, Norwich, and other provincial newspapers'. The stranglehold of London sources of news for non-local items in the provincial press was thus being broken, a process that owed much to the developing sophistication and range of these papers, so that they offered items that were of interest to other newspapers, such as complaints by the Leeds Chamber of Commerce over Spanish tariffs, reprinted in the *Newcastle Courant* on 15 January 1791. Elections to local offices increasingly attracted attention. Thus the *Taunton Courier* of 12 March 1828 reported at length on the election of the county coroner, a report on the celebrations following a week later.

If more local and more non-metropolitan items were being carried in the provincial press by the end of the eighteenth century, the dominance of the London press as a source for all British newspapers remained strong throughout the period, and was indeed a continuation of the situation that had pertained from the origins of the non-London press. Dutch newspapers were used as sources of information in Bristol in the 1740s by Hooke's short-lived *Oracle*, but, in general, until the development of telegraphy, non-metropolitan British newspapers did not enjoy independent access to foreign news, with the important exception of the receipt of American newspapers in ports trading across the Atlantic. In addition, although Scottish and Irish newspapers do appear to have had particular correspondents in London, their provincial counterparts did not, so that the London items in non-metropolitan newspapers were generally drawn from London papers, whether attributed or not. Under the heading 'Breaking Up of the Ministry', the *Taunton Courier* of 16 January 1828 carried items from *The Times, Globe, Morning Chronicle, Morning Herald*, and *New Times*. This situation did not constrain the reporting of London news or the publication of national, i.e. metropolitan, opinion, and in these spheres the provincial press expanded its coverage in the first half of the nineteenth century.

In the eighteenth century, the social position of the owners and printers of provincial newspapers was generally not that of the urban elite, as Flindell noted. Furthermore, their local agents were important to networks of trade, information and credit, but not at the most exalted level: the agents named in the *Leeds Mercury* of 28 November 1721 included booksellers in Halifax, Leeds and Ripon, a livery-lace weaver in Manchester, a cutler in Wetherby, a clockmaker in Skipton, a postmaster in Pontefract, and a grocer and mercer in Otley. By the mid-nineteenth century, however, the leading provincial papers were more heavily capitalized and their proprietors and editors in part members of more influential and socially more prominent circles.

Provincial newspapers stressed the importance of the freedom of the press, *Felix Farley's Bristol Journal* of 2 August 1783 writing of a constitutional entitlement to 'speaking and writing', but, in general, such claims had no specific political resonance. Opinions played a secondary role to the publication of news, not, of course, that news and opinion were always differentiated, or can be today. The *Cumberland Pacquet* was launched in time to report the 1774 general election, and the first issue included nearly two columns, starting with a message from 'A Freeholder' that included the customary reference to impartiality which, misleading as it could be, highlighted a stated objective of provincial newspapers:

> The ensuing election for this country engrosses the greatest part of a conversation in these places; most people know the general proceedings in the canvass, but the letters published since the Wigton meeting have not come to the hands of all the freeholders; therefore as it coincides with that impartiality which, by your advertisement concerning the Whitehaven news paper, you profess to observe on every occasion, I send you a copy of each of these letters which I desire you will insert at large.

Though local items increased, the provincial press continued to be dominated by London newspapers in its news coverage. The rise in the number of columns in individual papers made it possible to carry more local and national news and also more advertising. The number of advertisements in the *Sherborne Mercury* rose from about 1,000 in 1740 to about 4,000 in 1790.

Newspapers brought fresh items of news and opinion, that were generally as reliable as they could be by the press standards of the period, on a regular basis to individuals and communities that had hitherto lacked such information or been dependent on the more expensive manuscript newsletters. The provincial newspaper world was divided into two spheres, the provincial press and the provincial circulation of metropolitan newspapers. The latter increased during the period, both in the counties near London, where the foundation of titles was limited, and further afield. Improvements to roads and postal services, and later the creation of rail links, enabled the London press to circulate more speedily. Whereas, in 1764, 1,090,289 London papers were sent into the country via the Post Office, in 1790 the figure was 4,650,000.[5] Many of the purchasers were presumably dissatisfied with the option of the available provincial papers: two readily apparent groups were readers in the Home Counties and those who wanted news more regularly than once a week. Others sought to take both the London and the provincial press. The

1826–37 journal and earlier correspondence of Robert Sharp, the village schoolmaster of South Cave near Beverley, reveals that he read the *Political Register* until the price went up to 1*s* in 1830, and *The Times*, but also the Hull press and occasionally its York counterpart.[6]

Provincial papers became more extensive in their reporting and more assertive in their editorializing. This was both self-conscious and trumpeted. The *Birmingham Commercial Herald* of 2 January 1809 declared:

> we fulfil our duty to our readers as amply by offering our own comments as by paying half-a-guinea, weekly, to an underling of a London news office, for the extract of a letter, containing nothing but the mere chit-chat of the day.

Thus, the issue of 2 January 1815 offered comments on the terms of the Treaty of Ghent with America. Economic development ensured that more parts of the country were integrated more closely into international trade and thus that news from abroad was of greater direct interest. The *Birmingham Chronicle* devoted much attention in 1823 to the crisis in Spain and to French intervention. This was seen as of direct relevance. The issue of 30 January noted 'The anticipation of war has created a lively sensation among the manufacturing interests of this town. There is an unusual bustle and anxiety in the workshops and warehouses of those connected with the gun trade.' The issue of 6 March carried an editorial noting the importance of the crisis for merchants, manufacturers and 'holders of foreign stock'. Original editorial comment in *Felix Farley's Bristol Journal* developed from 1811, the *Bristol Gazette*, and *Bristol Mercury* following in 1817 and 1818 respectively.[7]

The very growth in the provincial press in the same period (as of provincial printing as a whole)[8] suggests that it is misleading to emphasize a rivalry between London and provincial newspapers. Both responded to, and sustained, a growing appetite for news and opinion in a broad range of society, although the public was presented as a narrower constituency by the provincial press than its metropolitan counterpart.[9] At the same time, it is necessary to recover the different constituencies of the provincial press. This was true not only in England but also in the wider reaches of the British newspaper world. The editorial comment in the first number of the *Cape Town Gazette, and African Advertiser* (16 August 1800) presented a varied readership that could not only be found there:

> In consequence of the non arrival of any ships from England for so long a time, we feel disappointed at not being able to lay before our readers, any thing particularly interesting, especially to those who reside in and about the capital of the Colony: at the same time we feel it a duty incumbent upon us to share our intelligence with that description of people who live in a more remote part of the Colony, and in a manner retired from the world.

The variety in the readership affected the response to the news, its content, tone, frequency and speed. More generally, the appetite for news, and its social and cultural causes and consequences, was an important development that created opportunities for entrepreneurs and others. Many of the factors that had discouraged use of the press[10] became less powerful with time. Print became more normative as a means of communicating information and ideas. The role of the press as a means of validating or denying reports, including those in other papers, can be seen in an item under a local by-line in the *Dorchester and Sherborne Journal* of 23 January 1801:

Paragraphs have lately appeared in several papers, and have been copied into many others, stating an intention on the part of government, to propose to Parliament to break up Friendly Societies, or to tax their funds, which have caused a considerable degree of alarm and uneasiness among members of such societies; we have therefore the sincerest pleasure in being able to assert, from an authority on which we can rely with the utmost confidence, that the statement is *utterly unfounded*; the Chancellor of the Exchequer never mentioned the Friendly Societies in Parliament except on one occasion, and then in terms of high commendation, with a view of extending the advantages of them to other descriptions of persons.

The wider process of the extension of print culture both made it more normative, and thus enhanced the value of the press, and also provided copy and comment for newspapers. The *Birmingham Commercial Herald* of 4 January 1813 drew on the visual possibilities from another dimension of news, that offered by maps:

Whoever will take a map of the Russian Empire and examine the space contained between Vilna, Riga, and the lately existing Moscow, will see how considerable a tract of country has within the last six months been subjected to all the horrors of war.

The increasingly authoritative character of print also created problems, as its authority potentially clashed with that of other sources of authority and expertise. Newspapers showed an awareness of this difficulty. The *Hampshire Chronicle* of 30 January 1779 reported,

Philanthropos's recipe for the prevention and cure of the hydro-phobia may, for anything we know, be very proper, not being competent judges of the subject; but to publish anything, from an anonymous correspondent, either as a preventative or cure for that dreadful malady might be attended with the most fatal consequences;

as persons, in that melancholy situation, instead of applying to an eminent physician, the proper resort, might be tempted to tamper with inefficacious medicines till it is too late to expect any relief from proper treatment.

Repeatedly, the press emerges as one aspect of change, rather than as a 'fourth estate' pressing for particular policies. Nevertheless, its role was still important. A greater sense of national consciousness was scarcely novel, but it was encouraged by the *regular* national news and opinion provided by the press, and newspapers were apt to treat public opinion as the 'sovereign tribunal'.[11] This situation was accentuated at times of national emergency. Thus, *Wheeler's Manchester Chronicle* declared on 29 December 1792:

> From the great importance of the debates of Parliament, it becomes an absolute duty to give such a sketch of them as our limits will allow; and the various association advertisements, which are of great length, claim an immediate publication. These circumstances confine us to the passing occurrences of the week, and have obliged us to omit many advertisements.

Advertisements, however, were costly to omit. The *Exeter Gazette, or Universal Advertiser for the West of England* of 26 December 1793 announced that its price was to rise to 4*d* an issue from 2 January 1794. Declaring its goal of giving 'our readers the earliest statement of political events, as well as to supply them with every entertainment a weekly register of occurrences would permit', it offered a 'statement, whereby the public will perceive that no provincial paper can with propriety be charged less than 4*d*.

	d
Stamp Duty	2
Paper	½
Expresses and Expenses in Printing	½
One Half-Penny for each Paper allowed to *Newsmen (exclusive of travelling Expenses)	½
	3½
Gains (bad debts not included)	½
	4

*The average expenses of collecting the monies of those papers that go through the Post-office, may be put down at the same calculation.

The chief advantage, therefore, likely to arise to the printer of a newspaper, is from the number of advertisements it contains.'

The consequences of advertising for the press have been described in terms of a consumer revolution, but the implications for politics were far greater: only a portion of goods and services were advertised, while most political groups and single-interest lobbies sought to use the culture of print in order to transmit their messages, and organize, encourage and recruit supporters. Thus, the lengthy resolutions of a meeting of Newcastle Methodists against Sidmouth's Bill for the registration of Dissenting Ministers were printed in the *Newcastle Chronicle* of 25 May 1811 which, in turn, was drawn to Sidmouth's attention.[12] The *Taunton Courier* was not alone in keeping readers and electors informed of the votes of their representatives. On 5 March 1828 the paper reported:

> The name of 'H. Seymour' appearing in the published lists both of the majority and minority of members who voted for and against the motion of Lord John Russell, for a committee to take into consideration the present state of the laws affecting Dissenters, we are requested, in order to prevent mistake, to inform our readers, that the respected representative of this town, Henry Seymour Esq. voted in the majority on that occasion.

In other words he voted for repeal of the Test and Corporation Acts. On 25 June 1828, the paper added that the London press had mistakenly omitted Seymour's name from the list of those who had voted against a Bill to authorize the Archbishop of Canterbury to grant a reversion to a sinecure. On 16 July 1828 the paper added:

> We are requested to state that Henry Seymour, Esq. voted in the minority, on the 10 inst., in favour of the proposed Bill to restrain corporate bodies from using their funds in electioneering purposes. His name is, for the second time within the last three weeks, omitted in the list published in the London newspapers. . . . The publication of the divisions in the House of Commons is frequently matter of important intelligence to the country, and therefore the accuracy of the lists is no less important both to the constituents and their representatives, and ought to be most carefully attended to by the London editors.

The *Devonshire Chronicle and Exeter News,* a keen supporter of parliamentary reform, sought to stir up a local response in its issue of 9 July 1831 by printing a list of how Devon, Cornwall and Somerset MPs had voted on the second reading of the Reform Bill. The previous year, Sir Gilbert Heathcote, a prominent Lincolnshire landowner, had sought to defuse discontent about the use of threshing machines by announcing in the *Stamford Mercury* his 'wish that his tenants shall not any longer use' such machines.[13]

As always, the role of newspapers can be understood best if they are not abstracted from their social, economic, cultural and political context, and treated as a force apart, that impacted upon society. Instead, they have to be seen in their contexts, as an interactive aspect of a complex situation, a society characterized by a symbiotic relationship of change and continuity. Furthermore, at the local level, the foundation and expansion of the press can be linked to that of a range of institutions that also reflected greater interest in the wider world as mediated through print. Thus, in Kendal, a book club was formed in 1761, a newsroom was founded in 1779, a subscription library in 1794, an 'Economical Library' for the less affluent in 1797, and a second newsroom in 1820; both were still operating in 1829. The foundation of newspapers was also linked to the interaction of towns within an urban system.[14]

The expansion of the provincial press continued in the nineteenth century. In part, this was a matter of expanded sales by individual titles, but there was also an important creation of new papers through England as printers probed market opportunities and it became the norm for towns of any size to have a newspaper. These newspapers primarily drew on the London press rather than on each other for news (although the latter process also occurred), and this limited the development of regional hierarchies of newspapers.

As an example of the growing density and localization of the press, newspapers established in Plymouth in 1718, 1758 and 1780 had all failed after a few years, but in 1808 two rival newspapers were founded there and continuous newspaper production in the town began. In 1824, the *North Devon Journal*, the first newspaper in north Devon, was founded in Barnstaple, and in 1839 the first in south Devon, at Torquay, and the first in Penzance. The density of publication in the south-west increased from 1847, with newspapers appearing in Teignmouth and Tavistock that year and in Sidmouth and Dawlish in 1850.[15] The presence in more localities of locally produced newspapers helped to develop the growing centrality of print to local consciousness. They also helped to sustain the print industry as newspapers were a regular product, whereas much other printing work was spasmodic in character.

The growing role of locally produced newspapers also helped to ensure that newspapers were both the most important form of political print and that they displaced, lessened or challenged other means of conveying information and opinion. In 1831, the people of Taunton followed news of the fate of the Commons hearing of their election petition in the press. The *Taunton Courier* of 16 March produced a full account of the result. In contrast, in the 1740s, news of the parliamentary discussion of the Weymouth charter had been conveyed there by letter.[16] Provincial newspapers in the first quarter of the nineteenth century increasingly adopted a more insistent politicized stance that can be linked to a shift in provincial opinion and political culture.[17] In addition, the greater density of the provincial press encouraged many (but by no means all) papers to emphasize their local character, or a region that was less far-flung than hitherto. This was not simply a matter of titles and areas of distribution, but also of contents. The relationship between the social contours described in the last chapter and the spatial pattern discussed in this was further complicated by the political issues probed in the following chapters. However, in large part due to the focus of the press on propertied society, there was less regional variety within the provincial press than is the case today.

NOTES

1. Exeter, Devon CRO, 48/26/13 DC. 6327.
2. G.A. Cranfield, *The Development of the Provincial Newspaper, 1700–1760* (Oxford, 1960); R.M. Wiles, *Freshest Advices: Early Provincial Newspapers in England* (Columbus, Ohio, 1965); H. Barker, 'Catering for Provincial Tastes: Newspapers, Readership and Profit in Late Eighteenth-century England', *Historical Research* 19 (1996), 42–61; G. Tatham, 'The Sherborne Mercury in the Eighteenth Century: A Regional Newspaper?' (unpublished paper).
3. D.A. Johnson, 'Joshua Drewry and the first Stafford Newspapers', in M.W. Greenslade (ed.), *Essays in Staffordshire History* (Stafford, 1970), pp. 187–9.
4. J. Feather, *The Provincial Book Trade in Eighteenth-century England* (Cambridge, 1985), p. 48; A. Sterenberg, 'The spread of printing in Suffolk in the eighteenth century', in M. Crump and M. Harris (eds), *Searching the Eighteenth Century* (1983), pp. 38–40.
5. M. Harris, 'The structure, ownership and control of the press, 1620–1780', in J. Curran, G. Boyce and P. Wingate (eds), *Newspaper History from the Seventeenth Century to the Present Day* (1978), p. 90.
6. J.E. and P.A. Crowther (eds), *The Diary of Robert Sharp of South Cave: Life in a Yorkshire Village, 1812–1837* (Oxford, 1997).
7. P. Brett, 'Early Nineteenth-century Reform Newspapers in the Provinces: The *Newcastle Chronicle and Bristol Mercury*', *Journal of Newspaper and Periodical History* (1995), 59.
8. C.J. Mitchell, 'Provincial Printing in Eighteenth-century Britain', *Publishing History* 21 (1987), 5–24.
9. Barker, *Newspapers, Politics, and Public Opinion in Late Eighteenth-century England* (Oxford, 1998), p. 177. Other recent work on the provincial press of the period includes M. Beaven, 'Warwickshire Provincial Newspapers in the Early 1750s', *Warwickshire History* 9 (1993), 12–34, and C.Y. Ferdinand, *Benjamin Collins and the Provincial Newspaper Trade in the Eighteenth Century* (Oxford, 1997).
10. J. Barry, 'The press and the politics of culture in Bristol 1660–1775', in

J. Black and J. Gregory (eds), *Culture, Politics and Society in Britain, 1660–1800* (Manchester, 1991), pp. 73–4.

11. *Birmingham Commercial Herald*, 2 January 1809.
12. Exeter, Devon CRO, 152 M/C 1811 OE.
13. S. Bennett, 'The Swing Riots in Lincolnshire', in S. and N. Bennett (eds), *An Historical Atlas of Lincolnshire* (Hull, 1993), p. 96.
14. On this general process, although not on newspapers, J. Stobbart, 'Regional Structure and the Urban System: North-west England, 1700–1760', *Transactions of the Historic Society of Lancashire and Cheshire* 145 (1995), 45–73.
15. I. Maxted, 'Printing, the Book Trade and Newspapers *c.* 1500–1860', in R. Kain and W. Ravenhill (eds), *Historical Atlas of South-west England* (Exeter, 1999), pp. 243–4.
16. Correspondence of John and Richard Tucker. Bod. MS. Don. *c.* 105–6. More generally, see B. Harris and J. Black, 'John Tucker, M.P., and Mid-eighteenth-century British Politics', *Albion* 29 (1997), 15–38.
17. D. Eastwood, *Government and Community in the English Provinces, 1700–1870* (1997), pp. 76–7; B. Harris, 'Praising the Middle Sort?', pp. 11–12, 17.

CHAPTER SEVEN

Politics 1750–1789

The printer of this paper, solicitous to observe the strictest impartiality in all matters relative to elections, begs leave to acquaint those concerned in them, that the Hereford Journal is equally open to all parties, while they endeavour to promote the interests of their respective friends by liberal and manly means. It being his opinion, that although the editor of a public paper cannot justly be debarred the common privilege of private judgment on political subjects, it should be one of the first objects of his care, that the sentiments which he adopts shall not be discernible in the publication under his management. They will also please to be informed that everything, written with a view to serve electioneering purposes, is inadmissible unless it be paid for.

British Chronicle or Pugh's Hereford Journal, 17 August 1780

While English became the language of profit, profit remained the purpose of most British periodicals. The public was willing to pay for political news, speculation and discussion. Newspapers were helped by the expansion in the range of public political news in the late eighteenth and early nineteenth centuries. This centred on the expansion of parliamentary reporting, but that cannot be understood on its own. Instead, it has to be treated as an aspect of change in attitudes to the press and of the political culture within which newspapers operated and which they helped to frame.

Public politics had been far from unimportant in the early decades of newspaper history,[1] but, in the early eighteenth century, there had been a change in the modes of political communication with the characteristic high political forms of private letter and, to a lesser extent, speech, supplemented, in the open forums of coffee-house, theatre, pulpit, and the expanding public spaces of Augustan England,[2] by public discourse. In this process, political printing – ballads, flysheets, caricatures, pamphlets and newspapers – played a major role, both articulating views and, themselves, providing subject matter for the world of print. Just as publishers sought the patronage of the public, so did politicians and political groups that sought to use the mechanism of print to their own profit.

This was taken further in the second half of the eighteenth century by the deliberate cultivation of the possibilities of print by political groups and, in particular, symbols of public politics, most prominently first the

London Patriots of the 1750s and then John Wilkes. This squinting anti-hero and entrepreneur of faction used the press, especially the *North Briton*, an essay-paper that he founded, to attack George III and his ministers in the 1760s.[3] This use of the press helped to ensure that the procedures of government regulation and intervention became more prominent, and this, in turn, sustained both newspaper comment and public interest in the press. Issues of press regulation had always been seen as part of a debate over the nature of the governmental system. In the 1760s, the political weakness of government, the coming of peace in 1763, the relative lack of other topics of comparable emotive interest, and the particular features of the *North Briton* affair, helped to ensure that issues of press regulation became symbolic of the essential public issues at stake in the struggle between ministry and opposition.

The 'public space' that the press could fill was a crucial point. The natural difficulties of regulation and the specific problems of securing convictions were exacerbated by judicial differences of opinion over the legal extent of government powers. These helped to make legal regulation a major issue and a widely accepted solution difficult. The Sardinian envoy, Scarnafis, reported in 1771 that he had been unable to obtain an elucidation of the legal issues at dispute, either from the Secretary of State for the Southern Department, the Earl of Rochford, or from several MPs, and that the freedom of the press was very hard to determine.[4]

Two major elements of the challenge to the government's position were the difficulties in securing convictions and the willingness of the opposition to contest legally the actions of the Secretaries of State. Had the major trials been held outside London, their course might have been different, for there was no doubt of the difficulty of obtaining convictions in the capital, but one significant aspect of continuity in the eighteenth-century struggle over the regulation of the press was that all major cases involved London papers and were held in London. Conversely, the prosecution of the *Stamford News* in 1811 was a testimony to the growing maturity, politicization, and importance of the provincial press.

In 1756, the First Lord of the Treasury, the Duke of Newcastle, had sought legal opinion for a prosecution of the printer of the *London Evening Post*, an opposition tri-weekly, that on 26 August had published a letter from 'Britannicus', asking 'Are not our rights, lives, and liberties, now brought into a very precarious situation by such unconstitutional measures, as introducing a foreign army, and neglecting our own militia?' Newcastle was advised that this was 'a direct and daring charge upon the Parliament of unconstitutional measures', but told that a prosecution was unwise because the paper had been printed in London and must therefore be tried there: 'The temper of the times must . . . be consulted in prosecutions of this nature, and from all I have heard and been informed it is at present in too inflamed and convulsed a state to advise any prosecution of this kind.'[5]

As most of the 1760s were 'inflamed', at least in so far as the opinions of many London jurors were concerned, prosecutions remained a problem. In 1770, the six newspaper printers who had printed Junius's attack on George III were all, bar one, acquitted, despite a major ministerial effort to secure convictions. Had the prosecutions all succeeded they may well have had a significant effect, at least in the short term, as the sole printer sentenced, John Almon of the *London Museum*, was forced to give sureties for two years.[6] 'Indignation', writing in the *Gazetteer* of 13 August 1770, linked the verdicts to a struggle to secure a public world of politics:

> The late decisions of the two very spirited London juries have given a mortal blow to the present despotic, feeble, and unprincipled administration. They had no chance to stand, but by keeping their actions, by the terror of law, a secret from the world. Now that an honest and indignant people have determined not to be longer the instruments of ministerial oppression, all men that can write will combine to expose the ignorant Goths in office.

As so often, the comment on press activity was correct in discerning a general expansion and inaccurate in its specific conclusions. An anonymous essay of 1769 on the liberty of the press claimed, 'It is a singular circumstance, but a real fact, that the Liberty of the Press has grown stronger from every attack on it; and that the situation of newspapers has become more flourishing in proportion to the increase of the duties imposed on them'; while, conversely, another item that year sought to demonstrate that the press was better treated under George III than under his two predecessors.[7]

Freer and stronger the press may have been, but it was to be no more influential in terms of having a direct impact on policy. In 1770, the Duke of Grafton, the ex-First Lord of the Treasury, who had been much harried by the press, dismissed the idea of making 'every impudent report, which may be circulated through the channel of our newspapers' a matter of parliamentary debate, and the ministry of his successor Lord North (1770–82) proved relatively impervious to press abuse. The direct political consequences of the legal battles over the press were far more limited than either successive ministries or their opponents had suggested.[8]

The indirect consequences, particularly the growth, despite attempts to prevent it, of parliamentary reporting, were more significant. This had been seen as a parliamentary privilege, and in June 1660 the Convention Parliament prohibited publication of parliamentary proceedings without the consent of Parliament. Newspapers that breached the regulations had been punished, most recently four in 1760, though more leniency had been shown towards the magazines, so that in the mid-1750s, when

Richard Beckford had wished to practise parliamentary oratory, he did so 'by studying magazines and historical registers', rather than newspapers.[9] In 1762, the Commons had reaffirmed its right to control the publication of its proceedings, and printers were accordingly punished in 1764, 1765, 1767 and 1768. The prominence of the Commons in expelling Wilkes and subsequently denying him election for Middlesex made reports of its activities ever more interesting and important, and the leading London papers sought to satisfy a demand, but, in doing so, they pressed against not only the privilege of Parliament, but also the monopolization of politics by the privileged. In 1771, reports about the reaffirmation by the Commons, on the motion of Wilkes' opponent George Onslow, of their prohibition of publication led to action against eight newspapers. The City of London, where Wilkes was now an alderman, gave shelter to the printers who refused to answer charges at the Commons, and a clash between the two jurisdictions vindicated the Commons, but made the political dangers of suppressing debates all too clear. As a result, from 1771, little attempt was made to limit reports, and they swiftly became a major feature of the press.[10]

The *Town and Country Magazine* claimed in 1782, 'The speeches and debates, in both Houses of Parliament, are of such importance, as to engross the greatest part of our newspapers, and necessarily become matters of the utmost consequence to all our readers'.[11] James Perry frequently widened the columns of the *Morning Chronicle* during the parliamentary session to ease the pressure on space caused by the fact, he noted in 1794, that advertisements were also most common at that period of the year. The development of parliamentary reporting underlined the influence of the metropolitan over the provincial press, as the latter eagerly devoted column after column to debates, taking its information from the London papers. The *Reading Mercury* obviously felt that this was what its readers wanted. Parliamentary items occupied a substantial portion both of the free sheets distributed occasionally with the paper and of the paper itself, notes on the front page drawing readers' attention sometimes to such items on the back page.[12] The arrival of such items helped to dictate the working arrangements of newspapers. The *Glocester Journal* of 24 January 1785 announced: 'As the meeting of Parliament will necessarily oblige us to reserve a greater portion of our paper for the last post, it is requested that those advertisements which require immediate insertion may be sent by the middle of the day on Saturday.' The following century, newspapers offered editorial comments on parliamentary news they reported, as, for example, in the *Birmingham Chronicle* of 17 and 24 April and 1 May 1823.

Parliamentary reporting offered the reading public a greater range of information than hitherto. Nine out of the sixteen columns of the *Courier* of 1 January 1795 were devoted to printing part of the Commons debate on the Address, and the opposition paper provided a list of the Foxite minority and their constituencies. Four days later, the *London Packet* printed a list of MPs who had abandoned support of the war with France. Many of the surviving division lists derive from press reports, both for the Commons and for the Lords.

There was criticism of some aspects of parliamentary reporting. Many debates did not seem to provide appropriate or attractive copy, but once newspapers had developed the practice of printing them during the session it was difficult to substitute other material speedily, while it was easier to fill space by this means than by any other, and once the paper had gone to the expense of obtaining parliamentary reports (for long the sole specialized reporters were the parliamentary ones) it was necessary to use the copy. In 1785 the first issue of the *Daily Universal Register* referred to readers facing 'long accounts of petty squabbles about trifles in Parliament, or panegyrics on the men and measures that he most disliked; or libels on those whom he most revered'. The prospectus for the *Star* in 1788 stated, 'The debates in Parliament, being subjects of universal concern, claim a respectable portion of this paper; but dull and uninteresting prolixity will be as carefully avoided, as affected and unmeaning brevity.'

Accuracy was another problem. It was not easy for parliamentarians in hot and stuffy chambers to provide accurate reports of proceedings. Comparisons between different accounts often reveal major discrepancies. Newspaper reporters were faced with additional problems. They were not allowed to take down notes until the 1780s and prior to that had to rely on their memories, William Woodfall excelling so far as to earn the name 'Memory' Woodfall. Reporters were not sure of a place, and from the back of the gallery they could not fully see the Commons. The gallery could be cleared whenever a member on the floor of the House chose to 'spy strangers', and the gallery was cleared automatically when a division was taken and then not reopened. There were no reliefs for the reporters in the 1770s. The situation improved with time and newspapers were increasingly able to plan their reporting. The *Morning Post* of 4 January 1798 noted that its arrangements for reporting the debate of the previous night 'were made upon the supposition that Messrs. Fox, Pitt, and Sheridan would rise late, and we therefore reserved some of our reporters and a part of this paper for their speeches'.

The *Morning Chronicle* of 8 January 1787 stated that 'the first aim of the reporter of parliamentary debates in this paper is, and ever has been, to evince the most unquestionable impartiality and fairness'. Despite such claims, there were frequent charges of inaccuracy in parliamentary reporting, and indeed the gallery was known as a place for drinking. William Hazlitt, parliamentary reporter of the *Morning Chronicle* in 1813–14, harmed his health by drinking there. In 1788, William Grenville, a confidant of William Pitt the Younger, told the Commons the 'newspaper misrepresentations of the proceedings of that House had of late been very frequently complained of'.[13] Aware of the importance of a reputation for accuracy, newspapers competed to stress their reliability, and to criticize that of their rivals. In 1817, the Whig-Radical *Tyne Mercury* and the Tory *Newcastle Courant* clashed over the accuracy of the former's report of Grey's Newcastle Fox dinner speech of that year.[14] The *Oracle* of 29 January 1795 declared 'The person who objects to our not having given Mr. Pitt's amendment on Mr. Grey's motion verbatim, will, however, feel, that our account contains the substance and purport of it, which are all that can be expected in a daily paper.' The *True Briton* of 2 February 1799 announced:

> We have great satisfaction in having received from various quarters, and particularly from several Members of Parliament, who were present at the debate on Thursday night, the highest commendations of our report of it; and particularly of Mr. Pitt's speech. Our reporters were peculiarly attentive to his statement, as we thought it essential that both *Ireland* and this country should know what were the precise grounds upon which it was intended the union should be established.

Public politics was therefore well established in the press by the close of the eighteenth century and politics had become public to a considerable extent, albeit not in all spheres. The press was both the principal medium of the new public politics and able to report and comment on it. The *Salisbury Journal* of 9 February 1795 reported 'On Thursday a general meeting of the inhabitants of this City, Close, and Neighbourhood was held at the Council Chamber, for the purpose of considering the propriety of petitioning Parliament for peace', and printed the petition. Reports of meetings played a major role in the press, providing national publicity for a myriad of causes. By providing information, the press played a major role in making the political process more accessible.

A greater awareness of the possibilities of print was part of a more widespread concern to influence public opinion and the opinion of those interested in politics. Public opinion developed as a category in political thought, although there was uncertainty about what constituted such opinion and about its impact on high politics. The press was central to politicization, the strengthening, sustaining and widening, if not of a specific political consciousness, then at least of national political awareness. In 1762, Elizabeth Montagu was depressed about Newcastle: 'There is an universal dejection among honest people. The public papers, absurd as they are, have made deep impressions.'[15]

As most local newspapers consisted largely of material from the London press, the 'provincial press' in its first flush was spreading metropolitan opinion rather than reflecting local views. Widespread printing played a major role in the development of national political campaigns, such as that of 1787–90 against the Test and Corporation Acts.

In general, in the reign of George III and especially (but not only) towards the end of the century, non-metropolitan papers became more active in their expression of distinctive opinions, and many of them more obviously partisan in their politics, although, in the case of some papers, this had been true from the outset. The populist opposition, and, in part, radical Wilkesite movement of the 1760s was much covered in the press and was adept in securing press interest and support. It did not prove a short-lived agitation comparable to that aroused by the swiftly repealed Jewish Naturalization Act of 1753.[16] Newspaper reporting also came to play a greater role in contested elections. To give a Scottish example, on 4 May 1768, the *Caledonian Mercury* devoted over two columns to the Cromartyshire election, accusing the sheriff of bias and William Pulteney, the victorious candidate, of misconduct. This was clearly unacceptable to Pulteney, and the next issue (7 May) carried a letter from him to the printer, Walter Ruddiman:

. . . I think it highly unbecoming in me to enter into a discussion of that matter in a news-paper, but judge it proper, in general, to declare that the anonymous account is not a just state of the case; many of the most material facts are omitted, and many others mis-represented.

He proceeded to enlarge on the charge. Pulteney was congratulated by James Crawford:

I see your letter in answer to Sir John's has been published. It was proper on many accounts to do so – 1st To stop the mouths of the public who were making a great clamour. 2ndly The Court of Session who may have taken an early prejudice which would not have been easily overcome and lastly the House of Commons, some of whom on seeing Sir John's side without an answer, might have engaged for him as believing all that he said to be true. No reply has as yet been published here nor do I think any will – If any is published, the publishers should be called to account if that can be done.[17]

Crawford was correct to draw attention to the attitude of the Court of Session and of Parliament. The election was referred successively to both, and Pulteney was vindicated. It is unlikely that the public discussion of the case in the columns of the *Caledonian Mercury* affected the outcome, but it is significant that politicians competing for the support of a tiny Cromartyshire electorate of fewer than twenty should also have felt it important to create a favourable impression in the world of print. The press reports, however, were designed not to persuade the electorate, but, rather, seen as crucial to shaping the national response to local events. This was a classic instance of the role of the non-metropolitan press as an intermediary between London and the localities. In some respects, this was true of the world of print in general. By its very nature, the immediacy of contacts in the localities lessened the need for written communication there, and thus offered less access for print.

Yet the situation was changing as reliance on the written word increased, with, for example, greater use of printed forms in bureaucracy.[18] Such forms were a type of serial publication, part of a regular process by which information was gathered and disseminated, and instructions transmitted. This could be directly linked to the press. The prospectus for the *Sherborne Mercury*, which was founded in 1737, promised that it would provide the information offered by 'all public notices that shall be advertised therein'.[19] The first issue of the *Cape Town Gazette, and African Advertiser*, that of 16 August 1800, carried an official notice:

> It is hereby ordered, that all Advertisements, Orders, etc. which appear under the Official Signature of either of the Secretaries in this Colony, or of any other Officer of Government, properly authorised to publish them in the *Cape Town Gazette, and African Advertiser*, are meant, and must be deemed to convey official and sufficient Notifications, in the same Manner as if they were particularly specified to any one Individual, or Others, to whom such may have a Reference.

The multi-faceted nature of print, however, ensured that, while the printed word continued to be associated with authority and its processes, it had other and different associations as well.

The deepening of a national political consciousness can be followed in the press. It is instructive to compare two speeches made by Dorset MPs in 1761 and 1789. At the electoral meeting held at the Crown in Blandford Forum on 13 January 1761 to introduce the candidates for the county at the forthcoming uncontested election, the politicians said little of policy and the surviving account is a manuscript one.[20] Twenty-eight years later, a meeting held at Dorchester to pass an Address of Thanks to William Pitt, for his conduct in the Regency Crisis, was reported at some length in the press. The politicized nature of the occasion and the extent to which the Dorset MPs were divided were clear from the account in the *Salisbury and Winchester Journal* of 2 February 1789. Like his father, Humphry, in 1761, Charles Sturt MP stressed his independency, but the changed nature of the political world, specifically the sharper awareness of politics and politicians, was indicated by the appearance of a reasonably lengthy account of his speech in print. The Foxite Humphry had been unexpectedly defeated in 1784.

Readers enjoyed a wealth of opinion that they would not have had earlier in the century. On 20 January 1780, the *British Chronicle or Pugh's Hereford Journal* printed a petition submitted to Parliament by the

Common Council of Hereford calling for the abolition of many posts at the disposal of government. The following week, an account of a meeting in Cumberland was published, as was the Gloucestershire petition and an account of that county's freeholders' meeting. The hostility to Lord North's ministry was obvious and British governments in the two world wars would not have permitted the publication of such speeches as that of George Berkeley, who 'lamented the many miseries in which this unhappy country was involved by a set of men, who, studying their own private interest only, were totally indifferent to the great concerns of the nation'.

Yet the expression of critical opinion was dominated by men of position. Berkeley, the son of an Earl, was an old Etonian naval officer, whose stand for the opposition in a 1776 by-election did not preclude eventual support for Pitt. A sense that conservative social assumptions resonated widely lay behind the attack on the opposition in the pro-government *Leeds Intelligencer* on 20 March 1781:

> There is an astonishing effrontery in many of the minority members who talk of independence and condemn pensioners and place men, when it is well known that these independent men don't enjoy an acre in land, nor a shilling in the funds, and that their whole subsistence depends on private pensions, which they receive from their employers.

There was no comparison in terms of sales or readership with the newspaper world of the late nineteenth century. The world of 'popular' politics made possible by the eighteenth-century press was very different from that of the age of Disraeli and Gladstone, and it is more appropriate to use the term 'public' politics for the earlier period; 'mass' politics is certainly inappropriate. A smaller scale of activity does not, however, suggest a lack of consequence, and the press played a major role in fostering and sustaining a political world very different from that of the calculations of borough patronage.

The press played a major role in the rise of petitioning.[21] In part as a result of the rise of extra-parliamentary associations, the presentation of petitions on national issues to Parliament rose considerably in the last quarter of the century. In the boroughs the number of signatories was almost double that of electors, a clear indication of the extent to which the 'political nation' was not limited to the electorate. Instead, politics encompassed a considerable amount of activity by the more humble members of the community (mostly men),[22] and, thus, to an extent, directed, expressed and contained their views.

There was therefore a symbiotic relationship between the press and public politics. The consequences of this nexus, sphere or space (terms vary) of opinion and activity are more problematic. It is necessary to free the concept of public opinion and the related treatment of the press from the teleological context in which they are commonly presented. The hold of the Whig myth of history ensured that the development of the modern political system, successively parliamentary government, democracy and democratization, seemed the major theme in British history and was thus automatically associated with progress. In such a schema, the 'long' eighteenth century was the period between the establishment of parliamentary government, thanks to the Glorious Revolution, and nineteenth-century extensions of the franchise, beginning with the Reform Act in 1832. The place of opinion 'out of doors', outside the world of Court and Parliament, was similarly clear. Its development indicated the limits of the representative system, and, in turn, helped eventually to secure its failure on the part of whichever groups are supposed to have displayed it.

Such an analysis was, in part, an aspect of the important role of history as public myth, a facet that the press readily lends itself to, but such an approach has grave limitations. Aside from teleology, there is the questionable attempt to treat a struggle for change in the political system as the central political issue. Rather than focusing largely on attempts to change the distribution of power within society as significant, important as these were, especially in the 1790s, it is more appropriate to understand the extent to which those active in politics chose to work within the system. This can be better appreciated if the absence of a revolutionary consciousness is not treated as a sign of failure.

The press was part of the process by which politics was channelled through the system, although it is clear that extra-parliamentary action was not simply a matter of popular mass activism and, anyway, that much of this activism can be defined as 'conservative'.[23] The elements of conservatism can be found in explicitly political action, most obviously the anti-revolutionary loyalism of the 1790s; and, also, in what has been presented as the 'moral economy' of the populace, their support for customary rights and charges.[24] Support for government policies could be just as significant and valid an expression of public opinion as opposition to them, and this became more clearly the case in the last quarter of the century, initially with backing for a firm line towards the American colonists.

Popular conservatism of an explicitly political character was a major feature of the public politics that received much press attention from the 1790s, in part thanks to its associational character in terms of organizations such as Constitutional Associations and Pitt Clubs whose activities provided copy.[25] If such bodies are a reminder of the diversity and complexity of public opinion, the press was similarly diverse. Direct financial pressures and inducements from government and other political bodies did not end this diversity; nor indeed were they intended to do so. Small-circulation papers were vulnerable, not least to pressure on their crucial advertising revenue, and their modest finances made subsidies, paid items and the provision of paid official notices valuable bait. In 1789, Thomas Wood, printer of the *Shrewsbury Chronicle*, explained to a government MP,

> the articles I have inserted in favour of Opposition. These articles have every one of them been admitted only on the footing of advertisements. And I could not refuse them. You know how I am surrounded with members who voted on that side, which are my customers . . . I have however received letters of thanks for my introducing so many articles in favour of Mr. Pitt which I have done gratis . . . I shall be happy to insert anything you or any other friend of Mr. Pitt's may send . . . without any fee.[26]

The profitability of small-circulation newspapers could be affected by even modest subsidies, and the potential for exercising such control was discussed in the press, the *Reading Mercury* of 10 December 1770 reporting that Lord North 'being lately told by a friend that his administration could not possibly last long, as Junius and all the good writers were against him, he replied that was certainly his own fault, for that he could have them all on his side whenever he wished'. It was certainly possible to purchase newspapers, the ministry buying the *Morning Post* in 1776. It has been suggested that an active press policy by Pitt the Younger between 1784 and 1790, including a marked rise in subsidies, played a role in improving press coverage of the ministry.[27]

Yet the effect, as well as the extent, of subsidies may have been exaggerated. Despite the extensive catalogue of papers that received ministerial inducements, the degree of influence enjoyed by the government was limited. The Secret Service accounts for 1784 list sums of only £100 each for five newspapers. Most papers and writers in receipt of government money in the 1780s and 1790s received less than £200 annually. Such amounts were probably too small to sway any newspaper's editorial viewpoint and they were probably spent in order to ensure favourable coverage of a particular issue.[28] If so, the situation seems to have been very different from that in the reign of Queen Anne, when, it has been recently argued, subsidies were required both to launch and to sustain newspapers.[29]

Alongside the dimension of variety provided by a diversity of views, there was another provided by the availability of news. This varied both between and within years. News was generally in short supply in the parliamentary recess and in peacetime. As the Seven Years' War neared its close, the *Bristol Journal* prepared to fill the likely gap by offering its readers another version of the war, the issue of 15 January 1763 announcing:

> As in times of peace a scarcity of news must consequently ensue, it is presumed a state of England, from the famous Peace of Aix-la-

Chapelle [1748] to the Declaration of War against Spain in the year 1762, will not be disagreeable to our readers, as it will include many interesting and curious particulars relative to this nation since that time: including The History of the Present War. To be continued weekly.

In fact, the political agenda shifted quite considerably in the post-war world. Whereas British politics had been dominated by war or the prospect of war since 1738, after 1763 domestic disputes came to the fore (although foreign affairs, albeit in an episodic manner, still received much attention). This was demonstrated by the press reports of the celebrations for the proclamation of peace which occurred as agitation over the new cider excise was sweeping the west of England. The *Bristol Journal* of 23 April described the burning of an effigy of the Prime Minister, John, 3rd Earl of Bute,

On occasion of the proclaiming of the peace last week at Stroud-water, an apple-tree, which had been cut down for that purpose, was carried in the procession, together with an effigy as large as life, with a B inscribed on the back. At the close of the cavalcade, the effigy was put into the stocks, then hung up by the common hangman, and afterwards, burnt to ashes. The same ceremony, we hear, was observed at Dursley, and other parts of the county of Gloucester.

The Wilkesite movement provided a more sustained and national subject for discussion and debate, and one that focused renewed attention on the identity of the public, the nature of representation, and the role of the press.[30] The outbreak of the War of American Independence in 1775 in part led to a shift back to foreign affairs, but the war was also a civil war within the empire that aroused considerable dispute within Britain, divisions that were covered in the press. The *Leeds Mercury* of 31 October 1775 carried, under the Leeds by-line, an account of a general meeting in Newcastle over the American crisis. To a far lesser extent, the war also affected advertisements with, for example, an increase in the number of those used to encourage recruiting.[31] There was also a more direct political relationship, in the shape of the argument that British press criticism of George III and his ministers influenced the American public debate. This was indeed the case, and led to bitterness about the criticism. Gage, the Commander-in-Chief in North America, observed to the Secretary at War in 1772: 'Your papers are stuffed with infamous paragraphs which the American printers, especially those of Boston, seldom fail to copy with American additions.' Two years after, he added from Boston, 'The seditious here have raised a flame in every colony which your speeches, writings, and protests in England have greatly encouraged.'[32]

Foreign news tended to accentuate the metropolitan focus of the English press, but not all items of American news came through the London papers. In 1747, *Felix Farley's Bristol Journal* had announced that it had engaged Boston and Philadelphia correspondents.[33] The *Leeds Mercury* printed items in late 1775 derived from a letter received by a gentleman at Berwick from his friend at Boston (18 July), a letter from Boston to someone at Halifax (1 August), a ship from Boston arriving at Liverpool (19 September), a letter from a soldier at Boston to his father in Chester (10 October), and a letter from Virginia to a correspondent at Whitehaven (24 October). In its issue of 24 November 1774, the *Cumberland Pacquet* had stressed the particular quality of its American reporting: 'A respectable merchant in this town has favoured us with several American news-papers, and particularly the *Boston Gazette*, *Pennsylvania Journal*, *Massachusetts Gazette*, and the *Virginia Gazette*, and provided some examples.'

Similarly, the *British Chronicle* published, under its Hereford by-line, items that were not received from the London press. On 20 May 1779, news of the Brest fleet was published from a Bristol correspondent, while on 8 July further maritime news appeared under a Bristol by-line as an 'extract of a letter from a gentleman of Plymouth to his friend in this city', and that September news of American privateers appeared from Cardigan, Haverfordwest, and Swansea. The *Glocester Journal* of 28 August 1780 printed news of the unsuccessful attempt to advance across Central America via Lake Nicaragua: 'By the Grantham packet which is arrived at Falmouth, we have the following accounts. From the Jamaica Gazette. Extract of a letter from Fort St. Juan, to a gentleman at Jamaica, May 18.' The *Birmingham Chronicle* of 26 February 1824 took its report of war with Algiers from an item in the *Royal Cornwall Gazette* based on a warship arrived in Falmouth.

In the period between the Peace of Paris in 1763 and Britain's entry into the Revolutionary War in 1793, the press was pulled towards a consideration of domestic affairs by two factors, first their intrinsic importance and, secondly, the need for copy. Newspapers had expanded in size during the period 1739–63 and the return of peace was not to be accompanied by any reduction in size. The absence of documentary evidence on this point necessarily makes it conjectural, but it appears that newspapers welcomed the rise in contentious 'public' politics in the 1760s. Dramatic political events provided not only points of reference in terms of public activity that could serve to explain, or rather provide an explanation for these developments, but also types of political activity that produced material for those who wished to report them. The appeal to a public wider than that customarily involved in political activity had to be striking and dramatic, comprehensive and swift, and this led both to the use of print and to the demonstrative politics of petitions, addresses, instructions, demonstrations and riots that could be reported readily.

Even without the latter, there was still a practice of appealing to public support, although this was more widespread in peacetime on the part of opposition than of government. For example, in 1768, when there was a parliamentary dispute over landownership rights in Cumberland which had implications for electoral and national politics, the press was more effectively used by Edmund Burke, a leading opposition figure who wrote three letters, two of which were published in the *Public Advertiser* and then reprinted for distribution in Cumbria.[34]

The provincial press divided markedly over the American War of Independence, newspapers such as the *Cambridge Chronicle, Leeds Mercury* and *Newcastle Chronicle* supporting the Americans, while others, for example the *Newark and Nottingham Journal* and the *Newcastle Courant*, were loyalist.[35] New papers founded during the conflict tended to take sides: the *Nottingham Gazette*, launched in 1780, supported the Americans. In addition, certain divisive local issues, for example the struggle between freemen and corporation in Coventry, interacted with newspaper rivalries.[36]

Political partisanship played a role in the increase in the number of titles, especially outside London, where the number of newspapers already reflected a range of opinion. These divisions in viewpoint were taken forward into the early 1780s as first political reform and then the fate of the Fox-North government in 1783 became central issues in political contention and public attention. The resolution of the political crisis with William Pitt the Younger's victory in the general election of 1784 was widely attributed to a shift in public opinion. The hostile William Eden referred to a 'frenzy of the people'.[37] The press had clearly played a role in this, although its extent is difficult to assess. Nevertheless, the degree to which the election was contested on national political grounds[38] in large part reflected the ability of the system of political communication to articulate such a contest. The press was central to this system.

NOTES

1. T. Harris, *London Crowds in the Reign of Charles II. Propaganda and Politics from the Restoration until the Exclusion Crisis* (Cambridge, 1987).

2. P. Borsay, *The English Urban Renaissance. Culture and Society in the Provincial Town, 1660–1770* (Oxford, 1989).

3. M. Peters, 'The *Monitor* on the Constitution, 1755–1765: New Light on the Ideological Origins of English Radicalism', *EHR* 82 (1971), 706–25, *Pitt and Popularity: The Patriot Minister and London Opinion during the Seven Years War* (Oxford, 1980), and '"Names and Cant": Party Labels in English Political Propaganda, *c.* 1753–1763', *Parliamentary History* 7 (1984), 103–27; P.D.G. Thomas, 'John Wilkes and the Freedom of the Press', *Bulletin of the Institute of Historical Research* 33 (1960), 86–98 and *John Wilkes: A Friend to Liberty* (Oxford, 1996); J. Brewer, 'The Number 45: A Wilkite

Political Symbol', in S.B. Baxter (ed.), *England's Rise to Greatness, 1660–1763* (Berkeley, 1983).

4. Scarnafis to Charles Emmanuel III, 29 March 1771, Turin, Archivio di Stato, Lettere Ministri Inghilterra 77.

5. Sharpe to Newcastle, 28 August 1756, BL, Add. 32867.

6. R. Rea, *The English Press in Politics 1760–1774* (Lincoln, Nebraska, 1963), pp. 177–87.

7. *Berrow's Worcester Journal*, 9 November 1769; *St James's Chronicle*, 4 May 1769.

8. Grafton, 5 December 1770, Cobbett, 16, p. 1309.

9. J. Brooke (ed.), *Horace Walpole, Memoirs of King George II* (3 vols, New Haven, 1985) II, 26.

10. P.D.G. Thomas, 'The Beginning of Parliamentary Reporting in Newspapers, 1768–74', *EHR* 74 (1959), 623–36; W.C. Lowe, 'Peers and Printers: the Beginnings of Sustained Press Coverage of the House of Lords in the 1770s', *Parliamentary History* 7 (1988), 241–56.

11. *Town and Country Magazine* 14 (1782), iii–iv.

12. *Reading Mercury*, 25 February, 25 March 1771, 22 February, 31 May, 21 June 1773, 21 May 1781.

13. Cobbett, 26, p. 1429.

14. P.D. Brett, 'The Whigs and the Newcastle Fox Dinners 1812–1820', *Durham University Journal* 83 (1991), 12.

15. Montagu to Earl of Bath, 23 October 1762, HL, Montagu papers 4592.

16. T.W. Perry, *Public Opinion, Propaganda and Politics in Eighteenth-century England: A Study of the Jew Bill of 1753* (Cambridge, Mass., 1962); Brewer, *Party Ideology and Popular Politics at the Accession of George III* (Cambridge, 1976), pp. 139–60.

17. Pulteney to Ruddiman, 6 May, Crawford to Pulteney, 11 May 1768, HL, Pulteney MSS 1905, fol. 121. The defeated candidate was Sir John Gordon.

18. M. Wilcox, 'The Rolls of the Glamorgan Court of Quarter Sessions', *Annual Report of the Glamorgan Archivist* (1992), p. 28.

19. C.H. Mayo, *Bibliotheca Dorsetiensis* (1885), p. 75.

20. Bod. MS, Don 20, b20.

21. J.E. Bradley, *Popular Politics and the American Revolution in England: Petitions, the Crown and Public Opinion* (Macon, Georgia, 1986).

22. P. Langford, *Public Life and the Propertied Englishman, 1689–1798* (Oxford, 1991).

23. C. Condren, 'Radicals, Conservatives and Moderates in Early Modern Political Thought: A Case of Sandwich Islands Syndrome?', *History of Political Thought* 10 (1989), 525–42.

24. E.P. Thompson, *Customs in Common* (1992).

25. J.J. Sack, *From Jacobite to Conservative. Reaction and Orthodoxy in Britain, c. 1760–1832* (Cambridge, 1993).

26. Wood to James Bland Burges, 23 January 1789, Bod. BB, 18 fols, fols. 40–1. For the attempt by both parties to influence provincial papers prior to the 1790 general election, D.R. McAdams, 'Politicians and the Electorate in the late eighteenth century' (Ph.D., Duke, 1967), p. 151.

27. J. Ehrman, *Pitt* (3 vols, 1969–96) I, 66.

28. Christie, *Myth and Reality*, p. 328; S. Lutnick, *The American Revolution and the British Press, 1775–1783* (Columbia, Missouri, 1967), p. 19; I. Asquith, 'The structure, ownership and control of the press, 1780–1855', in Boyce *et al.* (eds), *Newspaper History*, p. 111; H. Barker, *Newspapers, Politics, and Public Opinion in Late Eighteenth-century England* (Oxford, 1998), p. 72.

29. J.A. Downie, 'Periodicals and politics in the reign of Queen Anne', in Myers and Harris (eds), *Serials and their Readers* (Winchester, 1993), p. 58.

30. P. Woodland, 'Extra-parliamentary political organization in the making: Benjamin Heath and the opposition to the 1763 Cider Excise', *Parliamentary History* 4 (1985); Brewer, *Party Ideology and Popular Politics at the Accession of George III* (Cambridge, 1976); R.L. Capraro, 'Typographic Politics: the Impact of Printing on the Political Life of Eighteenth-century England, 1714–1772' (Ph.D., Washington University, St Louis, 1984).

31. S. Conway, 'The Politics of British Military and Naval Mobilization, 1775–83', *EHR* 112 (1997), 1186.

32. Gage to Viscount Barrington, 2 September 1772, 18 July 1774, BL, Add. 73550.

33. D. Milobar, 'Aboriginal Peoples and the British Press 1720–1763', in S. Taylor, R. Connors and C. Jones (eds), *Hanoverian Britain and Empire* (Woodbridge, 1998), p. 68.

34. F.P. Lock, *Edmund Burke I* (Oxford, 1999), pp. 245–6.

35. J. Bradley, *Religion, Revolution and English Radicalism. Nonconformity in Eighteenth-century Politics and Society* (Cambridge, 1990), pp. 378–9; S. Lutnick, *The American Revolution and the British Press 1775–1783* (Columbia, Miss., 1967); J. Sainsbury, *Disaffected Patriots: London Supporters of Revolutionary America 1769–1782* (Kingston, Ontario, 1987).

36. J. Money, *Experience and Identity. Birmingham and the West Midlands 1760–1800* (Manchester, 1977), p. 61.

37. Eden to Lord Sheffield, 10 April 1784, BL, Add. 45728.

38. M.W. McCahill, *Order and Equipoise. The Peerage and the House of Lords, 1783–1806* (Woodbridge, 1978), pp. 31–6; J. Cannon, *The Fox–North Coalition. Crisis of the Constitution* (Cambridge, 1969), p. 225; F. O'Gorman, *Voters, Patrons and Parties. The Unreformed Electorate of Hanoverian England, 1734–1832* (Oxford, 1989), pp. 295–6. For other factors at work in the elections, T.R. Knox, '"Peace for Ages to Come": The Newcastle Elections of 1780 and 1784', *Durham University Journal* 84 (1992), 13–15; P.D.G. Thomas, 'The Rise of Plas Newydd: Sir Nicholas Bayly and County Elections in Anglesey, 1734-84', *Welsh History Review* 16 (1992), 174–6.

CHAPTER EIGHT

Reporting the Revolution

Where the spark of freedom has not yet blazed forth, the folly of the potentates of the Earth, by the severity of their judgments, are working the work of God and Reason, and forcing their subjects to feel the insulted dignity of men, to act like men, and to support the rights of men.

Newark Herald and Nottinghamshire and Lincolnshire General Advertiser,
26 October 1791

The French Revolution was the biggest single challenge to the European *ancien régime* and a transformation that had many major repercussions in the British Isles. It was particularly important for the press not only as it set the challenge of reporting and explaining a rapidly changing and unpredictable situation, but also because the response to the Revolution revealed and accentuated fault lines within British public culture and led to a new emphasis on a politics of class.

For British newspapers, the Revolution presented an opportunity and a challenge. It offered a series of dramatic and interesting events taking place just across the Channel. In contrast to the American Revolution, when distance had posed major problems of reporting and, especially, of verification, reports about events in France were relatively easy to check, even if their significance might be contested. French was also the foreign language that was least problematic for British newspapers.

These opportunities also posed a challenge. Precisely because such news could be provided and because there were known to be important and interesting events taking place in France, newspapers covered the Revolution at length. The 1780s and 1790s were years of increasing competition for the British press, with more titles crowding the market. The general trend for increased sales did not necessarily help individual titles. In part, this was a feature of what has been termed the birth of a consumer society.[1] A larger, more cash-oriented and more changeable market was bound to offer more opportunities and challenges. Inevitably this was most acute in London, where a large number of printers ensured a particularly competitive atmosphere. The *World* warned on 27 February 1792:

As a small lesson to such as are inclined to speculate upon this property, it may not be amiss to know that from the short credit given by the STAMP OFFICE, compared with what may be necessary to give to trade in general, a paper of established consequence is obliged perhaps to be from £1,500 to £2,000 in advance.

Despite this, there was a large number of newspapers, matched by a genuine diversity of opinion, content and style.

In competing for readers, newspapers had traditionally cited the accuracy and speed of the news. The Revolution fitted into this pattern by providing a steady stream of news which papers wished to report as fast, as fully, and as accurately as possible. Individual titles boasted of the particular quality of their French news. As the major item in such news was the proceedings of the successive national representative bodies, newspapers did not, in general, stress unique sources of information. Instead, they prided themselves on their speed. Thus, the *Oracle* claimed on 14 February 1792: 'As a proof that the *Oracle* still retains its boasted superiority in point of continental intelligence, yesterday's paper contained two entire days of the proceedings of the National Assembly later than any of our contemporaries.'

Speed was not the sole point upon which the newspapers prided themselves. On 6 January 1792 the *Morning Chronicle*, a leading London opposition paper, declared:

The important advices brought by the French mail of yesterday, opens to us a new field of speculation, and now the value of the correspondences that we have formed on the Continent will be truly ascertained. It shall be our daily care to present to our readers the most faithful statements, and they may be assured that we shall never from the affection of superiority give the imposing air of official documents to papers, of which we cannot pledge ourselves for the authenticity. Paris has been for some time overrun with diplomatic forgeries, and we have no doubt but they will be made an article of our import trade.

There was not on Monday last any genuine copy of the *official note* of Prince Kaunitz printed in Paris – For the precise terms so essential to political men, our readers must have patience.

Competitiveness explains why papers adopting broadly similar viewpoints still criticized each others' reporting. Nevertheless, the relationship with British political divisions took precedence. The claim that accuracy was sacrificed for political purposes had surfaced in every conflict in which Britain had been involved during the century. Thus, on 20 May 1781 the *Leeds Intelligencer*, an enthusiastic supporter of the North ministry, accused the opposition of spreading false news about enemy successes.

The French Revolution posed a different problem. The accuracy of news reports was less contentious than in the case of distant America, and on the 'push' or supply side of the newspaper provision of information it was simple to report developments in Paris, particularly once the vast expansion of the Parisian press and the meeting of a constitutional assembly provided a mass of information. However, the opportunity for criticizing aspects of newspaper comment was greater, both because of the complexity of the issues and because once the Revolution became radical, by British standards, there were no agreed criteria by which it could be judged. Initially, the Revolution could be located in an historical context as the French parallel to the British rejection of Stuart authority. The press could be placed in the same fashion, with the expansion of the French press in 1789 related to that which had followed the Glorious Revolution. The *Oracle* of 6 August 1789 employed historical examples in its search for extenuating comparison:

> The violence at present exercised in France is not peculiar to that people: – on the contrary, it is common to every nation struggling for its rights. Did the English constitution acquire permanency, and in some degree perfection, by the defeat of Charles I and the Royalists without bloodshed? . . . Would the accession of William III, that glorious epoch in the history of our freedom, have been unattended with slaughter and confusion, if it had not been for the peaceable abdication of that silly and superstitious monarch James II?

However, Louis XVI's flight to Varennes in 1791 rudely shattered the hopes of those who believed that change and continuity could be peacefully reconciled, that France could experience a Gallic version of the Glorious Revolution, and that violence would be of little consequence. The flight was given extensive coverage, including three-and-a-half of the sixteen columns in the *Salisbury and Winchester Journal* of 4 July, 'on account of the extreme length of the late very important intelligence from France, we are under the necessity of omitting many advertisements this week'. The *Public Advertiser* of 18 February 1792 was more hopeful than accurate in discerning a moderate consensus in Britain:

> The political discussions to which the French Revolution has given occasion in this country, though carried to the most extravagant heights of theoretical refinement, and the most desperate excesses of republican absurdity have at least produced some general good, as the public mind has been rendered more firm in the adoption of temperate principles steering clear of Tory superstition on the one hand, and equally avoiding the dangerous extreme of popular enthusiasm.

In fact, by early 1792, there were considerable differences between the newspapers in their attitude towards France, reflecting four developments.

The growing radicalism of French changes that Edmund Burke had warned against in late 1790, was now readily apparent. In late 1790 it was still possible to argue that, irrespective of his general intellectual and ideological arguments, Burke was inaccurate in his description and prognostication of French developments. In contrast, by early 1792 the accuracy of Burke's account of French developments and of his warning about possible repercussions in Britain was conceded more widely, although without shaking the views of radicals. Second, as the Revolution became more radical, it posed a more exciting and threatening example for British observers. Third, it became clear that the Revolution was going to lead to a major European conflict. Fourth, the Revolution became the leading item in the news. In 1790, Britain had come close to war with Spain and in 1791 to Russia. Thereafter, there was no long-lasting issue that could challenge the Revolution for a major share of newspaper space.

As French developments became a more prominent subject in the press, so they became more divisive, and the different views of newspapers became more apparent in their reporting. The conservative note to which Burke had given voice resonated widely. In February 1792 the anti-slavery campaigner, William Wilberforce, received a pessimistic letter from a supporter who, having informed him that a local anti-slavery resolution had been printed in Joseph Gales's *Sheffield Register* (a paper that was to end after its printer fled abroad in 1794 to avoid trial),[2] expressed doubt as to the chances of parliamentary repeal:

> The St. Domingo business, though it certainly ought not, has and will affect the sentiments of many in the House, as it has certainly done of many out of it. . . . To strike the moment the iron is hot, is the only time to strike, and that moment is unhappily over . . . the flimsy prate of a Scotch reviewer, or a mercenary paragraph writer in the newspapers, will outweigh evidence brought before Parliament.[3]

The radical *Argus of the Constitution* had no doubt that there was a close correlation between a paper's position in the world of British politics and its views of France. On 1 May 1792, it claimed, 'The less change there appears to be of a counter revolution in France, the more inveterate and abusive are the ministerial hirelings in this country against that generous and enlightened nation.' Six days later, the *Argus* reported increased sales, adding that it would tell the truth about the Revolution: 'here shall be no garbelling of the proceedings in France, no crying down of freedom'. It is, in fact, unclear whether the definition of a particular political viewpoint on French developments really affected sales, either for the *Argus* or for other newspapers. In an age before market research, newspapers were dependent on the personal impressions of their proprietors and the comments of correspondents and subscribers. These were necessarily of limited value. The element of choice was central. The number of papers readily available in London was such that, other than with regard to marginal or 'extreme' political opinions, it was very difficult for any individual paper to define a market in distinctive terms. In general, newspapers could try to stress the unique quality of their French news, because it was especially fast or full, but they had little to say about the particular quality of their accompanying comment. The principal exceptions were the radical papers.

These were not the only papers that criticized Burke's ideology and the Pitt ministry's decision in late 1792 to confront the developing French new order for the Low Countries, a decision that was to lead to war early the following year. The Foxite press, among whom the *Morning Chronicle* was most prominent, also did so but was faced with a more difficult task.[4] They had to cope with the disintegration of the Whig party in the face of the challenge of Revolutionary France and indigenous radicalism, and they faced the problem of deciding how far they could continue to defend the Revolution at a time when it was becoming less attractive in British eyes. Sales of the *Morning Chronicle* had benefited from the dispatch of its owner-editor, James Perry, to Paris in 1791, in his capacity as a 'deputy' of the English Revolution Society, the paper announcing on 12 July that it had established 'an arrangement of correspondence which will enable us to give an earlier account of what is passing there than any of our competitors'.

However, it rapidly became clear that the Foxite position was under serious challenge from radical and conservative viewpoints. The Birmingham riots sparked off by a Bastille dinner on 14 July 1791 appeared to provide hard evidence of the domestic volatility and instability that the Revolution might arouse in Britain. A letter in the *London Chronicle* of 26 July used a French phrase, presumably deliberately: 'the most recent popular transactions at Birmingham call for the most serious attention, as both the cause and effect were the spontaneous awful proceedings of the Tiers Etat'.

The summer of 1791 witnessed an increase in press coverage of French news. The parliamentary recess always posed a problem for a press that, in the absence of reporters, was dependent on the ready supply of large quantities of material, and which had, during the session, become used to printing the debates *in extenso*. In 1789 and, to a greater extent, 1791 and 1792 events in France helped to fill the gap. However, French news was more than simply a space-filler.

Increasing interest in French news can be seen not only in the London papers but in the far more numerous provincial newspapers. These commonly contained very little international news other than the mass of material that they reprinted from the London press. A change occurred in the summer of 1791. To take the example of the *Glocester Journal*, a well-established paper, this carried very few items of national news under its Gloucester heading, still less any relating to France. However, on 27 June the Gloucester column informed its readers:

In our last paper, by the mistake of some of the figures in our letter from London, the sum for which the estate of the French clergy had been sold was erroneously stated. Instead of 410 million livres, it should have been 147 million.

A literary reference followed the next week:

Many of the circumstances connected with the late revolution in France appear to have been a long time in a state of progressive increase. The late Dr. Smollett so long ago as the year 1765, in one of his letters, speaking of France, observed that that government may be said to be weak and tottering, which finds itself obliged to connive at the oppressions of the officers of its revenues – From the relaxation he remarked in the reins of the French government, he foresaw that at some favourable juncture it would be taken advantage of.

On 5 September the reference was to Burke, the dissemination of whose writings on the Revolution owed much to the press, but on 3 October the paper sought to avoid controversy:

We feel equally disposed to promote a spirit of moderation and forbearance with our correspondent, who signs himself a Citizen of the World, in respect to opinions on the important affairs of another country; but we conceive a letter, parts of which might lead to some extent of discussion, better calculated for the use of the London publications than a provincial paper, that has to relate occurrences of a week's accumulation.

Whatever the reason for this hesitation, the *Glocester Journal* was prepared to print under the Gloucester heading letters from London, anonymous in the fashion of the period, that were clearly critical of France. To give two examples that illustrate the tone of the reports about France in a major provincial newspaper at the end of 1791, the issue of 24 October reported:

The new National Assembly is said to be much less respectable on all accounts than the last; and their debates are carried on with such noise and confusion, as to have occasioned them to be hissed, more than once, by the people, when they broke up. They are chiefly composed of low advocats; many of them men of indifferent characters – A very sensible nobleman from hence, who has been lately to reside in Paris for ten weeks, making his observations on the state of affairs there, assured a friend of mine that out of the 800 members who compose the present National Assembly there are not above 36 individuals who have a property equal to £120 a year – so that the wise principle of our constitution, which obliges its Members of Parliament to be qualified with a real estate of £300 a year, as a pledge of the interest they take in the welfare of the state, is not at all observed in the new system of government in France.

A week later, there was reference to the St Domingo rising, an event that was widely taken in the press to illustrate the real dangers of the Revolution:

> The misfortune will expose to all the world the miserable incompetence of the National Assembly, to manage the interests of so great a nation, and do much to forward the views of those who are aiming to bring about a counter revolution. All the people of property there, indeed, begin to be very apprehensive of bad consequences, from the present situation of matters; and I have heard of one rich individual, who had vast concerns in France, that has lately remitted . . . above £200,000 to this country, to be invested in the stocks, merely with a view to draw his property from the dangers in which it is invested there, and to secure it, at any rate, in this country of true liberty and protection.

On 5 October 1791 the first issue of the *Newark Herald* devoted nearly one of its sixteen columns to an item beginning:

> The affairs of France having for some time past been the subject of general conversation, it may afford pleasure to a numerous class of our readers, to lay before them the following account of the mode of conducting the election of representatives to the National Assembly; it having been so much misunderstood, and so essentially differing from our method of electing Members of Parliament.

In the next issue, a generally favourable account was published beginning 'Our correspondent in France gives us the following account of the new National Assembly'.

Controversy about the Revolution was regarded as sufficiently interesting to attract flagging. Thus, in its issue of 21 February 1791, the *Salisbury and Winchester Journal* inserted as a notice in the local news, 'For Dr. Priestley's celebrated letter to Edmund Burke Esq. see our last page'.

By the end of 1791, the Revolution and its consequences were clearly the centre of attention for the press. As the *Glocester Journal* put it on 26 December, 'Expectation is awakened by the appearance of an approaching crisis in the affairs of France.' Furthermore, there was an element of *Schadenfreude* and national pride in the reporting. The *St James's Chronicle* devoted two-and-a-third of the sixteen columns in its issue of 3 January 1792 to news under the by-line 'From the Correspondent of the St. James's Chronicle, resident at Paris'. His tone was smug:

While England, generously scorning to stoop to mean and unworthy revenge, gives the admiring world a glorious example of magnanimity in not profiting from the distracted state of this country, the French, in our opinion, deserve not a little credit in doing justice to her sentiments – Britons are at this moment considered by the people here, as they should be, mortals of a superior kind.

The same issue also contained more critical passages:

The French have lost every idea of humanity – the evil has been contagious among them, and we believe it can be accounted for – formerly the French were attached to their religion (which, with all its superstition, was preferable to impiety), because they had some morals, and they are now without virtue, because they have sacrificed their religion.

In the same issue, the paper's Paris correspondent expressed an oft-held, but inaccurate, view, 'the sun of France will continue long eclipsed'. This ensured that for most conservative British commentators France in the winter of 1791–2 was a warning, not a threat, a situation that was to be reversed the following winter. On 5 January 1792, the *Public Advertiser* claimed that:

The political degradation of France, however lamentable to the people of that country, will have a beneficial influence upon other states, by affording an instructive lesson that must operate as a powerful check against that spirit of innovation, and that mad desire of impracticable liberty, which began to prevail in the world before the revolution in France took place, and which derived considerable strength from the commencement and progress of that extraordinary event. The great body of the people in all countries, will now be forcibly sensible of the danger of over-throwing the salutary restraint of long-established laws, and of the confusion and misery that must ensue from an attempt, to maintain order, tranquillity, and strength, in a state of impossible equality.

All countries in Europe are profiting by the consequences of the Revolution in France, while she herself is involved in the deepest misery and wretchedness. Her commerce is nearly at a stand, and the channels through which it was abundantly active and successful are getting into other hands, who, having no internal obstructions, are able to push their advantages with vigour, and who of course will be gradually obtaining such secure hold, that if France should recover from her political infirmities, it would be hardly possible for her to retrieve her commercial weight and prosperity. This is the blessed effect of popular insurrection in the vain pursuit of delusive freedom, and this is the great example of national outrage, which the worthy *Patriots* on this side of the water would recommend to honest and contented John Bull.

The use of France and French principles to discredit the parliamentary opposition and their supporters became a major theme in pro-government publications. Criticism of domestic supporters of France was far from novel. Indeed, the tradition that their preferences, whether for Catholicism, absolutism, French food or actresses, posed a threat to the health of the British body politic was a long one, and Burke's *Reflections* was effective in part because it drew on it. The idea that the opposition were really enemies of the country was scarcely novel, but the Revolution introduced the added charge that they were enemies not simply because they supported a foreign state, but also because they wished to change British society accordingly. As such, there was a revival of some of the themes present in criticism of the Jacobites.

In 1791 and during the parliamentary session of 1792, the claim that the opposition was disloyal was pressed home with reference to Foxite encouragement of Catherine the Great in her confrontation with Britain in early 1791. On 4 January 1792, the *Public Advertiser* claimed the opposition

sacrifice their country, its connections, its wealth, its safety, its happiness, its interests to their own hopes of being able to dispossess the ministry of their power. This indeed was too evidently seen during the late negotiation with the court of Russia.

Nevertheless, there was no suggestion that the Foxites wished to introduce Russian methods of government. The contrast with the charges brought against the actual and alleged supporters of France was readily apparent. The internationalization of the French Revolution was far more potent than that of its American predecessor. The *Public Advertiser* informed its readers on 7 January 1792:

The fate of France now hangs upon a thread, and will very soon be decided; for though our modern tribe of patriots approve of daring attempts to overturn the established government of a country in order to substitute principles of the most gross and impracticable republicanism, the powers of Europe will not look tamely on, and suffer a seditious delirium to proceed without obstruction, till it spreads its baneful infection to their own respective states, and threatens the danger of an universal spirit of popular insurrection. A powerful confederation is therefore certainly formed, that will speedily step forward to relieve the degraded monarchy of France, and, by punishing the lawless rabble who have usurped the dominion of that country, impress upon the people of every other state, the necessity of obedience to the laws, and respect to the general happiness of society.

The growing realization that the Revolution might lead to war added the dimension of British national interests to the press debate. The question of what Britain should do, was in part expressed in terms of the ideological debate substantially begun by Burke, but, in part, a pragmatic geopolitical attitude predominated. That Britain was not to be a member of this confederation until 1793 led to a certain measure of confusion in the press in 1792, as newspapers that opposed the Revolution found themselves obliged to defend British neutrality. However, the essential division within the press was already clear by the start of 1792. Though certain newspapers retained some sympathy for developments in France, many wanted the Revolution to fail and, no longer convinced that it would collapse of itself, they hoped for foreign intervention to achieve this end. None guessed that this would lead to over twenty years of conflict. This period was to be of considerable importance for British politics, not least with the consolidation under the pressure of war of a new conservatism in reaction to a radical challenge seen at home and abroad, and also with the transformation of the reforming pressures of the 1780s as their political edge was discredited by alleged links with radicalism. The press was no mere register of this shift. Instead, it was to be affected by it. The 1790s saw a revival of the marked ideological partisanship that had characterized the struggle with Jacobitism, an assault upon the radical press, the development of government sponsorship, and an increased politicization of the provincial press. The role of the press, and, more generally, of other aspects of the political culture of print, such as cheap tracts, can also in part be located within a broadening out of what has been termed the 'public sphere', as social groups whose role in public politics had hitherto been episodic sought to have their voice heard. In addition, the quantity and importance of the material available encouraged interest in the news, at the same time as it provided the means for meeting this demand.

Politicization can be seen for example in the rise in what were termed leading articles,[5] and in the extent to which provincial newspapers printed more items that they had obtained themselves. Under the local by-line, the *Chelmsford Chronicle* of 11 May 1792 printed three such items that revealed their sources for French news:

1. Two gentlemen of this country passing the week before last from Ostend to Dunkirk, were taken up as spies, and not liberated till the most perfect assurances were obtained of their being 'Good Men and True'.
2. A letter from Paris, dated the 1st inst. Says, that scarce a morning appears without some massacred body being taken out of the Seine.

3. A gentleman from the French army, who was witness to the horrid barbarities near Tournay, says that the treatment of poor Dillon[6] has so much alarmed the officers that several have already sought an asylum in this land of freedom, happiness, and security; and some of their families are arrived in this country.

A week later, the paper published an ironic letter from a pseudonymous correspondent, indicating the extent to which France and sympathy for her could be used to discredit by association:

Last week a patriotic meeting was held at Colchester, for the laudable purpose of amending and improving the constitution of this kingdom, and so eminent were the abilities displayed on the occasion, that they reflected the highest disgrace on the present and every former administration; and clearly evinced that tradesmen and mechanics, in consequence of their liberal education, were capable of becoming far better legislators than all the Pitts, Norths, and Foxs of the present, or the Chathams and Rockinghams of former days. It was proved to demonstration, that as this country was at present suffering under all the horrors of poverty, distress and civil war, and that as France was in a state of peace, happiness and perfect tranquillity, in consequence of the late Revolution, a similar change in government was not only desirable, but absolutely necessary. It was also asserted that although a change of kind might produce at first some disagreable effects, by raising the price of provisions, producing private quarrels, and public animosities, and teaching the industrious poor to subsist without eating or drinking, yet in return for all this, we should possess the rights of man, and be enabled to bequeath to our children, instead of rotten buildings, paltry estates and dirty farms, the more solid and perfect inheritance of universal liberty – a liberty of seizing on the goods of our richer neighbours, and of wreaking our revenge indiscriminately, without the trouble of law, equity, or even common justice.

In the following issue, two letters were published denying that the meeting used as a basis for this crude warning of class warfare had taken place. 'A Friend to Truth' declared that the paper had 'been made the vehicle of public slander'. The previous month, *Wheeler's Manchester Chronicle* had expressed suspicion of French foreign policy, while on 5 May it announced:

We on Thursday received a letter from an avowed partisan of the French Revolution, in which he threatens to chastise us, if we publish our sentiments any more on French affairs. Besides the threat, the letter is extremely scurrilous – and gives a very forcible idea of the similitude and dangerous tendency of the French free opinion here, and their acts in their own country.

Developments in France were generally regarded critically. The *Westminster Journal: and London Political Miscellany* of 26 January 1793 wrote of Louis XVI's execution: 'as a murder we are confident it will be felt in the heart of every Englishman'. One item blamed the execution on Orléans, 'the issue of a criminal connexion between his licentious mother and a coachman', according to a writer who had not lost the ability to include the detail that readers apparently relished.

The Revolutionary crisis was to be important to the social politics of the British press, but the actual reporting of France can be seen as more interesting for perception than for objective assessment. It is not surprising that the press essentially viewed events in France in British terms. In order both to comprehend and to be comprehensible, foreign events had to be presented by the press in recognizable terms. This was exacerbated by the shortage of foreign correspondents and the importance of items submitted by unpaid writers. The former removed the consistent focus of a coherent and informed approach, and reflects the conservatism in reporting technique that characterized most of the press. The role of unpaid correspondents in Britain increased the stress on comment, because it was that in which they were principally interested. This comment centred on British politics and tended to treat French developments in a simplistic fashion, either as a dreadful warning or as a source of inspiration. Neither approach benefited from detailed attention to events in France and knowledge of these was useful only in so far as it could be fitted into these established interpretations. The principal shift in the reporting of the Revolution thus occurred in response to Burke because he defined a substantially new interpretation and essentially began not a debate but an increasingly acerbic reiteration of views. This could vary in its fury, with events in France, such as the September Massacres in 1792, encouraging fresh vigour on the part of the critical tradition, but there is little sign that individual writers or newspapers altered their views in accordance with these events.

The massacres and other violent acts served an important function in that they provided the specificity that newspapers lacked in their reports and which form so obvious a contrast to the very general nature of much comment. Specificity, concrete examples that could apparently make events more comprehensible, were not restricted to atrocities. Under a local by-line, the *Chelmsford Chronicle* of 21 September 1792 reported:

> such great advocates are the French for the levelling system, that they cannot, nor will suffer anyone to appear in the nation above a common man; an English gentleman, well known in the county of

Essex, being one day at Paris with his usual attendant servants, he attempted to ride in his phaeton through the streets.

According to the account, he was nearly hanged as a consequence, an example that may have been more meaningful to many readers than Burke's diatribes. Similarly, the impact of war with France from 1793 was to be brought home to readers by the extensive reporting not only of the conflict but also of the local activities of volunteer forces, whether a mock landing at Swansea, manoeuvres on the Haldon Hills or reviews.[7] These were interesting in their own right, not least as events that helped rank the locally prominent, both literally and metaphorically, and also underline their right to rank. Furthermore, such reports were examples of the role of emulation in the press and of the specificity that news provided.

Reports of events in France in 1789–93 had exaggerated the role of individuals and concentrated on developments in Paris. They also appeared to underline a precariousness of order, government and society that could be readily translated as a lesson for British readers. This class dimension had not been present in the press discussion of Jacobitism. Crowd or 'mob' violence helped to accentuate its impact. In the *London Chronicle* of 26 July 1791 'Quidam' argued that:

> The recent popular transaction at Birmingham calls for the most serious attention, as both the cause and effect were the spontaneous proceedings of the Tiers Etats. There are men enough ready at all times and in all countries, ambitious to raise themselves into consequence upon the shoulders of the people . . . may God in his mercy give the good people of Britain sense enough to know the due value of a constitution that has long been the admiration of the whole world; and to be warned by the horrors of the perilous experiment of refining systems of government above the standard of humanity, and then with stern despotism exacting conformity to them! We have had occasional specimens among ourselves of the government of mobs, when they take it in their heads to burst loose from the restraint of laws, which fit as easy upon them here, as laws ought to do: and the arbitrary acts of their majesty the People are infinitely more intolerable and dreadful, than those of any individual majesty whatever.

The expression of radical sentiments led to conservative disquiet and government action from 1792, when a substantial section of British society began to fear indigenous revolution. Action against radical newspapers was more than episodic. In 1792, the *Argus*, a radical London paper, was brought to an end, its printer Sampson Perry having been outlawed when he fled to France to avoid trial for libel, and the presses were used for the pro-government *True Briton*, founded in January 1793. The *Sun* had been funded with government support the previous October. The printer and editor of the *Morning Chronicle* were tried and acquitted of seditious libel in 1793, the year in which the *Leicester Chronicle* and the *Manchester Herald* ended as a result of government action. Daniel Holt, the printer of the former, was convicted of seditious libel and sent to Newgate Prison. Thereafter, however, there was a marked slackening in action, though that did not save the *Sheffield Register* in 1794, nor prevent the imprisonment of James Montgomery, the conductor of the radical *Sheffield Iris*, for political libels in 1795 and 1796.

Nevertheless, radical opinions were still expressed in the press by, for example, the *Bury and Norwich Post* and the *Cambridge Intelligencer*, and pro-government papers, such as the *True Briton* of 4 April 1799, criticized their opponents as pro-French.[8] The radical London bookseller and publisher Daniel Eaton hit back with his satirical *The Pernicious Effects of the Art of Printing upon Society, Exposed* (1794).[9] Two major London newspapers, the *Morning Chronicle* and the *Morning Post*, were seen as pro-French by the ministry and its newspaper supporters. Yet, disillusionment with France and concern about the tendencies of radicalism in Britain and Ireland helped lessen the expression of radical sentiment in a number of papers including the *Morning Post*. The *Morning Chronicle* continued to criticize the war, not least its rationale, cost and economic impact.

Far from the government trying to limit press readership by raising Stamp Duty, it was not raised until 1797, though that was by 1½*d*, the largest rise in the history of the tax. This led to a sharp increase in prices, the *Hull Advertiser*, for example, raising its cost from 4*d* to 6*d* a copy. The cost of the *Ipswich Gazette*, which had risen to 2*d* in 1725, 3*d* in 1776 and 3½*d* in 1789, now rose to 6*d*. The *Morning Post and Gazetteer* carried a notice in 1798: Price in 1783 3*d*, Taxed by Mr. Pitt 3*d*, Price 6*d*. Having raised £70,000 by adding ½*d* to Stamp Tax in 1789, the government now gained over £100,000.[10] Wartime circumstances exacerbated the price of paper: the *Dorchester and Sherborne Journal* of 26 February 1801 complained that the tax was 'laid at a time when, through the effects of the war, in depriving us of the raw materials, it has risen above 30 per cent'.

At least one important proposal for systematic government action, however, was not followed up. In 1799, the writer John Adolphus drew attention to the weakness of the current regulatory system. He pinpointed the difficulty of obtaining convictions in actions brought against newspapers, and drew attention to the increased and profitable publicity that prosecutions brought. Considering it impossible to return to the pre-1695 system of pre-publication censorship, Adolphus proposed instead a regulating office.[11] The recipient of John Adolphus' proposal, the conservative MP William Windham, blamed parliamentary reporting for the serious naval mutinies of 1797 and argued that it 'would essentially change the relations of the People with that House' as it gave, the People an opportunity of sitting in judgment every day on the measures under discussion in that House, tumultuously to express this disapprobation or approbation – and favoured the propensity of all vulgar minds, perhaps also of minds of no mean endowments, to form premature and intemperate decisions upon the whole matter, long before the detail of its parts and the character of its principle could be discussed and unfolded by the Legislature'.[12]

Windham was substantially correct. The publication of parliamentary debates gave the 'People' an opportunity to sit in judgment, episodically by making more informed electoral decisions, and continuously by enhancing the political applicability of the public discussion of policy. These processes were mediated through the newspapers, and that explains why there was a greater ministerial interest in influencing the press (as opposed to responding to particular attacks) in the 1790s and during the early nineteenth century than there had been from the mid-1730s to the late 1780s. Nothing came of Adophus' plan, but it is of interest because it reveals the extent to which the critical situation of the 1790s, defeat abroad and radicalism at home, led to the airing of new views on press supervision, and also indicates the cautious government response to the publication of opposition material. Despite the neutering of much of the radical press, there was no reign of terror in Britain. The government provided no support in 1799 for Lord Belgrave's motion in the House of Lords for the suppression of Sunday papers and it was defeated.[13] Six years earlier, no action was taken on the suggestion that the ministry purchase the *Birmingham and Stafford Chronicle* in order to prevent a possible acquisition by 'violent supporters of Priestley and Paine'.[14] Action in 1789 against the renting of newspapers by street hawkers was taken at the behest of proprietors concerned to close an alternative to purchase, and not as a political measure.

Clearly the ministry could live with a degree of criticism from a legal press that was greater than was commonly the case in Europe. The cause for that has to be sought not in the British press of the period, but in British history, specifically political culture. Though the Revolutionary period was a serious challenge to the assumptions of the political elite, not least in the creation of a language of class conflict, this challenge was substantially faced using traditional methods. Indeed the very conservatism of the response to Revolution, and the stress on continuity, precedent, privilege and law as (with the crucial addition of religion) the ideological focus of nationhood and counter-Revolution, made the development of new practices, institutions, ideas and notions unlikely. The libertarian heritage shared by all members of the political class was also important.

For a country in the throes of war and facing the prospect of revolution, the extent of new regulatory legislation was remarkably limited. In 1799, under the Seditious Societies Act, it was made compulsory to record the names and addresses of printers and publishers on every copy of a paper, and a compulsory registration of printing presses was introduced.[15] These were not, however, comparable to Continental repressive techniques and objectives. At least one-sixth of the journalists known to have been active in Paris in 1790–1 were executed during the Terror. The Revolutionary crisis, in contrast, led in Britain neither to a dramatic change in the press nor to sweeping attempts to repress it.[16]

Despite this, there was still concern in both governmental and conservative circles about press radicalism and this was strengthened in the 1810s as economic difficulties brought an upsurge of political and social radicalism. Charles Dibdin Junior, the proprietor of Sadler's Wells, claimed in 1813 that

> there really is an impudence in the press of this age that does the country more disservice in disorganising the people than all the democratic leaders can do, I think; and I'm afraid it is sowing the seeds of a commotion that our children or grandchildren will feel the dire effects of.[17]

The Revolutionary/Napoleonic period also witnessed an upsurge in conservative propaganda, as in the *Star, Sun, True Briton, Observer* (launched in 1791), *York Courant, Liverpool Phoenix, Manchester Mercury, Leicester Journal, Newcastle Courant, Caledonian Mercury* and *Edinburgh Herald.* Loyalist periodicals, such as the *British Critic, Anti-Jacobin, Anti-Jacobin Review and Magazine, Loyalist, Anti-Gallican* and *Annual Register*, thrived. In Leicester, Manchester and Newcastle, where there were both radical and conservative newspapers, the latter triumphed.[18] Both the *Leeds Intelligencer* and the *Leeds Mercury* were loyalist in the 1790s, although in 1801 the latter moved under new ownership towards the Whig camp. The reality of war took precedence for many papers. The *Glocester Journal* of 22 February 1796 declared:

> there never was a period that called more loudly upon the understanding and prudence of the nation for a suspension of narrow party hostility, for the sacrifice of every private view. . . . Nothing can be more vain than still to discuss the merits or demerits of the war, or the propriety of its prosecution, if we have no alternative, but must fight our way into peace.

The pattern of government action seen with the foundation of governmental papers, such as the *Sun* and the *True Briton*, in the 1790s, was not to be one that characterized the nineteenth century, but the other socio-political developments of the early 1790s were important. The typecasting of unacceptable reform as class-based accorded with a long tradition of differentiating between the people and the mob, but also gave it a new clarity. This helped to create a nexus that was to continue to be influential after war with France ceased in 1815, one in which the populist press was associated with a bitter critique of government *and* society, while ministerial protagonists emphasized the threat to ministry *and* society. This duality can be seen variously, but it was certainly a potential threat to the *ancien régime* in England, not least as the growing and increasingly urban population explored new practices of political power. That affected (and was expressed in) the press and will be probed in the next chapter. First, however, it is necessary to conclude with a methodological point. Alongside the emphasis on long-term trends in history, and of developments essentially reflecting these trends, it is also possible to stress the importance of changes in particular periods that can indeed be seen as discontinuities. One such was the response to the French Revolution, especially in 1790–3. That was a discontinuity in political and social positioning, but not in technology or in fiscal context. To turn to the other discontinuities, and to see how they interacted with this positioning, it is necessary to move forward to the mid-nineteenth century.

NOTES

1. N. McKendrick, J. Brewer and J.H. Plumb, *The Birth of a Consumer Society* (1982).
2. W.J.G. Armytage, 'The Editorial Experiences of Joseph Gales', *North Carolina Historical Review* 28 (1951), 332–61.
3. W. Mason to Wilberforce, 20 February 1792, Bod. MS, Wilberforce d 17/1, fol. 23.
4. I.R. Christie, 'James Perry of the *Morning Chronicle*, 1756–1821' in Christie, *Myth and Reality in Late Eighteenth-century British Politics* (1970), pp. 334–58; I.S. Asquith, 'James Perry and the *Morning Chronicle* 1790–1832' (Ph.D., London, 1973).
5. D. Liddle, 'Who Invented the "Leading Article"?: reconstructing the history and prehistory of a Victorian newspaper genre', *Media History* 5 (1999), 10.
6. A general murdered by his troops.
7. For example, *Bristol Gazette and Public Advertiser*, 26 April, 12 January 1804; *Birmingham Commercial Herald and General Advertiser*, 2, 16, 30 January 1804.
8. T.M. Blagg, *Newark as a Publishing Town* (Newark, 1898), p. 57; W.H.G. Armytage, 'The Editorial Experiences of Joseph Gales', *North Carolina Historical Review* 28 (1951), 332–61; R. Read, *Press and People 1790–1850: Opinion in Three English Cities* (1961), pp. 69–73; D. Fraser, 'The Press in Leicester *c.* 1790–1850', *Transactions of the Leicestershire Archaeological and Historical Society* 42 (1966–7), 59; M.J. Murphy, 'Newspapers and Opinion in Cambridge, 1780–1850', *Transactions of the Cambridge Bibliographical Society* 6 (1972), 41; M. Happs, 'Sheffield Newspaper Press . . . 1787–1832', (B.Litt.,

Oxford, 1973); J. Wigley, 'James Montgomery and the *Sheffield Iris*, 1792–1825: A Study in the Weakness of Provincial Radicalism', *Transactions of the Hunter Archaeological Society* 10 (1975), 173–81; C. Emsley, 'An aspect of Pitt's "Terror": prosecutions for sedition during the 1790s', *Social History* 6 (1981), 155–84; G. Bage, 'A Provincial Reaction to the French Revolution: Radical politics, social unrest and the growth of loyal opinion in East Anglia at the end of the eighteenth century, with special reference to the county of Suffolk' (M.Litt., Cambridge, 1983), pp. 5–6; Emsley, 'Repression, "Terror" and the rule of law in England during the decade of the French Revolution', *EHR* 100 (1985), 801–25. The extensive literature on the subject can be approached through C. Emsley, *British Society and the French Wars 1793–1815* (1979) and M. Philp (ed.), *The French Revolution and British Popular Politics* (Cambridge, 1991).

9. On Eaton and the radical publishing milieu of 1794–5, including the journals the *Citizen* and the *Philanthropist*, M.T. Davis, '"That Odious Class of Men Called Democrats": Daniel Isaac Eaton and the Romantics 1794–1795', *History* 84 (1999), 74–92.

10. A. Aspinall, *Politics and the Press* c. *1780–1850* (1949), p. 18.

11. Adolphus to William Windham, 25 March 1799, BL, Add. 37878, fols. 82–5.

12. *St James's Chronicle*, 1 January 1799.

13. Cobbett, 20, p. 621; Christie, *Myth and Reality*, p. 328.

14. Money, *Experience and Identity*, p. 62;

15. Aspinall, *Politics and the Press*, pp. 34, 38–40; D.W., 'On the Press', BL, Add. 33124, fols. 78–81.

16. Popkin, *Revolutionary News. The Press in France 1789–1799* (Durham, North Carolina, 1990), pp. 53–4.

17. G.C. White (ed.), *A Versatile Professor. Reminiscences of the Rev. Edward Nares, D.D.* (1903), p. 177.

18. H.T. Dickinson, 'Popular Conservatism and Militant Loyalism 1789–1815', in Dickinson (ed.), *Britain and the French Revolution 1789–1815* (1989), pp. 110–11; R. Hole, 'British Counter-revolutionary Propaganda in the 1790s', in C. Jones (ed.), *Britain and Revolutionary France: Conflict, Subversion and Propaganda* (Exeter, 1983), pp. 53–69; D. Herzog, *Poisoning the Minds of the Lower Orders* (Princeton, NJ, 1998). For loyalist constructions, M. Morris, *The British Monarchy and the French Revolution* (New Haven, 1998).

CHAPTER NINE

Politics 1800–1833

Notwithstanding the town of Shaftesbury has so often been exposed to the auctioneering hammer, and repeatedly sold to speculating jobbers, to the honour of the electors, they will soon be free, and once more relieved from Asiatic bondage. Richard Messiter, Esq. . . . has been indefatigable in driving the locust of the constitution from the borough, and there is no doubt but Edward Loveden Esq. of Buscot Park, and Robert Hurst Esq. of Horsham Park, will be returned to the new Parliament, in opposition to all the property late Benfield's – May the electors of every borough feel their own consequence and do likewise.

Dorchester and Sherborne Journal, 2 July 1802;
Asiatic was a reference to the Indian source of the wealth
of Paul Benfield the recent MP who was notoriously corrupt

The present state of public feeling, which has been most triumphantly manifested by the recent repeal of the odious Test Act, appears to us so favourable an omen, as should encourage every friend of civil liberty to use his utmost exertions to obtain the emancipation of 800,000 of our fellow-men and fellow-subjects, now held in an abject state of slavery in the British colonies.

Taunton Courier, 18 June 1828, pressing for petition
to Parliament

The editorial in the *St James's Chronicle* of 2 January 1800 stressed the political attitude as well as the political news of the paper:

Through the whole of the contest hitherto, it has been the endeavour of the St. James's Chronicle to persevere in the support of order and good government; to show an uniform detestation of the French usurpations; and to resist every attempt, open or secret, towards the overturning of our valuable constitution at home. In this line of conduct we are resolved to persevere, and though we are determined, with candour and impartiality, to afford truth every opportunity of justifying itself, we do not thereby find ourselves called upon to be the advocates of folly, treason, or atheism, however disguised.

On the following 1 January, the paper declared that it could look on the steady course it had run:

> amidst all the collisions of party, the vicissitudes of public opinion, and the horrors of revolutionary violence. It was originally published on the best maxims of the best constitution, and uniformly devoted to the real interests of society, religion, morality, and rational liberty.

There was a fresh burst of loyalist press activity in 1803–5 in response to the danger of invasion. Newspapers emphasized popular zeal[1] and the extent to which everything held dear was at stake.[2] The *Dorchester and Sherborne Journal* of 22 July 1803 declared:

> It is not a dispute about the possession of a foreign island, but we are to decide whether we shall be free – and *Britons never will be Slaves!* . . . what Englishman would basely remain and witness the plundering of his country, his sisters dishonoured, and the murder of his friends?

Papers, such as the *Birmingham Commercial Herald* on 2 January 1809, used the declaration of intent in the first issue of the year that was common to much of the press, to declare their loyalty.

> Despising all sneaking attempts to please all parties, we stand forth . . . the firm advocates of Church and State. . . . The insidious hand of innovation on the established constitution of our country is actively, though silently, at work. The ramifications of faction extend themselves, in various shapes, throughout the kingdom; and every country town has its weekly oracle, through which the poison is disseminated in a greater or less degree . . . these pests of society.

This custom of addressing readers at the beginning of the year was a testimony to the links between the two and reflected an understanding that readers were entitled to an explanation of policy. It was a development of the face-to-face culture in which printer-proprietors had originally launched and conducted newspapers. The *Birmingham Chronicle* of 1 January 1824 noted that it provided 'a declaration of the principles by which the publisher professes still to be governed, and thus gives a standard by which may be measured the character of the journal as it has been displayed in its conduct through the preceding year'.

Although the process is complex, the extent of wartime loyalism and the role allocated to it can both be seen as aspects of what has been presented as a more favourable response towards the notion of public opinion.[3] This had major implications for newspapers, although the press was not seen as co-terminous with public opinion. Aside from a changing assessment of the place of newspapers in society, there was also a marked shift in style. Newspapers had initially adopted many of the stylistic conventions of manuscript newsletters, not least an epistolary manner. The reader was addressed as if an individual, a method sustained in the magazines. The conventions of author–reader relations were different in the early nineteenth century, although the epistolary manner was maintained by the large number of contributions sent in to newspapers.

War was the focus of news in the first fifteen years of the century. The war abroad provided both the spectacle and the pressure of rapidly changing news from outside the community that could only be accessed through the newspapers. The excitement can be grasped in the head-lines, for example 'Entrance of the Russians into Vilna' and 'Destruction of the Remains of the French Army' in the *Birmingham Commercial Herald* of 18 January 1813. The progress of British forces, both in the Peninsular War and elsewhere, was extensively covered. Dispatches were printed, so that operations could be followed despite the absence of war reporters. Thus, for example, the *Courier* of 27 February 1811 printed dispatches from Wellington that covered the pursuit of French cavalry near Evora. Operations further afield were covered in a more episodic manner, because reports were less regular, but were still dramatic. The issue a fortnight earlier reported the surrender of Mauritius.

Most news of the war came via the London press, but provincial news-papers also sought to benefit from their own sources. Those on and near the south coast carried items based on reports brought by ships and contributed by correspondents in the ports. Thus, the *Dorchester and Sherborne Journal* of 16 January 1801 carried under a Weymouth by-line a very vigorous account of a struggle between the *Constitution* armed cutter and two large French privateers off Portland. The paper's printer directly profited from the war by launching a scheme to insure against militia service. More generally, there was an emphasis on early and particular news sources. Thus, *The Times* of 26 April 1804 noted that the previous day it alone had reported the surrender of Curaçao to British forces.

Accuracy could be a problem. Sergeant Thomas Morris threw light on both this and on newspaper sources in 1814:

> The drum-major of a regiment in our brigade, who, though he had not been within the smell of powder, wrote an eloquent and affectionate letter to his wife in London, giving her a detailed (but purely imaginary) account of the affair, describing very minutely his own exploits . . . highly pleasing to the good wife, who took occasion to show it to some of her friends, who advised her to send

it to the editor of one of the daily papers, who immediately gave it insertion.[4]

Nelson's victory at Trafalgar (1805) greatly lessened fears of invasion and the death of Pitt (1806) was followed by a period of protracted ministerial instability. There was a revival in opposition journalism, some of it manifested in new periodicals, such as the *Edinburgh Review* founded in 1806. The 'language of patriotism remained hotly contested even at the height of the Napoleonic War', as shown, for example, in the call for change in the *Examiner*, a highbrow weekly launched in 1808 that may have had a circulation as high as 8,000 by 1812. Far from war leading to a 'hegemonic' patriotism replicated in the press, there was a bitter contesting of principles and policies. This, for example, led the government of Spencer Perceval (1809–12) to step up legal action against the radical press.[5]

William Cobbett offered a populist voice in his *Political Register* founded in 1802; 'a more hardy and blackguard libeller probably never existed' according to one opponent.[6] He attacked the 'funding system' which he believed was hitting the social fabric and the poor. Cobbett focused on government corruption, for example in 1809 the sale of army commissions by the Duke of York's mistress, and allied with the London radical Sir Francis Burdett who pressed for parliamentary reform.[7] When Burdett was arrested in 1810 there was an upsurge in opposition press activity.

In 1812 Brougham told Leigh Hunt that the press was the real opposition to Lord Liverpool's government. In the provinces, the demand for peace was led by the *Leeds Mercury* under Edward Baines and prominently supported by several other papers such as the *Nottingham Review*, which was founded in 1808 by a Methodist printer Charles Sutton. Other newspapers argued that Napoleon could not be trusted, and thus, by extension, that those who called for peace were foolish and dangerous. Religious dissenters were prominent in several opposition papers. Most of those who funded Baines' acquisition of the *Leeds Mercury* in 1801 were dissenters, while Unitarians were prominent in the *Manchester Guardian*, which was founded in 1821. The Toryism of the *Royal Cornwall Gazette* led in 1810 to the launching of a rival *West Briton* edited by Edward Budd, a reformer and Wesleyan lay preacher.[8] Other papers critical of the government included the *Leicester Chronicle*, *Liverpool Mercury* and *Manchester Exchange Herald*. John Drankard, who emphasized political news in the *Stamford News*, which he edited, was imprisoned in 1811 as a result of his attack on flogging in the army.[9]

The very expression of radical sentiments clearly alarmed many, not only because of national circumstances, but also because they were being propagated in many provincial centres where there had been no earlier precedents for such action. This led to the active sponsorship of conservative papers, such as the *Nottingham Gazette* (1813–15), designed to stem 'the torrent by which the minds of the lower classes were being overwhelmed',[10] the *Yorkshire Gazette* founded in 1819, the *Leeds Patriot* begun in 1824, the *Newcastle Journal* launched in 1832, and in Salisbury in 1833 the *Wiltshire Standard*, which declared in its foreword, 'We unfurl our standard – no tricoloured bunting stained with the "blood and dirt" of Revolution – but an honest Union Jack bearing upon its ample surface, in language which all who run may read, the glorious motto of Church, King and Constitution'. Pressing in 1810 for active intervention in American domestic politics, John Henry contrasted British policy with that of 'the French party' which, he claimed, had

> first excited the common people, in a mode corresponding with its views of influencing the national policy; and in this mode, has seldom been unsuccessful. Newspapers are the engines which have been employed for that purpose; and in America are the true state levers which can pry any party out of its orbit.

Henry urged the appointment of British consuls able to fight for public opinion, not least by 'lessening the expense of certain newspapers to the common reader'.[11]

The defeat of Napoleon in 1815 made the situation in Britain more volatile by ending the external threat and leading to demobilization and serious post-war economic problems. This affected the press in a number of ways, not least by lessening reader interest in foreign and military news, a reminder of the extent to which circumstances changed the press, rather than the press changing the circumstances.

The press became more polarized in post-war Britain. When, for example, the *Lincoln Herald* was founded in 1828, it was politically neutral, but in 1830 it turned Tory in response to the launch of a paper in Lincoln in favour of reform.[12] The *Halifax Guardian* was started in December 1832, apparently in an attempt to counteract the reformist slant of the *Halifax and Huddersfield Express*, which had been launched in February 1831.[13] Linda Colley has drawn attention to the role of press expansion and parliamentary reporting in creating 'a unitary political discourse',[14] but the interplay of opinion inside and outside Parliament did not lessen serious divisions in opinion.

One government response, in keeping with the general policy of reaction in the late 1810s, was to tighten the fiscal regime. Stamp Duty was raised in 1815 to 4*d*, double the level to which it had been raised in 1789 and more than half the cost of a newspaper. Due to successive rises to a normal price of 7*d* from 1815, at a time of limited inflation, the real cost of a newspaper had increased substantially. Advertisement Duty was also increased to its highest level that year.

Stamp Tax and Advertisement Duty

	Stamp Tax	Duty per advertisement
1712	½d or 1d according to size of sheet	1s
1757	1d	2s
1776	1½d	2s
1780	1½d	2/6d
1789	2d	3s
1797	3½d	3s
1815	4d	3/6d
1833	4d	1/6d
1836	1d	1/6d
1853	1d	abolished
1855	abolished	

Such duties did not win the government support in the press, not least because the same ministry remained in office until 1827. High duties and ministerial continuity interacted with both the end of the Napoleonic War and a growing trend of political independence in the press to help encourage newspaper attacks on the government.

The duties also encouraged the revival in the 1810s of an unstamped press, though, whereas that of the early eighteenth century had not been primarily political, this was no longer true. The radical press of the 1810s also marked the revival of the essay-sheets that had been so influential in the eighteenth century. Such periodicals had continued to appear during the Revolutionary/Napoleonic period, when indeed they could attract greater sales and more sponsorship than had been the case during more quiescent times. The appearance of a political weekly with few or no advertisements, devoted in whole or part to an editorial essay, was not therefore novel, but what was distinctive about the new essay-journalism of the 1810s, led by Cobbett's *Political Register* (launched in 1802), was its determination both to adopt a popular approach and to secure substantial sales, a contrast to most earlier essay-weeklies. In 1816, Cobbett began to produce an edition of the *Political Register* containing only the essay, and, by dispensing with the news, thus avoiding Stamp Duty. He claimed massive sales: 44,000 copies of the first cheap issue, while by 1817 contemporaries estimated sales of the weekly at 60–70,000. Cobbett wrote in a readily grasped style, without the complicated sentence structure and opaque meanings that had characterized so many of his predecessors. The Prince Regent's chief equerry, Major General Sir Benjamin Bloomfield, complained, 'the Commissioners have suffered Mr. Cobbett and his inflammatory Register for three months to delude and incite the people to rebellion and acts of outrage'.[15]

Cobbett had already been imprisoned for two years and fined £1,000 in 1810 for an attack the previous year in the *Political Register* on the flogging of militiamen at Ely. The experience had ruined him financially and it is not therefore surprising that the suspension of Habeas Corpus led him to flee to America in 1817. His position was, however, filled at once by Thomas Wooler's weekly, the *Black Dwarf* (1817–24), which called in clear and ringing tones for political and social justice. Launched before Cobbett fled, the *Black Dwarf* was far more aggressive in its attacks on the establishment.

Other newspapers imitated the style and agenda of the *Black Dwarf* and the *Political Register*: including the *Manchester Political Register*, William Hone's *The Reformists' Register* (1817), the *Republican*, which soon became *Sherwin's Weekly Political Register*, and then the *Republican* again (1817–26), the *Medusa; or, Penny Politician* (1818–20), the *Cap of Liberty* (1819–20), the *Briton* (1819), and the *White Hat* (1819). In combination, this appeared a formidable armoury for radicalism, one that challenged the *modus operandi* of the Whig opposition nearly as much as the government, for the pretensions and prerogatives of the entire landed order were called into question in the assault on 'Old Corruption'.[16] The 'Peterloo Massacre' of 16 August 1819, the violent dispersal of those demonstrating in Manchester for political reform, aroused sustained controversy and provided a concrete focus for press attacks on the government. Newspaper reports were given particular vividness by the presence of a number of reporters on the platform. They included John Tyas of *The Times*, who reported

> . . . a cry was made by the cavalry, 'Have at their flags'. In consequence, they immediately dashed not only at the flags which were in the wagon [the speakers' platform], but those which were posted among the crowd, cutting most indiscriminately to the right and to the left in order to get at them. This set the people running in all directions, and it was not till this act had been committed that any brick-bats were hurled at the military. From that moment the Manchester Yeomanry Cavalry lost all command of temper. A person of the name of Saxton, who is, we believe, the editor of the *Manchester Observer*, was standing in the cart. Two privates rode up to him. 'There,' said one of them, 'is that villain, Saxton; do you run him through the body.' 'No,' replied the other, 'I had rather not – I leave it to you.' The man immediately made a lunge at Saxton, and it was only by slipping aside that the blow missed his life. As it was, it cut his coat and waistcoat, but fortunately did him no other injury. A man within five yards of us in another direction had his nose completely taken off by a blow of a sabre . . . we saw a constable at no great distance, and thinking that our only

chance of safety rested in placing ourselves under his protection, we appealed to him for assistance. He immediately took us into custody, and on our saying that we merely attended to report the proceedings of the day, he replied, 'Oh! oh! You then are one of their writers – you must go before the Magistrates.'

The government responded to press criticism by sponsoring its own papers, including *Anti-Cobbett, or, Weekly Patriotic Register* (1817) and Gibbons Merle's *White Dwarf* (1817–18), by changing the legal and financial context of press activity through legislation, and by a series of prosecutions. The Blasphemous and Seditious Libels Act (1819) ensured that libellous pamphlets could be seized. By permitting seizure, the Act prevented them from benefiting in their circulation from the publicity brought by convictions, and decreed banishment for second offences. The Publications Act (1819) extended the Stamp Duties by defining as a newspaper any periodical that contained news or remarks thereon, fixed the size of the sheet, and decreed that newspapers and publishers had to enter into recognizances.[17] Prosecutions included Charles Sutton of the *Nottingham Review* who was sentenced in 1816 to a year's imprisonment and a surety for good conduct thereafter of £500. In 1823 the proprietor of the *Sunday Times* was fined £200, imprisoned for three months, and had to provide sureties of £2,000 for good behaviour, for claiming that George IV was insane. However, in 1817, Hone was acquitted on three charges arising from his attacks on Christian doctrine.

Pro-government newspapers condemned the methods of the opposition. Thus, the *Birmingham Commercial Herald* of 4 December 1819 printed a rhyme attacking Paine and Cobbett and supported the Seditious Meeting Bill, although it hoped that it would not be perpetual: 'the assumed right of mob-meetings is a pretence of a very recent date . . . the malignant expectations of the disaffected should be extinguished by a law which shall endure as long as their acts of mischief continue in successful activity'. On 2 January 1819 the paper had urged the need to get accustomed to peace: 'our minds have so long been stimulated by strong excitements, that a degree of discipline may be necessary to curb our expectations'. 'The Liberty of the Press without its Licentiousness' was a regular toast at Pitt Club dinners, for example those in Birmingham in 1823 and 1824.

In 1820 the controversy surrounding Queen Caroline, the estranged and allegedly disreputable wife of George IV, offered profitable scandal. Newspapers required an unfolding story, rather than an episode to analyse or debate endlessly, and that was certainly provided by the controversy as Caroline returned to England and the ministry countered with a retrospective Bill of Pains and Penalties in the House of Lords to dissolve the marriage and deprive her of her royal title. The press lapped up the sexual details, and engaged in a vicious and personal debate as to whether Caroline was a wronged woman or a disgrace to her sex. As support for Caroline was a popular cause, and a useful means of attacking the libertine ways of the king, the entire debate lent focus and interest to political controversy, and it did so with profit, causing a boom in sales. The major dailies took sides, *The Times* supporting, the *Morning Post* attacking Caroline.[18]

The episode was, however, an unusual one in that it bridged the gap between the worlds of scandal and high politics, the subject matters of the Sundays and of the established dailies. It was not that the latter did not discuss scandals, such as the sale of posts or abuses by poor-law administrators, but rather that these scandals were generally political in both content and focus, lacking the visceral appeal of more salacious items. These worlds were generally separate, and the major dailies commonly concentrated on a drier diet of political news and speculation.

The legislation of 1819 had led to an increase in prices and a decrease in titles. The radical press were marginalized until the 1830s. They were overshadowed by the Sunday press, which offered crimes, sport and titillation, the sensational and the salacious, and by less radical but, nevertheless, reformist papers. These included the long-standing *Leeds Mercury* and the newly launched *Sheffield Independent* (1819) and *Manchester Guardian* (1821),[19] all of which gave long-standing calls for moral improvement a pointedly political content and energy. This has a wider significance because it was through their newspapers that the major cities of the north came to express political and economic opinions.[20]

In contrast, in most of provincial England, newspapers had developed in a context of shire and borough institutions and political communities with well-developed practices of discussing and contesting policy. In the latter case, the press had adapted to this world, not least because the small-scale printers and booksellers responsible for publication and distribution lacked the resources and, in most cases, the will to follow a completely independent path. There was a continuum in circumstances and goals as well as a contrast within the provincial press, but the latter became more pronounced in the early nineteenth century as the sales of major provincial papers rose.

The growing reading public read chapbooks, ballads and cheap periodicals more than newspapers, but there was still a growing popular market for the latter. The number of newspaper stamps issued for London and the provinces rose from 16.0 million in 1801 to 24.7 million in 1821. Economic growth helped reduce social tension and thus radical criticism in the mid-1820s. The *Birmingham Chronicle* of 12 February 1824 suggested that prosperity was leading to a general 'apathy' about Parliament. Furthermore, several of the campaigns of the period, for example in favour of the Greek struggle for liberation and against slavery, did not lead to serious political divisions. The newly appointed Home Secretary, Robert Peel, decided in 1822 to stop press prosecutions as counter-productive. This helped reduce tension with the press. An easing in political tension had definitely reduced interest in political publishing for a popular market in the 1820s, but the situation altered in the late 1820s and early 1830s as religious issues and then parliamentary reform came to the fore.

The repeal of the Test and Corporation Acts in 1828 was a contentious step, not least because in many localities relations between the Church of England and Dissenters were difficult. Thus, the *Taunton Courier* of 9 January 1828 devoted over two columns to a public meeting held on the 7th about establishing a school on the principles of the Church of England, with an additional letter of over a column on the matter; at this stage the paper consisted of eight pages, each of three columns. A week later, two letters followed, and on 23 January the paper sought to draw the issue to a close with two more letters, only for another of two columns to follow on 30 January.

Catholic Emancipation led to much greater controversy, in which the press played a major role.[21] The *Standard* was founded in 1827 to oppose Emancipation. Wellington's eventual decision to support Emancipation in 1829 divided the Tories and shattered the cohesion of the conservative press. The Ultra Tories who rejected Emancipation were an important group in 1828–34 and, thereafter, remained an important ideological wing of the Tories. The Ultras were supported by some important London and provincial papers, including the *Standard*, *St James's Chronicle*, *Age* and *Morning Journal* in London, and the *Brighton Gazette*, *Felix Farley's Bristol Journal*, the *Carlisle Patriot*, the *Royal Cornwall Gazette*, the *Leeds Intelligencer*, and the *Liverpool Standard*. These papers benefited from inside information, corrected speeches, advertisements, and in some cases donations. Wellington himself read papers, but was against the press, irrespective of its political slant. This was an aspect of his hostility to the party system and to popular pressure groups, and played a role in the weakness of the ministerial Tory press during his ministry.[22]

Wellington's opposition to parliamentary reform was unacceptable to important circles of opinion. Aside from the issue of a change in the franchise, there was also the question of a redistribution of seats. This was particularly sensitive in London, which felt under-represented, and even more in the major northern commercial and industrial cities, such as Manchester and Leeds, which lacked seats of their own and were subsumed in the county electorate. The issue was important in shaping the contours of local political activism, not least because enhanced national representation was believed important in order to secure local goals. As these cities were the bases of the northern press, there was an important conflation of political opinion and newspaper campaigning, a process aided by the active political role of many newspaper figures and their central place in public political consciousness within their communities. Joshua Drewry of the *Staffordshire Advertiser* was one of

Stafford's leading men and its mayor in 1818–19. William Bird Brodie, proprietor of the *Salisbury Journal* from 1808 to 1847, was a keen politician and ardent reformer, mayor in 1812, Lieutenant-Colonel of the Salisbury Volunteer Infantry 1830–40 and MP for Salisbury 1832–43. John Edward Taylor, a key writer for the pro-reform *Manchester Gazette* and in 1821 founder of the *Manchester Guardian*, was a prominent critic of the role of the magistrates and yeomanry at Peterloo. His paper helped to influence local feeling towards political reform.

In the case of pro-reform newspapers, local identity was linked clearly to a determination to ensure change at the national level. This was related to a process of social identification, as a self-conscious middle class was articulated and the opponents of reform stigmatized as a redundant *ancien régime* caste.[23] In the *West Briton*, which by 1831 had an annual circulation of 50,900, there were repeated attacks on Cornish borough corruption, pressure for parliamentary reform, condemnation of high levels of government expenditure, taxation, local rates and tithes, and support for farmer activism.[24] However, reform papers, such as the *Sunderland Herald,* founded in 1831, and the *West Briton*, did not support 'the unlimited extension of the elective franchise'.[25] Other new papers of the period included the *Bolton Chronicle* in 1831.

The protracted nature of the parliamentary reform crisis, at once national and local, high political and electoral, led to sustained excitement and a situation in which newspapers were obliged to take sides.[26] Their employment of descriptions such as 'crowd' or 'mob' revealed newspaper sympathies and was important in creating a perception of particular events.[27] Such descriptions were an aspect of the debate over the character and role of public opinion that played a major part in the press, an important aspect of its self-referential nature. Some newspapers reported as if revolution was a danger, discerning an apparent threat that they could then employ as a basis for commentary pressing the need for reform.

In addition, events such as the agrarian Swing riots of 1830 or the Bristol riots of 1831, provided much copy for the press.[28] Reports of reform agitation elsewhere in the country served to build up support. Thus, the pro-reform *Taunton Courier* reported on county meetings to present petitions in, for example, Berkshire (26 January 1831) and Cornwall (9 February), threw critical light on local MPs who were against reform (23 March), and supported the election of reforming MPs in Taunton itself (27 April). A partisan approach was the purpose of some papers, and it could also serve to underline the stress in the press on the value and role of newspapers: a politicized society thus seemed to require a political press and that was certainly the case in the early 1830s, although Tory papers did not favour many aspects of this politicization. The *Western Luminary and Family Newspaper: Agricultural, Commercial, and Literary Advertiser* of 4 January 1831 commented:

It will be observed by a paragraph in another column, that one of the rioters who was convicted of setting fire to a barn at Battle, and sentenced to death, has left it on record, in the confession of his guilt, that he ascribed his untimely end to Cobbett, who instigated him and others to these practices by his inflammatory lectures; and declares that but for this turbulent vagabond, he believed that there would have been neither fires nor mobs in that neighbourhood. We fear Cobbett has not been the only means of bringing about the disgraceful outrages which have been committed throughout the country. The fact is, the radical portion of the press have been labouring in their seditious vocation with increased fury, and wherever they have disseminated their doctrines, a spirit of insubordination and discontent has been conjured up which threatens to become fatal to existing institutions, and which even the Whigs will find exceedingly difficult to lay. It is impossible the country can enjoy peace unless the libellous demagogues Cobbett, O'Connell, and Carlile and such like are put to silence.

A series of unstamped radical papers, including the *Prompter* (1830–1), *Republican* (1831–3), *Poor Man's Guardian* (1831–5), *Radical* (1831), *Working Men's Friend* (1832–3), *Reformer* (1832), *Cosmopolite* (1832–3), *Destructive and Poor Man's Conservative* (1833–4), and *Man* (1833),[29] produced by bold and energetic publishers such as Richard Carlile (1790–1843),[30] publisher of the *Gorgon*, the *Lion* (1828–9) and the *Prompter*, and Henry Hetherington (1792–1849), publisher of the *Poor Man's Guardian*, launched sweeping attacks on the establishment, its pretensions, prerogatives, privilege and personnel. Instead, there was a call for action on behalf of the working class, including the vote for working men. Popular demand sustained this burst of radical publishing.

The government responded with prosecutions, not least of the vulnerable news-vendors. Hetherington was imprisoned in 1832, and in 1834 convicted and fined for publishing another unstamped newspaper, the *Destructive and Poor Man's Conservative*, a defence of trade unionism. However, the expression of working-class radicalism was not staunched, while the appearance of unstamped papers helped both to put the legitimate press at a comparative disadvantage, as Bloomfield pointed out in 1817,[31] and to focus attention on the Stamp Duties. This encouraged their reduction in 1836. Not all the unstamped papers were primarily political.

By the 1830s the role of the press as the prime forum for the expression of political opinion, radical or conservative, local or national, working-class or establishment, was clearly established, although many papers continued to strive for neutrality, for example the *Bristol Mirror* and the *York Courant*. Despite this, newspaper proprietors and writers were more prominent in politics and played a more active role than the majority of their eighteenth-century predecessors. This was true of national figures, such as James Perry of the *Morning Chronicle,* and of local counterparts, such as Edward Baines of the *Leeds Mercury* and Archibald Prentice of the *Manchester Times.* Baines used the *Leeds Mercury* in 1830 to promote Brougham's successful candidacy for Yorkshire. During the riots that led in 1832 to the burning of Nottingham Castle, the windows of the office of the Tory *Nottingham Journal* were broken.[32] Editorializing encouraged both a stronger definition of newspapers in political terms and also responses from rival papers. Rising political figures, such as Disraeli, wrote for newspapers. In 1835, the young Richard Cobden wrote a series of letters to the *Manchester Times* urging that the town petition for local self-government.[33] The extent to which the press was increasingly used by significant political and economic groups was a testimony to their realization that it represented an effective way of conveying a message to those interested in national or local concerns. This was part of the process in which the flow of information increased in the early nineteenth century.[34]

Effectiveness in conveying a message was not the same as successful persuasion, but in many instances the intention was rather to preach to the converted than to convert the opposition. The widespread printing of addresses, instructions and similar material by political and economic groups was intended to encourage the initiation of similar action, to maintain morale and to create the sense of a powerful and popular interest. The extent to which newspapers reflect opinion and how far they influence it, consciously or otherwise, is a perennial question. Some papers hoped to achieve both sales and reputation (not necessarily the same) by pursuing both purposes, as the early *Manchester Guardian* did so successfully, always taking care not to get too far ahead of opinion. In the same city, Prentice's *Manchester Times* never prospered because he was too pedagogic in trying to lead, and consequently failed to hold enough readers, either middle class or artisan.

The use of newspapers to popularize the idea of the representative nature of MPs was but part of a significant theme in the press, the public discussion of issues of policy. Readers were kept in contact with the activities of politicians, including local municipal officials and MPs. The *Country Spectator,* a radical magazine-type weekly published in Gainsborough, claimed on 6 November 1792 that without the press few would 'know that our representatives are acting in Parliament, nor should we be able to gain any genuine political information, unless from the *Rights of Man,* and one or two other good books, which are sold cheap . . . for the benefit of the poor'. Public criticism led to debate; few were prepared to suffer attacks in silence. The *Leeds Intelligencer* of 15 November 1785 printed a letter beginning, 'Much has lately been said respecting the water-works in this town – and since my conduct has been blamed, I take this method of laying the following state of the business before the public.' Five years later, the then-retired Lord North told the French ambassador that he had never seen a British government strong enough to be able to ignore what was said in print, and that it was necessary for ministries to reply to printed criticism in order to avoid unpopularity.[35]

NOTES

1. E.g. *Dorchester and Sherborne Journal*, 29 July, 5, 19, 26 August 1803.
2. E.g. *Ibid*, 12 August 1803.
3. J.A.W. Gunn, *Beyond Liberty and Property. The Process of Self-recognition in Eighteenth-century Political Thought* (Kingston, Ontario, 1983), p. 89.
4. J. Selby (ed.), *The Recollections of Sergeant Morris* (Moreton-in-Marsh, 1998), p. 33.
5. P. Harling, 'Leigh Hunt's *Examiner* and the Language of Patriotism', *EHR* 111 (1996), 1159–81, quote p. 1160.
6. Heriot to Addington, 17 August 1802, Exeter, Devon CRO, 152 M/C, 1802, OZ128.
7. The extensive literature on Cobbett includes I. Dyck, *William Cobbett and Rural Popular Culture* (Cambridge, 1992) and K.W. Schweizer and J.W. Osborne, *Cobbett in his Times* (Leicester, 1990).
8. E. Jaggard, *Cornwall Politics in the Age of Reform 1790–1885* (1999), p. 36.
9. D. Fraser, 'The Nottingham Press 1800–1850', *Transactions of the Thoroton Society* 67 (1963), 54–5; J.R. Dinwiddy, *Radicalism and Reform in Britain, 1780–1850* (1992), pp. 129–30.
10. Fraser, 'Nottingham Press', p. 48.
11. Henry to Marquis of Wellesley, 4 December 1810, BL. Add. 37292, fol. 207.
12. F. Hill, *Georgian Lincoln* (Cambridge, 1966), pp. 292–3.
13. E.Webster, 'The Halifax Guardian and Halifax Courier: Newspaper Rivals in the Nineteenth Century', *Transactions of the Halifax Antiquarian Society*, new ser. 4 (1996), 58.
14. L. Colley, *Britons. Forging the Nation 1707–1837* (New Haven, 1992), p. 363.
15. Bloomfield to the Home Secretary, Sidmouth, 4 April 1817, Exeter, Devon CRO, 152 M/C, 1807/OH76.
16. I. McCalman, *Radical Underworld. Prophets, Revolutionaries and Pornographers in London 1795–1840* (Cambridge, 1988); M. Wood, *Radical Satire and Print Culture, 1790–1822* (Oxford, 1994); K. Gilmartin, *Print and Politics: The Press and Radical Opposition in Early Nineteenth-century England* (Cambridge, 1996). For the background, J.A. Hone, *For the Cause of Truth: Radicalism in London 1796–1821* (Oxford, 1982).
17. For draft bills in the Sidmouth papers, Exeter, Devon CRO, 152 M/C, 1818 (OH).
18. E.A. Smith, *A Queen on Trial: The Affair of Queen Caroline* (Stroud, 1993).
19. D. Ayerst, *Guardian – Biography of a Newspaper* (1971).
20. J. Feather, 'The Merchants of Culture: bookselling in early industrial England', *Studies on Voltaire and the Eighteenth Century* 217 (1983), 20.

21. G.I.T. Machin, *The Catholic Question in English Politics 1820 to 1830* (Oxford, 1964).

22. J.J. Sack, 'Wellington and the Tory Press, 1828–30', in N. Gash (ed.), *Wellington: Studies in the Military and Political Career of the First Duke of Wellington* (Manchester, 1990), esp. pp. 159–61; D.G.S. Simes, 'A long and difficult association: the Ultra Tories and "the Great Apostate"', *Wellington Studies* 3 (1999), 79–80. For the impact of tensions within the Tory press on reporting, A. Heesom, 'The Duke of Wellington's Visit to the North-East of England', *Durham County Local History Society Bulletin* 60 (November 1999), 24, 35.

23. A. Briggs, 'Press and Public in early nineteenth century Birmingham', *Dugdale Society Occasional Papers* 8 (1949); Fraser, 'Nottingham Press', 'Press in Leicester' and 'The Editor as Activist: Editors and Urban Politics in Early Victorian England', in J. Wiener (ed.), *Innovators and Preachers: The Role of the Editor in Victorian England* (Westport, Connecticut, 1985), pp. 121–42; M. Milne, 'The *Tyne Mercury* and Parliamentary Reform, 1802–1846', *Northern History* 14 (1978), 227–42; D. Read, 'Reform Newspapers and Northern Opinion *c.* 1800–1848', *Proceedings of the Leeds Phil. and Lit. Soc.* 8 (1959), 301–14 and *Press and People* (1961). For an important recent account, P. Brett, 'Early Nineteenth-century Reform Newspapers in the Provinces: The *Newcastle Chronicle* and *Bristol Mercury*', *Studies in Newspaper and Periodical History* (1995), 49–67.

24. Jaggard, *Cornwall Politics*, pp. 39–40.

25. *Herald*'s prospectus, cited in M. Milne, 'Survival of the fittest? Sunderland newspapers in the nineteenth century', in J. Shattock and M. Wolff (eds), *The Victorian Periodical Press: Samplings and Soundings* (Leicester, 1982), p. 197.

26. N.D. Lopatin, *Political Unions, Popular Politics and the Great Reform Act of 1832* (1999).

27. M. Harrison, *Crowds and History: Mass Phenomena in English Towns 1790–1835* (Cambridge, 1988).

28. A.P. Hart, 'The Bristol Riots and the Mass Media' (Ph.D., Oxford, 1979).

29. P. Hollis, *The Pauper Press: a Study in Working-class Radicalism of the 1830s* (Oxford, 1970), pp. 319–27; J. Wiener, *A Descriptive Finding List of Unstamped British Periodicals, 1830–1836* (1970); J. Holstead, '*The Voice of the West Riding*; Promotion and Supporters of an Unstamped British Newspaper, 1833–34', in C. Wrigley and J. Shepherd (eds), *On the Move: Essays in Labour and Transport History Presented to Philip Bagwell* (1992), pp. 22–57.

30. J. Wiener, *Radicalism and Freethought in Nineteenth-century Britain: the Life of Richard Carlile* (Westport, 1983).

31. Bloomfield to the Home Secretary, Sidmouth, 4 April 1817, Exeter, Devon CRO, 152 M/C, 1807/OH76.

32. Fraser, 'Nottingham Press', p. 51.

33. N.C. Edsall, *Richard Cobden. Independent Radical* (Cambridge, Mass., 1986), p. 34.

34. D. Eastwood, 'The Flow of Information and the State in the Early Nineteenth Century', *Historical Journal* 62 (1989), 276–94.
35. Luzerne to Montmorin, French foreign minister, 31 May 1790, AE, CP, Ang. 573, fol. 202.

CHAPTER TEN

A New World of Print

The effort is now made to please the multitude, since they may be properly considered as the dispensers of rewards.

Oliver Goldsmith, *Public Ledger*, 22 August 1761

Life at the Australian Gold Diggings.
Douglas Jerrold edits Lloyd's Weekly London Newspaper.
The number for Sunday next, July 4, (Price Three Pence, post-free), contains Sixty Large Columns of the Latest Intelligence (to the Moment of Publication), from all parts of the world, by express, Electric Telegraph, and other means, regardless of expense. The number for Sunday next will also contain:– Editorial Articles: Church Lights; or, Roman Wax, and Pusey Dips; A House of Commons to Let; The Finsbury Folly; The Police and the People; A Letter from the Black Beggarman's Dog to Ladies in General; The Happy White-bait Family, etc. – Fatal No-popery Riots in Stockport – Dreadful Murder of an Old Woman: Remarkable Capture of the Murderer – Death of 274 Persons on Board a British Ship – Emigration: Gratuitous Advice to Emigrants; Emigration Schemes; Shipping Intelligence; Farming in Port Phillip, Wages, etc. – The Dissolution of Parliament – Wreck of an Australian Emigrant Ship: Loss of Life – Infringement of Public Liberty: Great Meeting at Bonner's Fields – Fatal Accident on the Great Western Railway – Monkery at Shoreham – The Crystal Palace and its Opponents – Pauper Emigration to Bermuda, etc. Lloyd's Weekly London Newspaper is Published every Saturday night in time for Post. Price only THREE PENCE!!! Post Free. Send Three Postage Stamps to Edward Lloyd, No. 12, Salisbury-square, London, and receive one Copy as a sample, or order off any newsvendor.

Advertisement, 1852

A memorandum of April 1836 from the newly launched Association of Working Men to Procure a Cheap and Honest Press offered both an account of social exclusion as a consequence of the 'taxes on knowledge', and a sense of the opportunities of print:

The working men of Great Britain live in a country remarkable for the extension and rapid circulation of intelligence and information:

177

yet they themselves are positively and in almost express terms, denied any participation in the benefits of the readiest, the commonest, the chief vehicle of knowledge – the newspaper.

A 'cheap and unshackled press' would, however, it was argued, offer grounds:

for improvement in their morals, for increased sympathy of the other classes of society, for a share in the formation of public opinion, and through these for all such ameliorations of their condition as would be consistent with the happiness of the community at large.[1]

Newspapers themselves supported such 'ameliorations', including the expansion of the social parameters within which readership developed. Under the heading Popular Education, the *Western Times* of 25 January 1851 declared:

We have only space to refer to the satisfactory Report of the meeting held at the Guildhall, to establish Public Libraries. We should prefer seeing a more direct effort to promote the education of the destitute youth and children of the city; but we receive the conclusions of the meeting as an admission of the public *duty* to provide a means of education for that class of Society whose means do not enable it to educate its offspring.

The paper's campaigning editor, Thomas Latimer, was a prominent radical, who was especially critical of what he saw as the abuses of established power in Church and State.[2]

Changes in the press were symptomatic of the modernization of the country. One of the many ways in which Victorian London was at the centre of British life was in the provision of news through its press. London created the image and idiom of nation and empire, and shaped opinions. Aside from this political function, the press also played a central economic, social and cultural role, setting and spreading fashions, whether through company statements or theatrical criticism. The press inspired emulation and fulfilled crucial needs of location -- of locating acceptable goals and ideas – for an anonymous and mobile mass-readership. The press was itself affected by change, by the energizing and disturbing forces of commercialisation and new technology.

It was to be legal reform and technological development that freed the Victorian press for major development. Newspapers had become expensive in the eighteenth century, in large part due to the successive rises in Stamp Duty. In the mid-nineteenth century, these 'taxes on knowledge' were abolished: the Advertisement Duty in 1853, Newspaper

Stamp Duty in 1855, and the Paper Duties in 1861. There had also been an important period of reduction in taxation in 1833–6, with the halving of the Advertisement Duty (1833) and of the Paper Duties (1836), and the reduction of the Stamp Duty from 4*d* to 1*d* (1836).

These cuts opened up the possibility of a cheap press, and that opportunity was exploited by means of a new technology centred on steam-powered printing presses, which spread in the 1830s. Latimer introduced one for the *Western Times* in 1835. The printer-proprietor of the *Staffordshire Sentinel* declared in his first issue (7 January 1854) that he had purchased a 'first-rate' Napier's 'Printing Machine', so as to be able 'to execute his work both expeditiously and at the cheapest possible rate'. High-speed presses permitted the printing of more copies and were therefore most in demand from newspapers with a large circulation. *The Times* commissioned Augustus Applegath to build an 'eight-feeder' rotary press in 1848. A decade later, it installed two ten-feeder Hoe rotaries; the first in England had been ordered for *Lloyd's Weekly Newspaper* in 1856. Web rotary presses which were able to print directly on to continuous rolls or 'webs' of paper were introduced in Britain from the late 1860s. The Walter press was first used by *The Times* in 1869 and by the *Daily News* in 1873, while the *Daily Telegraph* purchased the American Bullock press in 1870.

New technology was directly linked to the change in the fiscal regime, because the Inland Revenue had insisted that the continuous 'web of paper' produced by the papermaking process be cut into individual sheets in order to facilitate the calculation of Paper Duty. This was no longer necessary when the Duty ceased. The fall in the price of paper as esparto grass replaced linen and cotton rags as the source of the pulp was also important. The manufacturing process became more systematized.

New technology was expensive, but the mass readership opened up by the lower prices that could be charged after the repeal of the newspaper taxes justified the cost. The consequence was more titles and lower prices. The number of daily morning papers published in London rose from eight in 1856 to twenty-one in 1900, and of evenings from seven to eleven, while there was a tremendous expansion in the suburban press. The repeal permitted the appearance of penny dailies. The *Daily Telegraph*, launched in 1855, led the way and by 1861 had a daily circulation of over 140,000 and by 1888, 300,000. The penny press was in turn squeezed by the halfpenny press, the first halfpenny evening paper, the *Echo*, appearing in 1868, and having a peak circulation of 200,000 in 1870. Halfpenny morning papers became important in the 1890s, with the *Morning Leader* (1892) and the *Daily Mail* (1896), which was to become very successful with its bold and simple style.[3]

The papers that best served popular tastes were the Sundays: *Lloyd's Weekly News* (launched in 1842), the *News of the World* (1843), and *Reynolds's Weekly Newspaper* (1850). *Lloyd's*, the first British paper with a circulation of over 100,000, dropped its price to 1 *d* in 1861, and was selling over 400,000 by 1862, over 600,000 by 1879, over 900,000 by 1893, and in 1896 rose to over a million. The Sundays relied on shock and titillation, drawing extensively on Police Court reporting. The production and distribution of so many copies was a major organizational achievement.

In comparison, an eighteenth-century London newspaper was considered a great success if it sold 10,000 copies a week (many influential papers then were weeklies) and 2,000 weekly was a reasonable sale. In 1792, James Bland Burges was pleased when the newly launched *Sun* sold over 1,000 copies.[4] There was also a contrast in the provincial press, although the scale of sales was more modest. The density of distribution coverage had increased greatly. For example, the *Birmingham Herald*, launched in 1836 as a free paper supported by advertising revenue in order to take advantage in the cut of duty, promised to print 4,000 copies weekly. Of these, 2,000 were to be distributed in Birmingham and the 'neighbourhood' and the rest sent 'to respectable and influential inhabitants, to banking houses, attorney's offices, inns, news rooms etc.' in an impressive list of towns in each of Warwickshire, Worcestershire, Herefordshire, Staffordshire, Shropshire, Cheshire, Derbyshire and Leicestershire, as well as in a list of towns elsewhere stretching from Plymouth and Haverfordwest to Newcastle, and 'to the exchanges, commercial chambers, banking houses, libraries, news rooms, coffee rooms, commercial inns, and other places of public resort' in London, Bristol, Gloucester, Hull, Leeds, Liverpool, Manchester, Sheffield and York. By January 1838 the free circulation was up to 5,000; the paper could also be obtained by subscription. The Stamp Returns for 1854 indicated that the five Bristol papers had a combined annual sale of 710,000.

Aside from lower taxation and more rapid production technology, the press also benefited from the communications revolution offered by railways and the telegraph. The former allowed London papers to increase their influence. They could arrive on provincial doorsteps within hours of publication. Provincial papers could also receive news more rapidly. Thus, *Besley's Devonshire Chronicle* of 25 January 1847 noted that the Queen's Speech opening Parliament had arrived by express train. The building of trunk lines out from London gave the capital a nodal position that it had not had in the canal system. The telegraph vastly speeded up the communication of news and thus expectations of prompt news.[5] The news of the birth of Queen Victoria's second son in 1844 was the first press telegram sent from Windsor to London: it allowed *The Times* to print the news in an edition that went to press 40 minutes after the birth. Telegraphy also made it easier to check items. The combined impact of the railways and the telegraph in speeding up communication amounted not merely to an improvement but to a transformation, the beginning of modern times. The railways transformed physical contact, the telegraph mental interplay, and contemporaries soon realized this, although some did not welcome it; this was not a development detected only by historians in retrospect.

The speeding up of the news combined with swifter production techniques ensured greater consistency within individual issues. In the past, one section of a weekly might well be contradicted by another section that was printed later. Thus, the *Birmingham Commercial Advertiser* of 2 January 1804 reported: 'Thomas Pyatt, advertised, in our first page, as having escaped from prison, has been re-apprehended since the first form of our Herald went to press.'

Telegraphy increased the importance of access to the network of news and further defined the latter in terms of *comprehensive* international information, but was also expensive. In 1851, when the Calais–Dover cable was laid, Julius de Reuter established the first international agency in London. Two years later telegrams from Reuter began to appear in the *Manchester Guardian, Manchester Courier* and *Liverpool Mercury*; and *The Times* with other London dailies following in 1858.[6] During the Crimean War (1854-6), telegraphic links had been established to the Black Sea, but all bar one of the famous reports of *The Times*'s correspondent W.H. Russell were posted back.[7] An attempt to create a submarine telegraph link to India failed in 1860, but it was followed in 1865 by an overland link much used by Reuter, and in 1870 by a successful British-controlled submarine cable.[8] By the 1870s *The Times* was spending about £40,000 a year on telegraphy. The telegraph also speeded the movement of news within Britain, offering a far faster alternative to the railway. Provincial papers were provided with news by the London-based Electric Telegraph Company which progressed from summarizing the London morning newspaper to employing its own reporters.

The railway began to have an impact on the press at the same time as the newspaper taxes were cut in the mid 1830s. Aside from providing a crucial means for the conveyance of news and newspapers, the railway also affected the worlds of work and leisure, as well as where people lived. Commuting, suburbs and suburban environments all developed. This created demands and opportunities for the press. In 1848, the first of what was to be the network of W.H. Smith railway bookstalls was opened at Euston Station. By the time William Henry Smith died in 1891 he had opened 150 station shops.

In the long term, better communications and the reduction in duties in the 1830s were to lead to consolidation in the press. That, however, was not the intention behind the reduction and eventual abolition of the duties. Instead, this has to be located in the world of politics. The reductions reflected pressure from radicals who saw them as another stage in the reform process that had scored a major victory in the 1832 Reform Act; although many of the working-class radicals who became involved in the campaign for a cheap press felt a sense of betrayal that, despite their role in the extra-parliamentary agitation in 1830–2, they had largely been excluded from the franchise.

The response of other politicians was of greater importance. The Grey ministry (1830–4) pressed on to pass a series of measures including the abolition of slavery, the New Poor Law and the Factory Act, although the second was not seen as a reform by radical critics. The Melbourne ministry (1835–41) passed another series of reforms, including the Municipal Corporations Act (1835), the Tithe Commutation Act (1836) and the Civil Registration of Births, Marriages and Deaths (1837). Thus the reductions in newspaper duties can be seen as playing a part in what was presented as measured reform. This was designed as much to contain radicalism as to advance reform, and the Melbourne ministry in particular was wary of radical demands, rejecting both the secret ballot and the removal of bishops from the Lords. Radical MPs who pressed for the complete abolition of newspaper duties were thwarted. They included James Silk Buckingham, MP for Sheffield, a seat created in the First Reform Act, who had a background in journalism in India and London, and had been expelled from India in 1823 for criticizing its government in the *Calcutta Journal*, which he had founded in 1818.[9] Buckingham was a pioneer temperance reformer and chairman in 1834 of the first parliamentary inquiry into drunkenness: the temperance cause depended very much on effective printed propaganda.[10]

Containment was a matter not only of placating reformers, but also of hitting at the radical press, because it lessened the value of being unstamped. For that very reason, the stamped press had called for a reduction in taxation, and there was a powerful commercial reason to act. In the Lords debate of 8 August 1836 on the Newspaper Stamps Bill, Melbourne declared that it was designed not only to encourage knowledge but also to undermine the unstamped press. Lord Lyndhurst agreed as to the need to attack the latter. Another aspect of control can be seen in support by many newspapers for the creation of effective police forces,[11] although that was also part of a reforming attack on the abuses and limitations of earlier practices. John Edward Taylor, the founder of the *Manchester Guardian*, was subsequently Deputy Chairman of the Improvement Committee of the Manchester Commissioners of Police. His colleague Jeremiah Garnett was one of the Commissioners. The relationship between press and police could be close in other respects. The *Birmingham Chronicle* of 27 November 1823 announced 'We beg to inform Agricola that we have handed his two letters over to the Police, in preference to publishing them; and we doubt not but they will exert their authority to put a stop to the riotous and disorderly proceedings of which he complains.'

The issue of cost and its restraints were addressed in the advertisements for the *Daily News* published in January 1847; the paper had first appeared the previous year. These argued that cost was responsible for a lack of expansion in the number of London dailies, but found factors other than taxation responsible:

> First, the capital required to be invested. Next, the various talents, knowledge and experience which must combine to produce the result. The number of the requirements have, in truth, occasioned something very like a monopoly – and monopoly always commands its own price. Thus, whilst capital and competition had been doing good service in all other things, nothing had been attempted for the political and social wants of three great nations; and a daily London newspaper remained, until the establishment of the *Daily News*, a costly luxury, in which only the wealthy could indulge. The *Daily News* looks for support, not to a comparatively few readers at a high price, but to many at a low price.

Education was also seen as a way to contain discontent. *Besley's Devonshire Chronicle* of 25 January 1847 carried an item from St Austell about a JP using coastguards to prevent demonstrating china clay workers from blocking the shipment of grain:

> we cannot be surprised that men, uneducated and ignorant as they are on subjects of political economy, should, when hunger presses on them and their families, adopt the first means that present themselves to make known their grievances.

Between 1836 and 1853, there were no further cuts in duty. The association of activists for repeal with Chartism did not encourage a favourable response. The Tory ministry of Robert Peel (1841–6) was not temperamentally inclined to support a press free of taxation,[12] while the Whig ministry of John Russell (1846–52) lacked a working majority and was concerned about the challenge from the radical Chartist movement. In addition, the taxable yield of the duties remained a factor.

Instead, it was the coalition (Peelite and Whig) ministry of George, Earl of Aberdeen (1852–5), that resumed the pace of reform, ending taxation on advertisements in 1853. The weakness of Chartism after its failure in 1848 made reform and a press free of taxation appear less threatening. The unpopularity of the decision by the Stamp Office to prosecute the *Potteries Free Press*, an unstamped penny weekly, which Collet Dobson Collet had deliberately founded in February 1853 as a challenge to the regulatory regime, was followed by an inconclusive court action. This encouraged pressure for a change in the system. The repeal of the Advertisement Duties in 1853 was carried by a Commons majority of thirty-one. Disraeli supported the measure, but Gladstone opposed it.

The expansion of war reporting in the Crimean War (1854–6)[13] also encouraged a public interest in the press that made continued restrictions appear undesirable. Politicians were more willing to seek press popularity. Many newspapers actively supported the Whigs, and/or subsequently called for a change of government during the Crimean War, and a return appeared necessary. On 3 July 1852, the leader in the *Western Times*, a free trade paper, declared:

> The Exeter Election is fixed for Wednesday and Thursday next. The crisis demands the earnest zeal and unabated exertions of every Reformer. The Enemy has been tampering with, and endeavouring to seduce the poorer voters by the usual profligate expenditure in intoxicating drinks. Many a poor family will lament the broken health of its Parent and Protector, ruined and debauched by the agents of the Protectionist faction – the pretended friends of religion and order. The honest and independent portion of the electors must endeavour, by all lawful means, to defeat the corruptors, by watching over the weak, and warning them of the consequences of accepting the Tory bribes, whether in drink or coin. Recollect, that all who hold back on an occasion like this, no matter what pretence, are enemies of the cheap loaf, of extension of the suffrage – of the BALLOT – of education for the poor.

The *Western Luminary* of 9 January 1855 commented on the widespread criticism of the Aberdeen government: 'The press has done its part. It only remains for the country to do hers.' The press could claim to have played a major role in the fall of the government. The Palmerston ministry which followed passed the Newspaper Stamp Bill, with a second reading majority of 215 to 161. There was concern about the radical religious and political views of supporters of reform, as well as that competition for cheapness would lower the general character of the press, and would produce newspapers addressed only to the 'lower orders' and thus 'ministering to their passions'.[14] In response to fears about the likely character of politics under a cheap press, Palmerston declared his confidence in the people, adding that he had 'no fears that the anticipated evils from the existence of a cheap press would be realised'.

The sense of release that followed the removal of Stamp Duty, and the feeling that it had led to a press newly open to all, was captured by the *Weekly Express and South Devon Advertiser* on 8 January 1857:

> When the legislators removed the obstacle which had so long precluded the realisation of the idea of a people's press – a press which should be brought within the reach of the working multitudes, to enliven their homes and to instruct their minds – the Cheap Press, which at once sprang into being, fully equipped to struggle with exclusiveness and error, as Minerva sprang fully armed from the head of Jupiter, was, of course, pronounced impossible. The Dear

Press, with a jealousy unworthy of it, decried this new phase of journalism carefully chronicled its occasional failures, magnified its errors, ignored its successes, and, in fact, in every way strove hard to throw discredit upon it.

But the cheap newspapers were not thus to be pooh-pooh'd into nothingness. Misrepresentations injured them not; the failure here and there of an injudicious attempt did not neutralize the many successes elsewhere. The covert sneers and the open attacks of the Dear Press alike fell harmless. Cheap newspapers increased and multiplied. Like the Israelites in Egypt, the more they were oppressed, the more they grew. And now we confidently ask these sneerers and cavillers to behold and see how the young giant has grown. We triumphantly assert . . . the Cheap Press is a great fact.

The power that has been growing and expanding this past year will be still more mighty in the year in which we have just entered. We have a mighty work before us which will require every agent we can employ. Political and social reform must be secured; crime must be repressed; education must be fostered; the moral elevation of the masses must be continuously aimed at; the sweet voice of Religion and Philanthropy have yet to secure a full bearing; hypocrisy must be unmasked; and vice must be shown in its own image.

For this good work the Cheap Press will be a powerful engine, and we have little fear that it will prove itself adequate for its fair share of the reformation of the world. Speaking for ourselves, we at least feel hopeful for the future. We shall do our best to aid all legitimate schemes of political and social amelioration. We want better modes of education and greater facilities for training for the practical purposes of life. We want greater facilities too, for locomotives – better and cheaper travelling for the poor; we want better books and more of them; we want a higher political tone and less apathy in politics; we want more genuine and less sham representation; and, neither last nor least, we want less taxation. For these and many other reforms the Cheap Press will uniformly strive. The sympathies of every cheap newspaper are with the people. It springs for the people, it lives and acts for them; it looks for support to them. If this support be withheld the people alone are to blame. Let every reader take the hint, and procure us, at least, one subscriber for 1857.

The Crimean War led not only to press attacks on the government, but also to an active use of the press by protagonists and opponents of British intervention. Thus David Urquhart, a critic of Palmerston, founded the *Free Press* in 1855 to advance his views. On 31 August 1855, under the headline 'The Birmingham Conference. Have the Members been bribed?', the *Birmingham Daily Mercury* reported a meeting held to refute charges in the *Birmingham Journal*:

> Mr. Langley rose to propose a resolution deprecating the system of anonymous correspondence in newspapers as being dishonest, and pledging the meeting to labour for its speedy abolition. He contended that as it was, it was opposed to the rules of justice in England. . . . People of Birmingham . . . had got rid of priestcraft, they must now get rid of presscraft (cheers) . . . those whom he termed the rats and spiders of the press.

Yet, this call for the signature of articles itself only had resonance because it appeared in the press.

The final repeal – that of the Paper Duties in 1861 – only passed with considerable difficulty. It is generally less controversial to cut taxes than to raise them, but this proposed cut of revenue by about £1 million was opposed by politicians who would rather have spent the money on defence and by others anxious about a less expensive press.

The measure was introduced by William Gladstone, the Chancellor of the Exchequer, and was one that was to keep him popular with much of the press until the 1870s, but was opposed by the Prime Minister, Palmerston, much of the Cabinet and many parliamentarians. The measure passed the Commons on 8 May 1860 by a majority of only nine, and was then rejected by the Lords by 193 to 104, much to the pleasure of both Queen Victoria and Palmerston. Lord Robert Cecil, later, as 3rd Marquess of Salisbury, Conservative Prime Minister, praised the Lords. He had attacked Gladstone in the Commons because the Chancellor proposed to compensate for the Duties by raising income tax by $1d$ in the £1. This, according to Cecil, was an attempt to subsidize the cheap newspapers of Gladstone's allies.

Gladstone thought seriously about resigning, but in 1861 he successfully reintroduced the measure: Palmerston abandoned his opposition. Rather than introducing a separate Bill, Gladstone included his proposal in the Finance Bill [Budget], a measure condemned by Salisbury as 'more worthy of an attorney than of a statesman'. This criticism was regarded as unacceptable: attorneys were often of questionable repute. Cecil followed this up by offering to apologize, but to the attorneys not to Gladstone. This sally had no effect. The Lords passed the Budget in June, and the Duties were repealed from 1 October 1861.

It has been argued that Palmerston accepted the removal of the tax only in return for support for rearmament and fortification that he believed necessary in response to the ambitious schemes of Napoleon III of France. Gladstone, however, would not hear of expenditure that would put the nation into debt. In 1860 Palmerston had done whatever he could to defeat Gladstone's tax measures, and in 1861 Gladstone faced opposition from politicians who disliked a $10d$ income tax along with the abolition of the tax on knowledge. Initially inflexible, Gladstone was persuaded that if he dropped the income tax from $10d$ to $9d$ his ministerial critics might meet him half-way. Acquiescence in the removal of the Paper Duties was the concession, although it was also understood that Palmerston would obtain money for fortifications even if it meant seeking loans. Palmerston's concession on the Paper Duties has to be viewed in the context of the need to respond to the French, the arms build-up, and the drive to keep the Liberal coalition cabinet afloat.

Palmerston himself was in some respects ahead of his time in his manipulation of the press, and, as a major politician, was in the vanguard of moving political debate from Parliament to the platform by using the press as his instrument for currying popular favour and for defining the nation's identity in the process. When he stood for Tiverton in 1837, Palmerston made arrangements for the press to come from London, be well sited during his speech, lodged for the night, and for their return to London. In 1847, when he was opposed by the Chartist Julian Harney, Palmerston's key speech was reprinted by the press in its entirety and later published as a pamphlet. In December 1851, when he was dismissed by Russell, the *Morning Chronicle* and the *Morning Post* organized a campaign in his defence, and Palmerston paid a journalist to write a pamphlet attacking Prince Albert for supporting his dismissal. Palmerston cultivated a friendship first with Peter Borthwick and then his son Algernon, editors of the *Morning Post*. Many papers backed Palmerston during the Crimean War. His enemies, such as Cobden and Bright, who thought that they spoke for the public, complained frustratingly that Palmerston commanded too much attention from the press.

What was the tax-free press to be like? First, the provision of news was very different from the situation in the eighteenth century. In place of a reliance upon voluntary correspondents and scissors and paste, there was an increased use of professional reporters. Employed by particular papers, the reporters helped to give them a distinctive character. They also encouraged a focus on scoops. As with much else in press history, the impact was accentuated by emulation. In addition, reporters developed their own specializations, principally City, foreign and parliamentary. As a parallel move, there was a process of increasing specificity in the production organization, with sub-editors developing particular skills and tasks.

The papers produced by mid-century were recognizably different from those of the eighteenth century. Advertising, news and comment were more clearly distinguished than in the past. Layout was clearer and more predictable, with more effective and consistent grouping of material.

The press remained dominated by *The Times*. Its circulation was far greater than any other paper's, and it helped to set the tone of success. Initially, *The Times* (founded in 1785 as the *Daily Universal Register* and renamed in 1788) had been one of a number of successful London dailies, but, during the editorship of Thomas Barnes (1817–41), the paper was able to rise above all rivals. Barnes helped give the paper a reforming direction. His predecessor, John Stoddart, had been more conservative and was particularly opposed to Napoleon, but Barnes directed the fury of *The Times* against the Peterloo Massacre, the Six Acts and George IV, and in favour of Queen Caroline and Catholic Emancipation. In 1830, the paper gained the nickname 'the Thunderer' and on 29 January 1831 it published a leader urging public pressure for reform: 'Unless the people – the people everywhere – come forward and petition – ay, thunder for reform, it is they who abandon an honest minister – it is not the minister who betrays the people.'[15] Throughout the Reform Bill crisis, Barnes pressed the cause.

Barnes's successor, John Thaddeus Delane (1841–77), was a more successful establishment figure and helped to secure the respectability of the paper. A man who laid down his stomach for the sake of his paper, Delane's access to high society secured *The Times* confidence and confidences. Despite his earlier criticism of Palmerston, Delane, by the late 1850s and 1860s, became his confidante and the recipient of inside information. He was also a guest at Palmerston's shooting parties at Broadlands. Thanks to the high sales of the paper, it was able to yield profits that permitted investment in new technology – steam printing, stereotyping and rotary printing – and more correspondents. The latter helped to secure the readership.[16]

Prior to the end of Stamp Duty in 1855, no other daily could match this circulation, investment or range of material and, whereas *The Times* sold 50,000 copies daily, its counterparts managed only 5–6,000 each. The *Morning Chronicle* printed Henry Mayhew's accounts of the London poor in 1849–50, but ceased publication in 1862. Edward Baldwin's attempt to make the *Morning Herald* better than *The Times*, in particular by creating an effective system of foreign correspondents, led him to bankruptcy and his papers were sold to James Johnstone in 1857. The *Morning Herald*'s average circulation had fallen to 3,700 by 1854. Doing badly, this paper was closed in 1869. It was not until the *Daily Telegraph* was founded as an inexpensive penny daily in 1855 that a successful daily rival to *The Times* was launched. Like *The Times*, the *Telegraph* was not dependent on outside support. Profitability ensured that their proprietors and editors could choose their politics.

Alongside *The Times* from the 1840s, the most vigorous London papers were the popular Sundays, which benefited in their sales from only costing their readers one weekly payment. Yet low cost was simply an enabler of purchase. It was also necessary to create a product that large numbers wished to buy. Here the Sundays drew on the popular unstamped press of the 1830s. The radicalism of that decade helped encourage the publication of more than 200 unstamped publications. Most were short-lived and circulations were often small, but the most successful, the *Poor Man's Guardian*, sold up to 15,000 copies. Described as 'A Weekly Newspaper for the People, Established Contrary to "Law" to

Try the Powers of "Might" against "Right"', this weekly ran from 1831 to 1835 and was published by Henry Hetherington. It called for universal suffrage and restrictions on working time in factories, and pressed for the repeal of the Stamp Duty and of the Poor Law Amendment Act of 1834.[17] The last was attacked not only by other radical newspapers but also by Tory papers, such as the *Leeds Intelligencer*, that adopted a paternalist approach.

Not all radical papers were unstamped. William Cobbett edited the *Political Register*, which he had launched in 1802, until his death in 1835, and, although his impact by his last years was less than in the 1810s, he contributed to the general pressure of criticism of the establishment.

The Chartist press also condemned the existing system. The central pledge of Chartism, the 'People's Charter', issued in May 1838, itself owed much to the London Working Men's Association, which owed its genesis to the Association of Working Men to Procure a Cheap and Honest Press. The leading Chartist paper, the *Northern Star or Leeds General Advertiser*, was launched in 1837 and had weekly sales of over 10,000 by the close of its first year. The initial focus of the paper was hostility to the Poor Law Amendment Act of 1834, with its replacement of home relief by workhouses, a move that was presented as harsh. Feargus O'Connor, MP for Cork 1832–5 and for Nottingham 1847–52, who was very active on public platforms, made the *Northern Star* the voice of Chartism, and thus gave the paper more of a national voice. He bitterly denounced Stamp Duty, stating in the first issue 'Reader behold that little red spot in the corner of my newspaper. That is the stamp; the Whig beauty spot; your plague spot.'

The *Northern Star* helped increase Chartist cohesion, and at the same time disseminated its message. It became increasingly successful and survived O'Connor's imprisonment in 1840 for seditious libels in the paper. The Stamp Duty returns indicated sales of 572,640 in the year ending 5 January 1839 and 1,851,000 and 976,500 in the two following years respectively. The paper also benefited from a move to London in 1843. Ironically, O'Connor lost a libel case against the fiercely critical and Conservative *Nottingham Journal* in 1850. The commercial success of the *Northern Star* allowed the employment of full-time political activists as its agents. This was an important strength for the Chartist challenge, quite beyond the possibility of earlier radical movements. It was also a role model for subsequent 'militant' tendencies.

Other Chartist newspapers included the *Northern Liberator*, the *Western Vindicator*, and the *Charter*, as well as a series edited by James O'Brien, who signed his articles Bronterre: *Bronterre's National Reformer*, the *Operative*, the *British Statesman* and the *National Review*.[18] In 1849–55, George Julian Harney edited the *Democratic Review*, the *Red Republican*, the *Friend of the People* and the *Northern Tribune*, and he subsequently continued his radical newspaper editing activities in Jersey.[19] Similarly, the Isle of Man had served as an important base for radical publishing. Free of Stamp, Paper and Advertising Duties, papers published there were entitled to free postage throughout mainland Britain.[20] Furthermore, a number of reforming papers, such as the *Birmingham Journal*, were sympathetic to the Chartists.

There was also a new working-class press in Wales. *Y Gweithiwr* was launched in 1834 and followed in 1840 by the *Merthyr Advocate and Free Press* and by *Udgorn Cymru (Trumpet of Wales)*. Other radical Welsh journals included *Y Diwygiwr* (1835), *Chronicl yr oes* (1835), *Y Cronicl* (1843) and *Yr Amserau* (1843). Although their emphasis varied, all shared a moralistic rejection of the political and ecclesiastical Establishment that stemmed from the fusion of Nonconformity with socio-political activism. Chartist papers were characterized by a degree of social hostility to capital that was lacking in those that might be termed reform newspapers; the latter, for example the *Leeds Mercury* and the *Manchester Guardian*, were critical of what they saw as the Establishment and of institutionalized abuses, but far less so of the play of entrepreneurial capital and the new world it was creating. This had led to savage criticism during the factory movement of the early 1830s, although pressure then for shorter working hours for women and children came also from Tory paternalists and from major papers such as *The Times*.

An editorial in the *Northern Star* of 16 February 1850 under the headline 'Timid Law Makers and Powerful Law Breakers' declared:

> The struggle for a Ten Hours Bill has to be renewed. After years of agitation, and large sacrifices of time, money, and health, on the part of its advocates, the legislature, three years ago, at length recognised the justice of the principle they contended for, and embodied it in an Act of Parliament . . . the millowners – who had resisted its enactment with all the strength of their party, while under discussion -- determined to evade its provisions by means of a technical quibble. Remembering the old saying, that there never was an Act of Parliament yet passed, through which a coach and six might not be driven by those who had sufficient wealth and influence, they set to work to find, or make, the loop-holes which the legal verbiage always offers to the rich law breakers . . . introduced what is now known as the 'shift system'.

The radical and Chartist press fed into the Sundays, which were generally critical of government. George Reynolds, an active and popular Chartist, launched *Reynolds's Weekly Newspaper* in 1850 as a 'Sunday' for the working man. His leaders included harsh attacks on social inequities.

Their style was particularly influenced by earlier popular journalism. It was less complex and more readable than other papers. There was far more human interest and sensationalism. Both can be seen as echoing the early eighteenth-century cheap press. For example, the *Penny London Post, or The Morning Advertiser*, a tri-weekly, devoted much of its coverage in January 1749 to the 'sufferings of Mr. Joseph Pitts, who was several years a slave at Algiers'.

Their style was not particularly, and certainly not only, appropriate for political criticism. Indeed, the Sundays showed that it could be more readily appropriate for police news, and also for sports reporting.[21] From the perspective of the radical, this opened up a damaging contrast. The political direction that the popular press could take, as suggested for example by the *Political Register* and the *Northern Star*, could be lost in a more diffuse message driven by the commercialism first of the Sundays and then of the dailies that cut their prices after the abolition of Stamp Duty, especially the *Daily Telegraph* (the first penny London newspaper of the period) and the *Standard*.

These dailies were not aimed specifically at working-class readers, but the Sundays sought to reach this market, and dropped their prices to $2d$ after the removal of Stamp Duty, thus creating a cheap press that was sold direct to purchasers, rather than being read by larger numbers in communal contexts, such as beer shops: this development increased the disposability of newspapers and thus news. Depending on one's perspective, the populism of the Sundays tempered their politics or contributed to making them more accessible. This helped make the style and type of news offered by the Sundays seem unrespectable. To be labelled as cheap and populist, or as it would later be termed 'down-market', was to be commodified for a particular part of the newspaper market.

It is probably unreasonable to focus on political message, at the expense of other aspects of individual papers, reader preference and the press as a whole. Edward Lloyd, who launched *Lloyd's Illustrated London Newspaper* in 1842 (it became *Lloyd's Weekly News*), had started the *People's Police Gazette* in 1840. Nevertheless, as a theme of this book is the political placing of the press, it is appropriate to underline the importance of the failure of the unstamped papers of the 1830s and of the Chartist newspapers to develop a powerful popular radical press (although radicalism was to reappear in an advanced liberal press). Sundays and the dailies of the late 1850s could be more readily assimilated by mid-Victorian society and its political system, although this was not a process free from tension. For example, accounts of crime served not only to provide interesting stories, but also to convey, suggest or elicit wider responses. These could range from the need for reforms to a sense of instability requiring order. The press coverage of crime was very varied. Putting on one side the sensationalism that surrounded some events, it is clear that the local press was an ideal forum for discussing a whole range of issues including the actions of the police. The *Middlesbrough Weekly News*, for example, contained editorials and letters critical of lawless Irish and the inactivity of the town's police, but also criticisms of over-zealous policemen who infringed the rights of the poor. Similarly, the *Leeds Mercury* carried an extensive debate about the wisdom or otherwise of prosecuting publicans in the notorious Castlegate area of the town in 1847.

More generally, there was a tension between attempts to offer a Victorian public sphere and espousal of the divergent interests of a divided community and culture.[22] Alongside this it is necessary to note the conclusion that the 'new [mass] culture of compensation through diversion: diversion of the kind to be had in popular pictorial magazines – compensation for what they failed to offer . . . little that actively fostered the social, political, and economic advancement of the majority of working people'.[23] Looked at differently, there was a major broadening out of public culture without any matching degree of articulation and popularization of radical languages or options.

A focus on London papers is as inappropriate for the mid-nineteenth century as for the eighteenth: in many respects it represents a retrospective projection of the situation today. If *The Times* towered over the provincial press as much as its metropolitan rivals, it was less of a threat to the former, because their traditional function, as weeklies published outside London, was different. The provincial press did not change rapidly until mid-century. Then again the combination of the financial regime made possible by the end of duties and the new productive capability arising from technological developments made possible a major shift. The development of provincial dailies was the most important change in the provincial press since its foundation.

Although not all advertisers were reconciled to the costs of daily advertising,[24] the opportunity in the market was rapidly probed. The *Manchester Guardian* had originally appeared in 1821 at 7*d*. In 1836 it became a bi-weekly and its price was cut to 4*d*. The paper was converted from a bi-weekly into a daily in 1855, and in 1857 its price was cut from 2*d* to 1*d*. The *North Shields and South Shields Gazette and Northumberland and Durham Advertiser*, founded as a weekly in 1849 in order to challenge Newcastle's control of the trade of the Tyne and to provide the Shields with a paper of their own, instead of such titles as the *Sunderland Herald*, added a one-sided daily quarto sheet priced ½*d* two days after the repeal of Stamp Duty; the weekly was discontinued in 1866.

The end of Stamp Duty led to the foundation of numerous titles and newspaper companies: diversification and intensification of publication by existing operators was matched by new investment. The first provincial dailies in Birmingham, Liverpool, Manchester and Sheffield appeared in 1855, and in Newcastle in 1857; the *Mercantile Gazette and Liverpool and Manchester Daily Advertiser* of the early years of the century did not compare. The *Saturday Evening Post* launched in Birmingham in 1857 was specifically designed to fulfil the needs 'of the great body of the working classes'. The first daily in the south-west, the *Western Daily Press*, was published in Bristol in 1858, with the *Western Morning News* following in Plymouth in 1860. Selling for 1*d*, the *Nottingham Daily Guardian* appeared in 1861. The *Leeds Intelligencer* became the daily *Yorkshire Post and Leeds Intelligencer* in 1866. The *Bradford Observer*, founded in 1834, had from 1868 to face the competition of a daily, the *Bradford Daily Telegraph*, and, in turn, became a daily. However, whereas in 1868 fourteen of the largest English provincial towns had daily newspapers, there were none as yet in East Anglia, the Potteries or along the south coast from Dover to Exmouth. By 1885 forty-seven English towns had daily papers,[25] although some medium-sized parliamentary boroughs did not obtain dailies until later, Halifax for example not until 1892 with the *Halifax Courier*.

In addition, the new fiscal regime also encouraged a fall in the price of established papers and the publication of more non-daily provincial newspapers. The *Salisbury Journal* had raised its price to 7*d* in 1815, but in 1836 it was cut to 5*d* and in 1854 to 4*d*. The *Halifax Guardian* cut its price from 4½*d* to 3*d* in June 1855. In the south-west, Kingsbridge, Dartmouth, Crediton, Bideford, Newton Abbot and Helston gained their first newspapers in 1854, followed by Camborne and Chudleigh in 1855, Ilfracombe and Liskeard in 1856, Tiverton in 1859 and Totnes in 1860.[26] This represented a major intensification of the density of the press, not least because such papers were themselves the focus of local news networks. For example, the Chudleigh paper was in fact the *Weekly Express and Advertising Medium for Chudleigh, Newton, Teignmouth, Dawlish, Shaldon, Torquay, St Mary Church, Ashburton, Totnes, Bovey-Tracey, Moreton-Hampstead, Christow, and adjacent places*. The paper, a weekly costing 2*d* or, if delivered by post, 3*d*, indeed carried news columns from most of these places. In the north-east, towns gaining their own newspapers included Hartlepool in 1855 and Stockton in 1857. In the north west they included Ashton (*Weekly Reporter*, 1855), Burnley (*Advertiser*, 1853), Bury (*Gazette*, 1853), Middleton (*Albion*, 1856), Oldham (*Chronicle*, 1854) and Rochdale (*Observer*, 1856).

The appearance of provincial dailies changed the character of the entire provincial press, affecting those papers that did not appear on a daily basis. They had to respond to a different competitive environment in which they were therefore less effective in providing prompt local news and in acting as the purveyor of information about the wider world. As a consequence, those provincials that did not appear daily eventually became more truly local newspapers, while the provincial dailies became regional in character. They were thus able to compete for a readership that was substantial enough to permit them to invest in new printing technology and in a staff of reporters. As a result, they mirrored the internal organization and developments of the London daily press. This facilitated the movement of individuals between the two, and also helped secure the position of the London press as a model to the rest of the newspaper world.[27]

It would, however, be misleading to present too schematic a picture and to suggest that change was as rapid or clear-cut as outlined in the preceding paragraph. Provincial dailies were not simply regional, but also provided local, national and international news. The same was true of provincial weeklies. The prospectus of Chudleigh's *Weekly Express*, given in the first issue, that of 11 July 1855, stated:

The repeal of the Newspaper Stamp, together with the rapid advancement of the age, have induced us to issue The Weekly Express. . . . We shall supply our readers with the latest news from abroad, details of the war, parliamentary and local news, with other matter of an interesting, instructive, and useful character. To our agricultural friends, we shall offer the advantages arising from the latest London and country markets, being published in time for the Newton Market.

To the tourist, we shall point out the many claims upon him, showing the chief attractions, beauties, and sublimity of scenery in our favoured county. In short, we shall omit nothing that will have a tendency to benefit every class of our readers, avoiding the clashings of party spirit, having for our motto 'universal weal'.

The paper indeed provided both local news and that from further afield. The two were linked in the Crimean War, as accounts of the conflict were matched by those of local military manoeuvres.

Provincial newspapers varied in their politics,[28] and the pattern of rivalry seen with the response to the American War of Independence and, even more, the French Revolution was sustained in the post-Napoleonic world, although it was reshaped by the politics of those years. Catholic Emancipation was a major issue in the late 1820s. However, the energy and certainty lent by opposition to Revolutionary and Napoleonic France and their apparent allies was lost and the press became more open to reforming sentiments, especially if focused on improving the particular community and thus divorced from grander struggles. Provincial papers took stands on the resulting policies, a role that could not be fulfilled by the London press. Reform was linked to the growth of middle-class culture and consciousness in the great northern cities such as Leeds, Liverpool, Manchester and Newcastle.[29] The basis of authority in such cities had moved greatly from traditional to innovative. Their newspapers played a major role in orchestrating opinion in favour of reform.[30]

At the local level the newspapers were behind Corporation reform, for example in Leicester and Nottingham, the public health movement from the 1840s, the creation of paid police forces, the laying out of public parks and the building of public libraries and prisons. Whereas health and medicine in the eighteenth-century press had been a matter of unregulated advertisements, by the 1840s it was a subject of report and comment. This helped educate readers, and provided a context within which individual experiences and local developments could be located, expectations articulated, and advertisements reconsidered. Ideas of reform and accountability were not only pushed in the newspapers produced in cities. Under the heading 'Reform Meeting at Lyme Regis' the *Sherborne Mercury* of 6 February 1837 reported:

> A public meeting was held on Thursday the 26th instant [January], at the Guildhall in this borough, the Mayor in the Chair, for the purpose of enabling their respected representative, William Pinney, Esq., to state his opinions upon the leading political questions of the day, and to take the sense of his constituents on his parliamentary conduct during the past session.

The article continued by providing details of the meeting.

At the national level, many papers actively pushed reform. Although Peelite conservatism appealed to an important segment of the middle class, the Anti-Corn Law League founded in 1839 was a symbol of middle-class aggression.[31] Many newspapers, for example the *Leeds Mercury*, were active supporters of the league, although others were critical and some papers were founded to defend protectionism, for example the *Nottinghamshire Guardian* in 1846. The mismanagement of the Crimean War (1854–6) helped to boost middle-class values of efficiency in politics at the expense of the aristocracy. This was linked to the movement of Whiggism to Liberalism in the 1850s and 1860s as, in acquiring middle-class support, the Whigs became a party fitted for the reformist middle class. Reform was central to their appeal.

However, the diversity of opinion offered by the press in major towns was such that it would be misleading to think of reforming newspapers leading public opinion, unless it is also accepted that there were choices offered by the press. In Manchester in the 1820s, the *Manchester Gazette* and then the *Manchester Times*, which were the leading champions of reform, and the *Manchester Guardian* less markedly so, faced the Tory *Exchange Herald*, the *Manchester Courier* and the *Manchester Chronicle*.[32] Ironically, papers of different political persuasions were still reliant on identical sources of information.[33] The provincial response to *The Times*' criticism of the management of the Crimean War was similarly varied. It was praised for example in the *Bristol Mirror*, which on 6 January 1855 referred to *The Times*'

> advocacy of the unbiased opinion of the English people versus flunkeyism, redtapeism, and every other 'ism' that represents official misrule and love of clique . . . has spoken the sentiments of nine-tenths of the British people . . . God help us if we were left alone to

the tender mercies of the government, and of that narrow social circle which thinks it is treason to say a word against a lord, especially if he belongs to a ducal house; and God help us if the free opinion of the country were to be stifled by the hangers-on of that circle – toadies who do not deserve the name of Englishmen.

In contrast, the *Bristol Gazette* of five days later defended Lord Raglan:

It is all very easy for the correspondents of the London papers who have nothing to do but find fault; upon whom rests no responsibility, and whose confidence and arrogance are in proportion to their ignorance and their vanity, to re-iterate that this should have been done, and that should have been accomplished . . . but the public will not be misled by their one-sided and distorted representations. . . . What sort of discipline is to be maintained in an army when every pert lieutenant, captious cornet, or envious ensign, takes upon himself not only to criticise the plans of his general, but to hold him up to the common soldiers as their tyrant and oppressor, careless of their comfort and profuse of their lives?

Aside from politics, the press responded to the demand for prompt and comprehensive information in a rapidly developing society. The third number of the *Birmingham Herald*, whose complete title added *Midland Commercial, Literary and General Advertiser*, informed its readers on 11 August 1836 that in order to render the paper

useful to the commercial, manufacturing, and agricultural interests, it is the intention of the proprietors (so soon as the reduction of the Stamp Duty takes place) to give a careful selection of commercial intelligence, – proceedings of commercial bodies, and of public companies, – a share list, – price current, – list of bankrupts, dividends, etc – the London and country markets, – with statistical and other tables: and, also, a register of the proceedings in Parliament, with abstracts of important acts, and other political information (but not political discussions): with extracts from new publications, especially those relating to commerce or trade, with lists of new works, and other literary intelligence. And, also, births, marriages, and deaths.

Furthermore, it would be misleading to neglect the extent to which other issues, that can not be so readily fitted into a reform agenda, played a major role in the press. One such was the controversy created by the Oxford Movement, and another that resulting from the re-establishment of a Catholic hierarchy. The two could be presented as aspects of a common threat. The first leader in the *Western Times* of 18 January 1851 declared:

. . . these dirty Tractarians – mean, sordid, treacherous, and sneaking! how every honest sentiment rises up in indignation against their dark and dirty ways! . . . The Roman Catholics charge us with bigotry in resisting their claims to spiritual supremacy. If, behind their pretensions they had not an Inquisition, and a staff of goalers – if in Rome, at the present hour, the Pope allowed a particle of liberty of conscience to his own subjects – we should allow him to claim any spiritual government here that he pleased. But as we know the end, we have a duty to resist the beginning – but to resist it in such a way as shall give his followers the benefit of that religious feeling which is essential to the exercise of their worship, notwithstanding that a Pope would deny it to us in return.

More generally, many of the reports on meetings carried in the press related to religious and confessional activism, while newspapers frequently clashed over church matters. The *Sherborne Mercury* of 30 January 1837 reported at length the meeting of the Bath branch of the British Society for Promoting the Religious Principles of the Reformation. Chudleigh's *Weekly Express*, in its issue of 18 July 1855, carried a report of the Chudleigh meeting of the British and Foreign Bible Society. The *Western Times* was a persistent critic of Tractarianism in the Church of England, while the *Western Luminary* defended the Church and attacked Dissent. Latimer of the *Western Times* was acquitted of libel after he described Henry Phillpotts, the authoritarian Bishop of Exeter, as a 'careless perverter of facts' in his paper on 25 July 1846.[34] In Anthony Trollope's novel *The Warden* (1855), *The Times*, in the guise of the *Jupiter*, used the uncovering of abuses as a way to attack the Church of England and thus make the voice, pretensions and prerogatives bow to the superior power of print. In its leaders,

which are generally furnished daily for the support of the nation . . . it dealt some heavy blows on various clerical delinquents; on families who received their tens of thousands yearly for doing nothing; on men who, as the article stated, rolled in wealth which they had neither earned nor inherited.

Newspapers shaped, but also responded to, such controversies in a society that had long taken political discussion and debate for granted even if it sought to contain, if not limit, participation by both women and the poor. Improving activities were part of this containment. At the 1852 Annual Meeting of the Darlington Horticultural Society, the Reverend H. Harries pontificated: 'this society . . . was calculated to improve and elevate the taste of all classes, especially the poorer classes, by withdrawing them in their leisure hours from grosser indulgences to a pleasurable and improving pursuit'.[35] The press was less safe than the peonies, and opinions varied on the desirable social and gender span of an improving discussion of public issues. Nevertheless, discussion was seen as part of active citizenship, as well as a popular hobby. Wilkie Collins referred to the appeal of politics in *The Moonstone* (1868):

> The guests present being all English, it is needless to say that, as soon as the wholesome check exercised by the presence of the ladies was removed, the conversation turned on politics as a necessary result. In respect to this all-absorbing national topic, I happen to be one of the most un-English Englishmen living.

Such discussion, like the press and citizenship itself (as established by the franchise), was not, however, equally open to all. Furthermore, press comments about excluded groups, such as the Irish in England, were frequently vicious.

The normative quality of print was enhanced both by the development of other aspects of print culture and by the expansion of public education, although the Education Act that divided the country into school districts and required a certain level of educational provision, introducing the school district where existing parish provision was inadequate, did not follow until 1870. Print culture expanded with the growth of the novel, which became more popular in the nineteenth century and was closely linked to serial publication as many first appeared in parts in magazines. Like novels, magazines both became far more widely read and were seen as benefiting particularly from the expansion of women readers.[36]

Charles Dickens was particularly active in the magazine world, although he also played a role in the overlapping one of newspapers. Dickens himself began his journalism as a parliamentary reporter on the *Mirror of Parliament* in 1831, his father had been a reporter on the *Morning Herald*, and his father-in-law, George Hogarth, was first editor of the *Halifax Guardian* and founder-editor of the *Evening Chronicle*. Dickens himself briefly edited the *Daily News* in 1846. He launched the weekly magazine *Household Words* in 1850 and in 1859 incorporated it into *All the Year Round*, a magazine that he edited until his death in 1870. The latter sold as many as 300,000 copies. His magazines were recorders of society and, in general, accorded with the principles he had outlined in his first leader in the *Daily News*: 'the principles of progress and improvement; of education, civil and religious liberty and equal legislation'.[37]

Yet he was not ignorant of the costs and problems of progress, as was shown in his short story about a return to childhood haunts, 'Dullborough Town', published in *All the Year Round* on 30 June 1860:

> Most of us come from Dullborough who come from a country town
> . . . the Station had swallowed up the playing-field. It was gone. The

two beautiful hawthorn-trees, the hedge, the turf, and all those buttercups and daisies had given place to the stoniest of jolting roads. . . . The coach that had carried me away, was melodiously called Timpson's Blue-Eyed Maid, and belonged to Timpson, at the coach-office up-street; the locomotive engine that had brought me back, was called severely No. 97, and belonged to SER [South Eastern Railway], and was spitting ashes and hot-water over the blighted ground.

Magazines became more popular in mid-century. This was part of a changing periodical world as they in part took over from the quarterlies. Yet magazines also created a new expanded readership, for the quarterlies had been more restricted in their readership. The best known, the Whig *Edinburgh Review* launched in 1802 and its rival, the Tory *Quarterly Review* (1809), for each of which major politicians wrote,[38] had a circulation that was high given their dry contents – a peak of 13,500 and 14,000 respectively in the 1810s – but this was a very different market in its scale from that of the mid-century magazines. It was also a different market in terms of place or space to use modern literary discourse. Although the quarterlies were purchased by private subscribers, they were also widely available in institutions, especially subscription libraries, clubs and literary and philosophical societies. Communal consumption was also important for newspapers, the coffee-shops maintaining their late seventeenth-century role. Public houses were also very important, especially for working-class readers. Mid-Victorian magazines were different. Whether available in such institutions or not, the vast bulk of their readership was individual, or rather family, and that explained the character of the magazines. The debating nature of the quarterlies, many of the articles of which approximated to speeches in print, was transformed into a more homely, even intimate, product.

The informed essayism of the quarterlies led towards the specialist publications that expanded greatly, especially from the 1840s. They were more frequent than the quarterlies, part of the 'speeding up' of society which affected the demand for news and comment. Specialist works ranged from semi-political journals, such as *The Economist*, founded in 1843 by James Wilson MP, a former Financial Secretary to the Treasury, to attack the Corn Laws,[39] to works that were more specific in their interests and readership, such as the *Builder* (1842) and the *Musical Times* (1844).

The variety of periodical works was further indicated by the appearance of *Punch* in 1841,[40] and of the *Illustrated London News* the following year. Both were successful weeklies that exemplified the importance of visual mediums, and the latter's success in dominating the illustrated news market was seen with sales that exceeded 60,000 copies an issue in the first year and 100,000 by 1852, and approached 200,000 in 1856: the paper's Middleton and Applegath presses were kept busy. Its advertisement soliciting subscribers for 1855 emphasized the number of the illustrations – 1,000 engravings of the Crimean War alone in 1854 – an 'impartial and consistent advocacy of the welfare of the public', and the size of the readership. The *Illustrated London News* was a specialized instance of a more general move towards more illustrations in the press.[41]

The press had become the prime source outside the family of ideas, images and comparisons through which people could understand and structure their experience. This process was accentuated by the tremendous mobility of mid-Victorian society as massive urbanization drew on extensive migration within the country. This challenged, indeed frequently broke down, earlier patterns of communal control or at least influence, not that these had been indefinite and without strain. A newly expanded urban world that owed little to traditional disciplines searched for new ways to communicate, and the press provided the news, comment and advertising material that was required. The fast tempo of the daily press with the resulting rapid changeability of news matched a swiftly altering society. The scale of demand for the press offered a prospect of profitability that encouraged investment.

The capitalization of both newspaper and periodical production increased greatly in the second half of the century. As equipment and staffing costs rose this was in part driven by the needs of the industry, but the opportunities for profit were also important, and this attracted share capital. For investment purposes, it was best to avoid radical political views, not least because they might inhibit advertisers, as the limited advertising yield of the *Northern Star* in 1838–40 indicated.[42] Nevertheless, it is wise to temper any quasi-conspiratorial account of capitalism by noting the degree to which much of the working class apparently sought the entertainment and human interest that was offered them, rather than campaigning commitment.[43]

Commercialization was scarcely new, and was not necessarily incompatible with the role of newspapers and other periodicals as vehicles for opinion and instruction. Yet, allowing for obvious differences, it is worth seeking a parallel with the impact on television of advertisements after the Television Act of 1954: commercial television transmissions began the following year. It might have been possible for a regulated society drawing on wartime practices of state control to contain consumerism, but, once television advertising was available, then it became difficult to prevent development of what was truly a consumer society. A century earlier, legislative changes had also combined with technology and economic expansion to create a major discontinuity in public culture. This can be exaggerated[44] and much was clearly an acceleration of developments that had been under way for several decades.[45] Yet it was still the end of the *ancien régime* of the English newspaper world.

NOTES

1. BL, Add. 27819, fol. 28.
2. R.S. Lambert, *The Cobbett of the West: A Study of Thomas Latimer* (1939).
3. J. Wiener (ed.), *Papers for the Millions: The New Journalism in Britain, 1850s to 1914* (Westport, Connecticut, 1988). For a wider context, G.J. Baldasty, *The Commercialization of News in the Nineteenth Century* (Madison, Wisconsin, 1993).
4. Burges to Anne Burges, 2 October 1792, Bod., BB 48.
5. M. Blondheim, *News over the Wires: the Telegraph and the Flow of Public Information in America* (Boston, 1994).
6. D. Read, *The Power of News. The History of Reuters* (2nd edn, Oxford, 1999), pp. 13–19.
7. R. Furneaux, *The First War Correspondent* (1944), pp. 39–40; C. Chapman, *Russell of 'The Times': War Despatches and Diaries* (1984).
8. P.J. Hugill, *Global Communications since 1844. Geopolitics and Technology* (Baltimore, 1998), p. 39.
9. For his demand for compensation, BL, India Office, MSS Eur, C 249.
10. B. Harrison, *Drink and the Victorians* (2nd edn, Keele, 1994), pp. 106–8.
11. D. Taylor, *Crime, Policing and Punishment in England, 1750–1914* (1998), pp. 78–9.
12. For Peel's use of the press, D. Read, *Peel and the Victorians* (Oxford, 1987).
13. A. Lambert and S. Badsey, *The War Correspondents: the Crimean War* (Stroud, 1994).
14. *Bristol Mirror*, 17 March 1855.
15. For the official history, '*The Thunderer' in the Making, 1785–1841* (1935). See also D. Hudson, *Thomas Barnes of 'The Times'* (Cambridge, 1944).
16. *History of 'The Times'. The Tradition Established, 1841–1884* (1939).
17. J. Wiener, *Unstamped British Periodicals 1830–1836* (Ithaca, NY, 1969); P. Hollis, *The Pauper Press* (Oxford, 1970).
18. J.A. Epstein, 'Feargus O'Connor and the *Northern Star*', *International Review of Social History* 21 (1976), pp. 51–97, and *The Lion of Freedom: Feargus O'Connor and the Chartist Movement, 1832–1842* (1982). For another aspect of radicalism, S.A. Mullen, 'Keeping the Faith: the Struggle for a Militant Atheist Press, 1839–62', *Victorian Periodicals Review* 25 (1992), 150–8.
19. G.I.T. Machin, 'George Julian Harney in Jersey, 1855–63: a Chartist "abroad"', *Annual Bulletin of the Société Jersiaise* 23 (1984), 478–95.
20. J. Belchem, 'The Neglected "Unstamped": The Manx Pauper Press of the 1840s', *Albion* 24 (1992), 605–16.
21. V.S. Berridge, 'Popular Sunday papers and mid-Victorian society' in G. Boyce, J. Curran and P. Wingate (eds), *Newspaper History from the Seventeenth Century to the Present Day* (1978), pp. 247–64; A. Humphreys, 'G.W.M. Reynolds: popular literature and popular politics', *Victorian Periodicals Review* 16 (1983), 78–89; J. Knelman, 'Subtly Sensational: A Study of Early Victorian Crime Reporting', *Journal of Newspaper and Periodical History* 8 (1992), 28–33.

22. For an earlier period, see the complex argument in J.P. Klancher, *The Making of English Reading Audiences, 1790–1832* (Madison, 1987).

23. P.J. Anderson, '"A Revolution in Popular Art": Pictorial Magazines and the Making of a Mass Culture in England, 1832–1860', *Journal of Newspaper and Periodical History* 6 (1990), 25.

24. M. Milne, 'Survival of the Fittest? Sunderland newspapers in the nineteenth century', in J. Shattock and M. Wolff (eds), *The Victorian Periodical Press: Samplings and Soundings* (Leicester, 1982), p. 215.

25. H.J. Hanham, *Elections and Party Management* (Hassocks, 1978), p. 109.

26. Maxted, 'Printing . . .', in Kain and Ravenhill (eds), *Historical Atlas*, p. 244.

27. For the conceptualization of centre/local relations in terms of regimes of power and knowledge, M. Ogborn, 'Local Power and State Regulation in Nineteenth Century Britain', *Transactions of the Institute of British Geographers*, new ser. 17 (1992), 215–26.

28. D. Read, *Press and People, 1790–1850. Opinion in Three English Cities* (1961); M. Winstanley, 'News from Oldham: Edwin Butterworth and the Manchester Regional Press, 1829–1848', *Manchester Region History Review* 4 (1990), 3–10.

29. D. Fraser (ed.), *Municipal Reform and the Industrial City* (Leicester, 1982); J.K. Walton and A. Wilcox, *Low Life and Moral Improvement in Mid-Victorian England: Liverpool through the Journalism of Hugh Shimmin* (Leicester, 1991). Shimmin was editor-proprietor of the *Porcupine* (1860–71).

30. A. Jones, *Powers of the Press. Newspapers, Power and the Public in Nineteenth-century England* (Aldershot, 1996), p. 155.

31. N. McCord, *The Anti-Corn Law League 1838–1846* (1958).

32. M.J. Turner, 'Manchester Reformers and the Penryn Seats, 1827–1828', *Northern History* 30 (1994), 143–55.

33. M. Winstanley, 'News from Oldham: Edwin Butterworth and the Manchester Press, 1829–1848', *Manchester Region History Review* 4 (1990), 3–10.

34. J. Leach, 'The Revd. James Shore of Bridgetown, Totnes', *Devon Historian* 57 (October 1998), 16. See also e.g., R.L. Greenall, 'Ancient Church: Urban Parish. St Peter's Northampton in the Nineteenth Century', *Northamptonshire Past and Present* 9 (1997–8), 380.

35. *Durham County Advertiser*, 13 February 1852, quoted in R. Hamilton, '"Substantial Good and Rational Pleasure". The Darlington Horticultural Society', *Durham County Local History Society Bulletin* 45 (December 1990), 53.

36. Anderson, '"Factory Girl, Apprentice and Clerk" – The Readership of Mass-market Magazines, 1830–60', *Victorian Periodicals Review* 25 (1992), 64–72.

37. M. Slater (ed.), *The Dent Uniform Edition of Dickens' Journalism. I. Sketches by Boz and Other Early Papers 1833–39* (1994); *Daily News*, 21 January 1846.

38. J. Shattock, *Politics and Reviewers. The 'Edinburgh' and the 'Quarterly' in the Early Victorian Age* (Leicester, 1989), and 'Paranoid Politics: The *Quarterly* and *Edinburgh Reviews*', *Prose Studies* 15 (1992), 319–43.

39. R.D. Edwards, *The Pursuit of Reason: The 'Economist' 1843–1993* (1993).

40. R.D. Altick, *Punch: The Lively Youth of a British Institution, 1841–1851* (Columbus, Ohio, 1997).

41. Anderson, *The Printed Image and the Transformation of Popular Culture* (Oxford, 1991); P.W. Sinnema, *Dynamics of the Pictured Page: Representing the Nation in the 'Illustrated London News', 1842–1852* (Aldershot, 1998).
42. E. Royle, 'Politics, Protest and the Press in the Early Nineteenth Century', unpublished paper, p. 8.
43. W.B. Stephens, *Education in Britain 1750–1914* (1998), pp. 153-4.
44. S. Koss, *The Rise and Fall of the Political Press in Britain*, I (1981), pp. 1–3.
45. M. Harris and A. Lee (eds), *The Press in English Society from the Seventeenth to the Nineteenth Centuries* (1986), pp. 107–8. More generally, see Lee, *The Origins of the Popular Press, 1855–1914* (1976), and A. Jones, *Powers of the Press. Newspapers, Power and the Public in Nineteenth-century England* (Aldershot, 1996). On the 'law of the suppression of radical potential', B. Winston, *Misunderstanding Media* (1986) and *Media Technology and Society. A History: from the Telegraph to the Internet* (1998).

Selected Further Reading

A good, though somewhat dated, overview is provided by J. Curran, G. Boyce and P. Wingate (eds), *Newspaper History from the Seventeenth Century to the Present Day* (1978). For the seventeenth century, James Sutherland, *The Restoration Newspaper and its Development* (Cambridge, 1986) is somewhat limited. For the period down to 1800 Jeremy Black, *The English Press in the Eighteenth Century* (1987) and Bob Harris, *Politics and the Rise of the Press. Britain and France, 1620–1800* (1996). On the provincial press, G.A. Cranfield, *The Development of the Provincial Newspaper, 1700–1760* (Oxford, 1960). See also J.A. Downie and T.N. Corns (eds), *Telling People what to Think: Early Eighteenth-century Periodicals from the 'Review' to the 'Rambler'* (1993), Charles Clark, *The Public Prints: the Newspaper in Anglo-American Culture* (Oxford, 1994), Christine Ferdinand, *Benjamin Collins and the Provincial Newspaper Trade in the Eighteenth Century* (Oxford, 1997) and Hannah Barker, *Newspapers, Politics, and Public Opinion in Late Eighteenth-century England* (Oxford, 1998), and *Newspapers, Politics and English Society 1695–1855* (2000).

For the nineteenth century, Lucy Brown, *Victorian News and Newspapers* (Oxford, 1985), Laurel Brake, Aled Jones and Lionel Madden (eds), *Investigating Victorian Journalism* (1990), and Aled Jones, *Powers of the Press. Newspapers, Power and the Public in Nineteenth-century England* (Aldershot, 1996).

The journal that has developed from the *Journal of Newspaper and Periodical History*, founded in 1984, to *Studies in Newspaper and Periodical History* (from 1993), which then became *Media History*, has much to offer in its articles and reviews.

Index

Aberdeen, George, Earl of 183
accident reports 57–8
Adams' Weekly Courant 12, 61
Addington, Henry 90
Addison, Joseph 29, 97
Adolphus, John 156
advertising 10, 13, 20, 60–5, 69,
    110–13 *passim*, 192
    tax on 62, 165–6, 178–9, 183
Agreeable Miscellany 61
All the Year Round 198–9
almanacs 3
Almon, John 129
American news/press 79, 82, 88,
    138–9, 143
Amhurst, Nicholas 34
Anne, Queen 26, 29, 65, 137
Anti-Cobbett, or, Weekly Patriotic Register
    168
Applebee's Original Weekly Journal
    55
Applegarth, Augustus 179
Argus 82, 146, 155–6
Aris's Birmingham Gazette 67
Ashburner, Thomas 61
astrology 3
Aurora and Universal Advertiser 65

Baines, Edward 164, 173
Baldwin, Edward 188
Baldwin, Richard 7, 8
ballads 3, 5
Barnes, Thomas 187–8
Barrington, George 57
Bath Chronicle 115
Bath Journal 57
Beckford, Richard 130
Bell's Weekly Messenger 81, 82, 83

Benfield, Paul 161
Berkeley, George 135
Berkenhead, Sir John 5
Berrow's Worcester Journal 21, 51, 79 *bis*,
    96
Besley's Devonshire Chronicle 67, 180,
    183
Bible 2–3
Bingley, Edward 31
Birmingham 9, 51, 73, 147
Birmingham Chronicle 54, 69, 76, 84,
    91–2, 100, 105, 115, 130, 139, 169
    quoted vii, 52, 55, 56–7, 101–2, 104,
    120, 162, 182
Birmingham Commercial Herald 76, 84,
    101, 106–7, 115, 120, 121, 162,
    163, 168, 181
Birmingham Daily Mercury 185–6
Birmingham Gazette 111
Birmingham Herald 66, 67, 99, 180, 196
Birmingham Journal 185–6, 190
Black Dwarf 167
Bolingbroke, Lord 29–30, 36
Bolton Chronicle 57, 171
Borthwick, Peter and Algernon 187
Boston News Letter 88
Bowyer, William 36
Bradford Daily Telegraph 193
Bradford Observer 193
Bray, Revd Thomas 30
Brighton Gazette 170
Bristol 9, 17, 64, 113, 171
Bristol Chronicle 79
Bristol Gazette 61, 120, 196
Bristol Journal 102, 115, 137–8
Bristol Mercury 75, 120
Bristol Mirror 172, 195
British Chronicle or Pugh's Hereford

Journal 105–6, 111, 112, 127, 134–5, 139
British Gazette and Sunday Monitor 74
British Mercury 65
British Observer 12
British Packet and Argentine News 89
Briton 59, 74, 167
Brodie, William Bird 171
Brougham, Lord 90, 164, 173
Buckinghamshire...Mercury 115
Budd, Edward 164
Burdett, Sir Francis 164
Burges, James Bland 180
Burke, Edmund 140, 146, 148, 151
Burney, Fanny: *Cecilia* 70
Bury and Norwich Post 113, 156
Bute, John, 3rd Earl of 16, 138

Caledonian Mercury 133
Cambrian 111
Cambridge Chronicle 140
Cambridge Intelligencer 83, 156
Cambridge Oracle 115
Campbell, John 77
Canning, Elizabeth 55
Canning's Farthing Post 55
Cap of Liberty 167
Cape Town Gazette 89, 120, 134
Carlile, Richard 172
Carlisle Chronicle 111
Carlisle Journal 111
Carlisle Patriot 170
Caroline, Queen 168–9
Caryll, John Baptist 40
censorship 6–8, 25–6, 28
Champion 36, 37, 61
Chandler, Samuel 87
Charles II 7–8
Chartism 183, 189–90
Chelmsford Chronicle 61, 66, 79, 111–12, 114, 117, 152–3, 154–5
Chester Chronicle 115
Children's Companion 87
Chudleigh *see Weekly Express*
Cinque Ports Herald 115

circulation 92, 110–16 *passim*, 119–20, 179–80
Citizen 65
City Intelligencer 65
Clifton, Francis 34–5, 58
Cobbett, William 58, 104, 164, 166, 167, 172, 189
Cobden, Richard 173
coffee houses 12, 62
Collet, Collet Dobson 183
Colley, Linda 165
Collins, Benjamin 99
Collins, Wilkie 198
Colman, George 59
colonial news/press 88–9, 120
Common Sense 12, 37
'corantos' 4–5
Corn Cutter's Journal 34
Cornwall Gazette and Falmouth Packet 110
Cosmopolite 172
Cotta, John 3
Country Oracle and Weekly Review 114
Country Spectator 173
County Chronicle and Weekly Advertiser 114–15
County Press for Hertfordshire... 115
Courier 57, 84, 130, 163
Covent Garden Journal 64, 97
Coventry Standard 17
Craftsman 18 *bis*, 28–37 *passim*, 44, 58–9
Crawford, James 133
crime reporting 54–7, 92
Cumberland 140
Cumberland, Duke of 39
Cumberland Chronicle 111
Cumberland Paquet 105, 111, 114, 119, 139

Daily Advertiser 42–4, 62, 64, 70
Daily Courant 9, 28, 37
Daily Gazetteer 37, 42
Daily Mail 179
Daily News 70, 179, 182–3, 198

Daily Telegraph 179 *bis*, 188, 191
Daily Universal Register 75, 131
Darlington Pamphlet 111
Darlington and Stockton Times 111
Defoe, Daniel 53, 68
Delane, John Thaddeus 188
Derby Post-man 9
Destructive and Poor Man's Conservative
    172 *bis*
Devonshire Chronicle and Exeter News
    123
devotional books 3
Dibdin, Charles Jr. 158
Dickens, Charles 198
Disraeli, Benjamin 173
Diverting Post 58
Dorchester and Sherborne Journal 51, 54,
    60, 99, 104, 114, 163
    quoted 66, 78, 101, 121, 156, 161,
    162
Dorset 134
Drankard, John 164
Drewry, Joshua 171
Drewry's Derby Mercury 3, 100–1
Drewry's Staffordshire Gazette 57
Dublin Evening Post 115
Dundonald, Earl of 42

Eaton, Daniel 156
Ecclesiastical Gazette 87
Echo 179
economic news 5, 65–6, 69–70
Economist 199
Eden, William 140
Edinburgh Review 164, 199
editorials 83
education 101–2, 198
English and French Journal 45
Eton Journal 41
Evening Chronicle 198
Evening Mail 82
Evening Post 28, 42
Examiner 26 *bis*, 164
Exchange Evening Post 65
Exchange Herald 195

Exeter 9, 10, 116
Exeter Gazette 54, 92, 122
Express 66

Family Magazine 87
Farley, Edward 32–3
Felix Farley's Bristol Journal 12, 119,
    120, 139, 170
Fielding, Henry 58, 64, 97
Flindell, Thomas 110
Flindell's Western Luminary 92
Flower, Benjamin 83
Flying Post 8, 37
Fog's Weekly Journal – see under
    Mist
Fox, Charles James 140, 147,
    151
Foxe, John: *Book of Martyrs* 3
France 20, 38, 68, 78, 84, 163–4
    French Revolution 143–59
Frearson, Michael 4
Free Briton 36, 37
Free Press 185
freedom of press 6–8, 26–7, 28, 29,
    46, 128–9
Freke's Price of Stocks 65
Friend of India 89

Gales, Joseph 83, 146
Garnett, Jeremiah 75
Gazette 6–7, 45, 63, 70
Gazetteer and New Daily Advertiser 62,
    129
General Advertiser and Morning
    Intelligencer 101, 115
Gentleman's Diary 53
Gentleman's Magazine v, 12
George I 26, 27, 31, 44
George II 26, 31, 32, 44
George III 128, 129, 138
George IV 168–9
Germany 20
Gifford, George 3
Gillies, John 87
Gladstone, William 186–7

Glocester Journal 12, 54, 57, 69 *bis*, 130, 139, 147–8, 148–9, 149 (*bis*), 158
Gloucester Herald 115
Goldsmith, Oliver 177
Gordon,George 38
Gordon, Thomas 34
Gorgon 172
Grafton, Duke of 59, 129
Gray's Inn Journal 74
Grenville, William 131–2
Gyllenborg, Count 27

Halifax Courier 193
Halifax Guardian 75, 165, 193, 198
Halifax and Huddersfield Express 165
Halifax Journal 111
Hampshire Chronicle 53, 102, 112, 117, 121
Harding, Mr (proprietor) 43–4
Harland, John 83–4
Harley, Robert 10, 26, 41
Harney, George Julian 187, 189
Harries, Revd H. 197
Hazlitt, William 131
Heathcote, Sir Gilbert 123–4
Henley, John 58 *bis*
Henry VIII 2
Henry, John 165
Hereford Independent 111
Hereford Journal 20, 111
Hereford Times 66, 111
Heriot, John 90
Hertford, Algernon Seymour, Earl of 42–4
Hertford, Frances, Lady 42–4
Hetherington, Henry 189
Historical List of all Horse-Matches Run 60
Hogarth, George 198
Holt, Daniel 156
Home Counties 114–15, 119
Hone, William 167
Honest True Briton 13, 18, 27, 33
Household Words 198
Hull Advertiser 156

humour 58, 70, 97
Hyp-Doctor 58

Idler 63
Illustrated London News 58, 199–200
index to newspapers 52
Ipswich Gazette 156
Isle of Man 190

Jackson's Oxford Journal 75–6
Jacobitism 27–41 *passim*
James II 7, 8
'James III' (Pretender) 31, 32, 38
Johnson, Dr Samuel 63
Johnstone, James 188
Jopson's Coventry Mercury 17, 67
Journey to London 19
'Junius' 58–9, 129, 137

Kelly, John 37
Kendal 124
Kendal Courant 111
Kendal Weekly Mercury 61, 111
Kentish Gazette 66, 76
Kentish Post 9

labour relations 103–4, 106–7
Larkin, George 7
Latimer, Thomas 178, 179, 197
Leeds 113, 170
Leeds Intelligencer 55, 79, 91, 144, 170, 189, 193
  quoted 54, 116, 135, 173–4
Leeds Mercury 9, 60, 62, 90, 91, 106, 118, 138, 139, 140, 158, 164, 169, 173, 190, 192, 195
  quoted 103, 108
Leeds Patriot 165
L'Estrange, Sir Roger 6
Leicester Chronicle 156, 164
Leicester and Nottingham Journal 113
Licensed Victuallers Association 64
Lilly, William 3
Lincoln Herald 165
Lion 172

Liverpool 69, 111
Liverpool Mercury 164, 181
Liverpool Standard 170
Lloyd, Edward (I) 65
Lloyd, Edward, (II) 191
Lloyd's Evening Post 19
Lloyd's News 65
Lloyd's Weekly London Newspaper (later
    Lloyd's Weekly News) 86, 179–80,
    191
lobbying and petitioning 68–9, 135
London 12, 80–1, 111, 118, 119, 178,
    192, 193
London Chronicle 58, 59, 81, 147, 155
London Evening Post 30, 41, 70, 128
London Farthing Post 44–5
London Gazette 6–7, 45, 63, 70
London Journal 33, 34, 37, 42, 45, 88
London Museum 129
London Packet 29, 131
London Post 53
Lower Bank Gazette 87

McCulloch, William 87
Mackinnon, William 91
mad dogs 99–100
magazines 12, 198–9
Maidstone Journal 51
Mainwaring, Arthur 26
Man 87, 172
Manchester 170
Manchester Chronicle 195
  see also Wheeler's...
Manchester Courier 75, 181, 195
Manchester Exchange Herald 164
Manchester Gazette 171, 195
Manchester Guardian 75, 83–4, 164,
    169, 171, 173, 181, 190, 192, 195
Manchester Herald 83, 156
Manchester Observer 167
Manchester Political Register 167
Manchester Times 173 *ter*, 195
Mannheimer Zeitung 20
Marlborough, Duke of 41
Mayhew, Henry 188

Medley 26 *bis*
Medusa; or, Penny Politician 167
Melbourne, Lord 182 *bis*
Mercantile Gazette 192
Mercator 68
Mercurius Aulicus 5
Mercurius Britannicus 5
Mercurius Politicus 5–6
Mercurius Pragmaticus 5
Merle, Gibbons 168
Middlesbrough Weekly News 191–2
Middlesex Journal 79, 101
Miller, Edward 60
Mirror of Parliament 198
Mist, Nathaniel 29–38, 41–2, 58, 98
  Fog's Weekly Journal 31, 33–4, 35–7
  Mist's Weekly Journal 31, 33–4, 97
  Weekly Journal 30, 37, 65
Mitre and Crown 40
Mohun, Charles, Lord 41
Monitor 26, 59, 74, 117
Montagu, Elizabeth 132
Montagu, Lady Mary Wortley 58
Montgomery, James 156
moral comment 91–2, 96–8, 105–7
Morning Advertiser 64, 90
Morning Chronicle 58, 60, 90 *ter*, 130,
    147, 156 *bis*, 187, 188
  quoted 131, 144
Morning Herald 75, 90, 188, 198
Morning Journal 170
Morning Leader 179
Morning Post 59, 60, 131, 137, 156 *bis*,
    169, 187
Morris, Sgt Thomas 163–4

National Journal 38, 39–40
Nedham, Marchamont 5–6
Newark Herald 76, 143, 149
Newark and Nottingham Journal 140
Newcastle 9, 17, 61, 116, 132
Newcastle, Duke of 32–3, 128
Newcastle Chronicle 123, 140
Newcastle Courant 12, 59, 63, 79, 88,
    117, 118, 132, 140

quoted 45, 53–4
Newcastle Gazette 9
Newcastle Journal 165
News of the World 86, 179
Norfolk Chronicle 117
North, Lord 129, 135, 137, 140, 174
North Briton 16, 58, 59, 74, 128
North Devon Journal 72, 124
North Shields and South Shields Gazette 192
North Wales Chronicle 111
Northampton 17
Northampton Journal 13–17
Northampton Mercury 13–17, 57, 115
Northern Star 189, 191, 200
Norwich 9, 17, 115
Norwich Gazette 9, 40
Norwich Post 9 *bis*, 88
Norwich Post-Man 9
Nottingham Daily Guardian 193
Nottingham Gazette 140, 165
Nottingham Journal 173, 189
Nottingham Review 164, 168
Nottingham Post 9
Nottinghamshire Guardian 195
Nutt, Elizabeth 33

O'Brien, James 189
Observator 32, 41
Observer 56
O'Connor, Feargus 189
Old England 28
Oracle 59, 60, 82, 84, 118, 132, 144, 145
Original Ipswich Journal 53, 112
Original London Post 53
O'Rourke, Owen 31
Owen, Edward 45
Oxford 9, 34
Oxford Gazette 6, 51
Oxford Post 35

Palmerston, Lord 184, 187, 188
pamphlets 4, 36–7, 51, 168
Parker's London News 10, 63

parliamentary reporting 129–32
Parrot 18
Partridge, John 3
Pasham, James 14, 16–17
Patriot 111
Pearson, Lt Hugh Pearce 89
Peel, Sir Robert 169–70, 183
Pelham, Henry 68
Penny London Post, or The Morning Advertiser 73, 88, 191
Penny Post 7, 8
People's Police Gazette 191
Perceval, Spencer 164
Perry, James 90, 130, 147, 172
Perry, Sampson 155–6
Peterloo massacre 167–8, 188
Phillpotts, Bishop Henry 197
Pitt, William 117, 131–2, 134, 137 *bis*, 140, 164
Plain Dealer 46
Playford, Henry 58
Plymouth 124
Political Register 120, 164, 166, 167, 189, 191
Poor Man's Guardian 172, 188–9
Portsmouth Gazette 114
Post Boy 8, 30, 41, 45
Post Man 8
Potter, John 25
Potteries Free Press 183
Prentice, Archibald 173
Preston Journal 20
Printing Acts 6, 7, 8, 73, 77
printing technology 72–5, 178–9, 188
Proctor's Price-Courant 65
Prompter 172
Protestant Courant 7
provincial press 12–13, 80, 110–25, 192–5
Public Advertiser 58, 77, 140, 150–1, 151–2
Public Occurences Foreign and Domestic 88
Publick Intelligencer 6
Publick Occurrences Truly Stated 7

Pulteney,William 29–30, 133
Punch 97, 199
Purser, John 37, 38

Quarterly Journal of Agriculture 99
Quarterly Review 199

Racing Calendar 60
Radical 172
railways 67–8, 77, 98, 180–1
Rayner, William 10
Reading Mercury 51, 54, 55, 60, 63, 67,
    130, 137
Reformer 172
Reformists' Register 167
religion 2–3, 30, 123, 170, 194, 196–7
religious press 87–8
Republican 167, 172
Reuter, Julius de 181
Review 9, 59
Reynolds, George 190
Reynolds's Weekly Newspaper 86, 179,
    190
Richmond, Duke of 34
Rider, Cardanus: *British Merlin* 3
Robe, Thomas 64
Robinson's Price-Courant 65
Royal Cornwall Gazette 110, 139, 164,
    170
Ruddiman, Walter 133
Russell, Lord John 123, 183
Russell, W.H. 181
Russia 30, 38, 117, 151

St James's Chronicle 57, 66, 68, 117,
    149–50, 161–2, 170
St James's Evening Post 8, 45
Salisbury and Winchester Journal 64, 69,
    75, 113–14, 115, 132, 134, 145,
    149, 171, 193
    quoted 50, 98–9, 100, 103–4, 104–5
Saturday Evening Post (Birmingham)
    192
Saxton (editor) 167
scandals 31, 58

Scarnafis (envoy) 128
'scissors and paste' technique 80
Scot, Reginald: *The Discoverie of
    Witchcraft* 3
Scotland 6
    see also Jacobitism
Scroggs, Chief Justice 7
Selby 67
Senator 26
Sheffield Advertiser 59, 84, 91
Sheffield Independent 76, 169
Sheffield Iris 156
Sheffield Mercury 100
Sheffield Register 83, 146, 156
Sherborne Mercury 51, 57 *bis*, 66, 67,
    100, 101, 110, 114, 119, 134, 195,
    197
Shipley, J.B. 59
Shippen, William 36
Shrewsbury Chronicle 113, 137
Sicily 34
size and format 50–2, 67, 75, 78–9, 81
slavery 103, 107, 117, 146, 182
Smith, William Henry 181
Smithson, Sir Hugh 42–4
Spain 68
Spectator 9
sport 59–60, 80
Staffordshire Advertiser 68, 111, 171
Staffordshire Sentinel 52, 179
Stamford Mercury 124
Stamford News 128, 164
Stamp Duty 9, 10, 11–12, 26, 50, 78,
    81 *bis*, 156, 165–6, 168
    repealed 178–9, 183, 184–7, 192
    unstamped press 10–11, 19, 166,
    172, 182
Standard 170, 191
Stanley's newsletter 33
Star 61, 82, 83
Starry Messenger 3
Stationers Company of London 6, 7,
    8
Steele, Sir Richard 27
Stoddart, John 188

Strahan, William 36
Sturt, Charles 134
Sun 82, 90, 156, 158, 180
Sun Fire Insurance Company 65
Sunday press 9, 74, 80, 86–7, 92, 169,
    179–80, 188, 190–1
Sunday Times 168
Sunderland Herald 171, 192
Sussex Weekly Advertiser 41
Sutton, Charles 164, 168
Swift, Jonathan 26, 29

Tatler 9, 97
Taunton Courier 57 *bis*, 67, 100 *bis*, 114,
    118 *bis*, 124, 170, 171
    quoted 54, 63, 65, 76, 105, 123, 161
Taunton and Somersetshire Herald 78
Taylor, John Edward 171, 182
Telegraph 66
telegraphy 180–1
television 200
Terrae Filius 34
Thompson, William 41
Thurtell (murderer) 55–7
Times 74–5, 75 (*bis*), 90, 163, 169, 179,
    180, 181, 187–8, 190, 192, 195–6
    quoted 167–8
Tipu Sultan 27
Tiresom, Thomas 46
Town and Country Magazine 130
Trevor, Robert 58
Trewman's Exeter Flying Post 54, 55, 98
Trollope, Anthony 197
True Briton (I) 40
True Briton (II) 74, 90, 132, 156 *bis*,
    158
Turner, Cholmley 41
Tutchin, John 32, 41
Tyas, John 167
Tyne Mercury 132

Union Journal: or, Halifax Advertiser
    111
United Provinces (Netherlands) 20
Universal Spy or, The Royal Oak Journal

Reviv'd 34
Urquart, David 185

war reporting 5, 78, 84, 143–59,
    163–5, 183–4
    propaganda press 158
Walpole, Sir Robert 18, 32, 33, 34, 41,
    58–9
  father 8
Walter, John 75
Webster, William 87
Weekly Dispatch 86
Weekly Express … for Chudleigh… 57, 68,
    101, 184–5, 193, 194, 197
Weekly Journal – see under Mist
Weekly Medley 35, 58
Weekly Miscellany (C of E) 87
Weekly Miscellany; or… Entertainer 51
*Weekly Miscellany for… Trade, Arts and
    Sciences* 65
Weekly Packet 65
Weekly Register 59, 85
Weekly Times 86
Wellington, Duke of 170
Welsh press 111, 190
Werkmeister, Lucyle 83
West Briton 164, 171
West Indies 34, 89
Western County Magazine 99
Western Daily Press 192–3
Western Luminary 96, 107, 171–2, 184,
    197
Western Morning News 193
Western Times 92, 178, 179, 184, 196–7,
    197 *bis*
Westminster Journal 88, 154
*Westmorland Advertiser and Kendal
    Chronicle* 111
Westmorland Gazette 111
Wheeler's Manchester Chronicle 50, 122,
    153–4
*Whiston's Merchants Weekly
    Remembrancer* 65
White, Robert 5
White Dwarf 168

White Hat 167
Whitehaven Weekly Courant 111
Whitfield, George 87
Wilberforce, William 146
Wilkes, John 58, 128, 130, 138
Willes, John 32
William III 8
Williamson, Joseph 6
Wilson, James 199
Wiltshire County Mirror 75
Wiltshire Standard 165
Windham, William 117, 156–7
Witches of Northamptonshire 3
Witches of Warboys 3
Wolfe, John 4, 33
Wolverhampton Chronicle 111, 114
Wood, Thomas 113, 137

Woodfall, William 131
Wooler, Thomas 167
Woolmer's Exeter and Plymouth Gazette
  60–1, 66, 105
Working Man's Friend 172
World 27, 59, 60, 87, 143–4
Worsley, Sir Richard 53
Wyndham, Sir William 36

York 9, 53, 67, 69, 113
York Courant 9, 41, 78–9, 172
York Gazetteer 9, 41
York Mercury 9, 12, 62
Yorke, Philip, 1st Earl of Hardwicke
  31
Yorkshire Gazette 165
Yorkshire Post 193